3/19/14

To Alberto - on
Congratulations
your beautiful new
granddaughter

Shana

FROM TERRA TO VERDE:
THE ART OF SHARON KOPRIVA

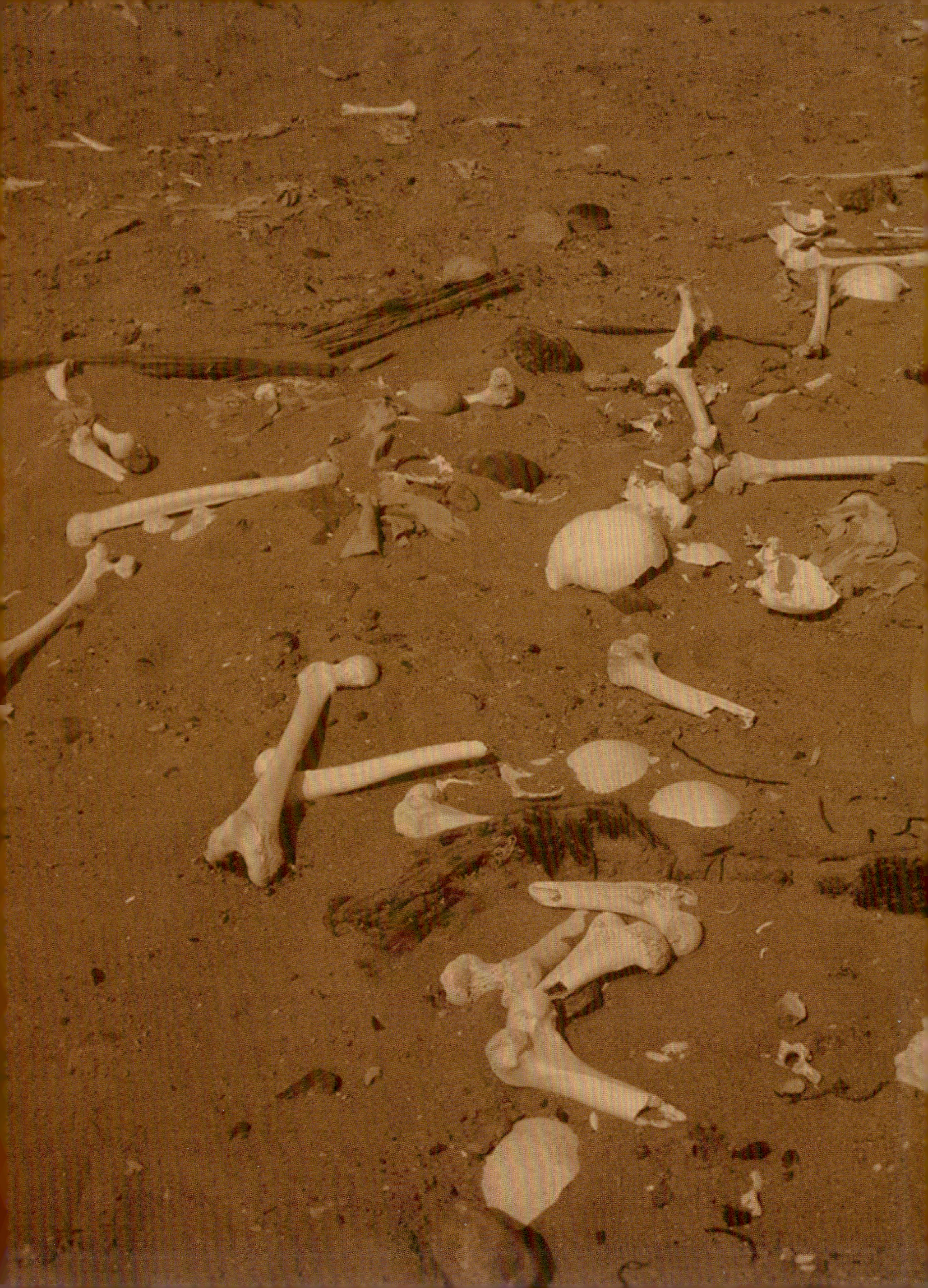

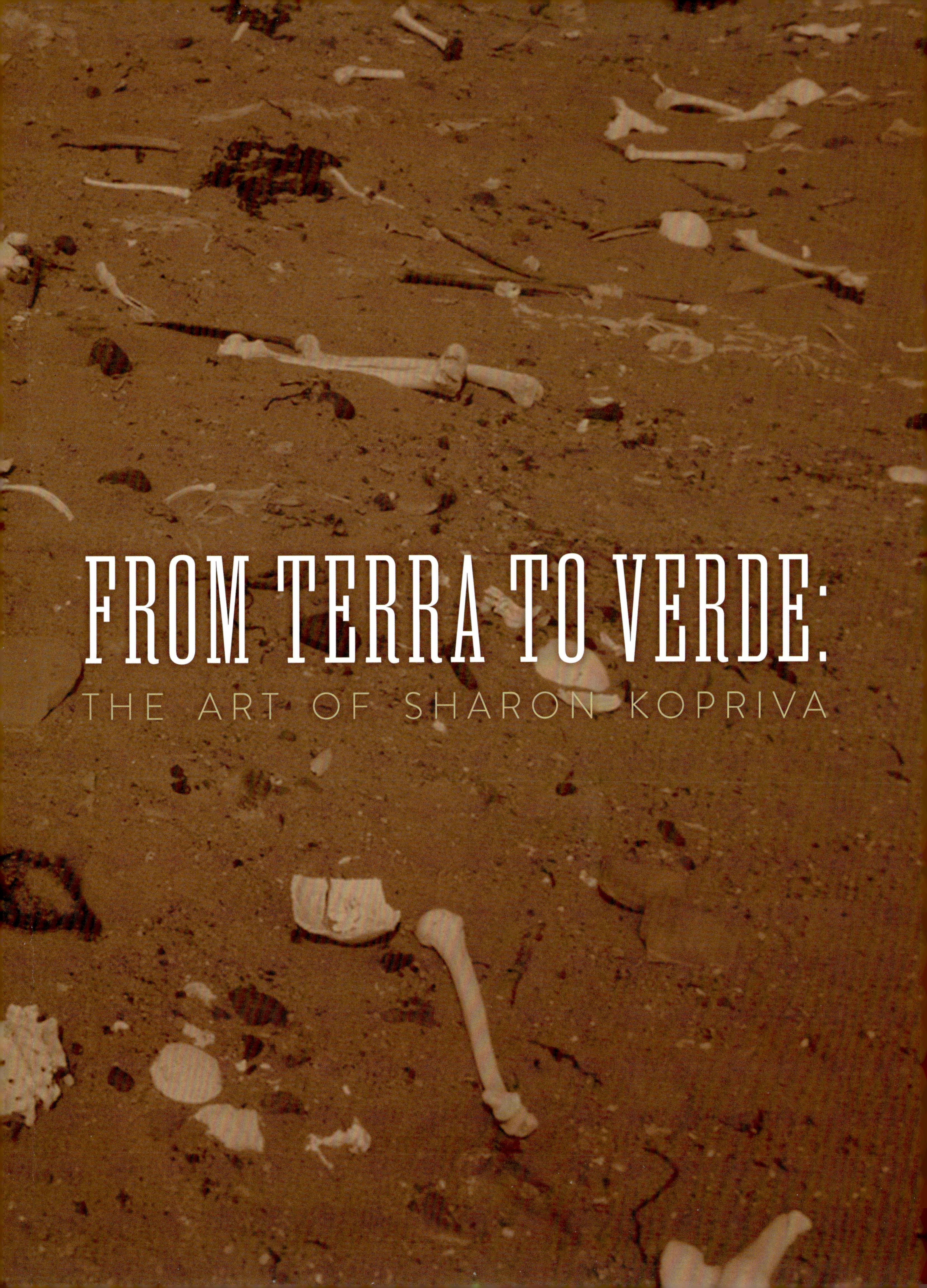
FROM TERRA TO VERDE:
THE ART OF SHARON KOPRIVA

This catalogue was published to coincide with the exhibition *From Terra
to Verde: The Art of Sharon Kopriva,* organized by the Ogden Museum of
Southern Art.

Produced by the Ogden Museum of Southern Art/University of New Orleans
Director: William P. Andrews
Chief Curator: Bradley Sumrall
Design: Dean Cavalier and Phillip Collier/Phillip Collier Design

ISBN 978-0-9772544-6-0

Library of Congress Cataloguing-in-Publication Data

Front cover:
Cathedral Green, 2012,
Oil and mixed media on photo canvas, 81 x 186 x 2.5 inches.
Collection of the artist.

Fin de Siècle, 1987-2001,
Oil and mixed media on canvas, 80 x 115 x 11 inches.
Collection of the artist.

Back Cover
Alchemist's Tree, 2011,
Oil and mixed media on photo canvas, 40 x 36 x 2 inches.
Collection of Gwen and Dwayne Ortman.

In the Name of the Father, and of the Son, and of the Holy..., 2003,
Papier-mâché and mixed media, 38 x 80 x 24 inches.
Collection of the artist.

Printed in United States of America (Garrity Printing, New Orleans, La.)

Ogden Museum of Southern Art/
University of New Orleans
925 Camp St.
New Orleans, La. 70130
504.539.9650
www.ogdenmuseum.org

Copyright and Photography Credits:
Dan Allison: p. 45,77,84-89,90-93,97,99,100,101
Gary Bunkhead: p. 28,37-39, 38,49,56,59,60-63.65
Ray Burnette: p. 102
Tom Callins: p. 17-19,27,40,41,57
Michael Collins: p. 14,58,64,68,69,79,80
George Craig: p. 36
George Hickson: p. 51
Gus Kopriva: p. 104
Bryan Kuntz: p. 54,70-72,76,78
Frank Martin: p. 13,15,16,20,30,35
Richard McCabe: p. 34
Suzanne Paul: p. 106
Bradley Sumrall: p. 111
Rick Wells: p. 10-12, 21-26,29,32,33,40, 42,43,44,46,53,73,74,75,81-
83,91,94,98,100,103

TABLE OF CONTENTS

FROM TERRA TO VERDE

What moves in grass I love—
The dead will not lie still,
And things throw light on things,
And all the stones have wings.
-Theodore Roethke, from "The Small"

Looking at the work of Sharon Kopriva over the last thirty years is to view a visual counting of a deeply personal and spiritual artistic life. From the early abstracted images of an imagined landscape where the earth itself has bones, through her sculptural interpretations of ethnographic imagery and the humanity within her Catholic faith, through explorations of iconography and universal truths, through the quiet and reverent portrayal of her forest, of her cathedral of green – she has always depicted the world around her – real and imagined – and has done so with a singular vision.

The Early Years

Born in 1948 in Houston, Texas, Kopriva started drawing as early as she can remember. Her mother, Rosalie "Rosy" Ortman was first-generation Italian-American and a devout Catholic. Her father, Lowell "Red" Ortman was a veteran of World War II – a navigator of thirty-seven missions in a B17 bomber – who operated a small boat and outboard-motor shop in the same building that now holds Kopriva's studio in the Houston Heights.

Her first eight years of school were spent under the guidance of the nuns at Christ the King Catholic School, an experience that continues to inform her work to this day. Although her core beliefs and the themes of her work were shaped in Catholic school, it wasn't until she entered public school that she received any formal art training. Field trips to Museum of Fine Arts, Houston and exercises in drawing, painting and papier-mâché kindled an interest that led her through a degree in education, through a decade of teaching in Texas public schools, and eventually to her acceptance into the Master of Fine Arts program at University of Houston in 1979.

In 1979, the Houston art scene was just beginning to break free of both the shadow of Texas Impressionism – think Julian Onderdonk, Edward Eisenlohr and fields of bluebonnets – as well as the dominance of the New York-driven aesthetics of minimalism and abstract expressionism – think Helen Frankenthaler and Kenneth Noland. It was an exciting place to work, with new voices like curators James Harithas and Jane Livingston spreading the gospel of a new regionalism. The faculty of the University of Houston had recently added James Surls and John Alexander to the staff, both artists working in highly original styles separate from the influence of established artistic trends. Add to this the fact that Houston was at the epicenter of the Texas oil industry's Gusher Age. The resulting swift cultural and economic changes helped to create an environment of patronage and opportunity for young artists working there. Kopriva desperately wanted to be part of this momentum. John Alexander remembers, "She didn't just break into the Houston art scene, she kicked its door in."

The Early Work - Terra

In the graduate program at University of Houston, Kopriva's work was focused on the landscape. Hers was a created landscape, an expression of how she envisioned the earth, the Terra. This was not the pastoral Impressionistic landscapes of the Bluebonnet School – although she would use the bluebonnet subject later, in a uniquely Kopriva way (pgs. 58, 63 and 65). Her early landscapes looked beneath the surface, at the bones of the earth. With graphite and oil she attempted to reveal the layers of humanity beneath the grass, in the cavities and crevices of the landscape. In umber and ochre, she depicted our own history of birth, death and renewal, often utilizing a womblike shape as a symbol of fertility. Her bones levitated from the landscape; her egg shapes transformed into vortexes.

During graduate school, Kopriva began her first true studies of early cultures, their beliefs and customs. Although deeply Catholic, she was searching for a broader understanding of spirituality, one that could encompass all of history and humanity. Her use of the egg or vortex as a primary symbol in her early landscapes shows this search for meaning in the most basic of forms. In the words of the great nineteenth century Russian Theosophist, Helen Brovatsky: "The symbol of an egg expresses the fact ... that the primordial form of everything manifested, from atom to globe, from man to angel, is spheroidal, the sphere being with all nations the emblem of eternity and infinity—a serpent swallowing its tail."

One of her painting teachers suggested that she attempt something different. "This landscape doesn't exist," she said. "Try moving in a different direction." The statement angered Kopriva. Thankfully, she did not abandon the development of her style, of her unique perspective. In June 1982, she hung her thesis exhibition on the walls of the University's Blaffer Gallery. Graduate school was over, and she made plans to visit Machu Picchu with her husband, Gus, and a few close friends.

Peru

In 1982, Sharon Kopriva entered Peru for the first time. She visited the museums and historical sites. She climbed Machu Picchu one year before it became an UNESCO World Heritage Site. Yet it was a visit to the remains of a culture much older than the Aztecs that had the most profound effect on her. When she visited the ancient burial grounds of the Nazca culture, she felt she had found the imagined landscape in her work. The dry climate of the Nazca desert and the ritual burial practices of the Nazca people allowed the necropolis to remain surprisingly intact. Looters – mostly searching for valuable textiles in which the dead were buried – had spread the bones of many open tombs onto the desert floor.

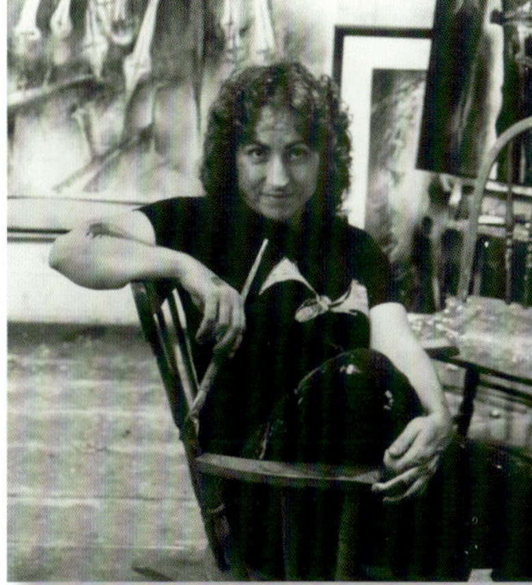

> "Standing in the Nazca Desert, I had an epiphany. I felt as if I'd stepped into one of my paintings, several of which were then on display in my graduate thesis exhibit in Houston. I had been told that what I painted did not exist. But now I saw it – I was a part of it. This wasn't a surreal vision but a physical reality. A sea of skeletal remains appeared on the ground before me as far as I could see. Bones washed white from exposure to sun and wind, so bleached they almost glowed against the soil.
>
> The bones did not levitate like they had in my paintings, but they seemed as if they had that capacity. I sensed an energy, something I had experienced before."

This experience not only deepened her interest in non-Western cultural traditions, mythology and history, but began a theme of memento mori in her work that was to be paramount for the next thirty years. She returned to Houston, not only validated, but energized to begin a new body of work.

Back in her studio, the first few years (1982 through 1984) were spent creating work in the same medium as her student work, oil and graphite on paper (*Impressions,* p. 11). The figure became more prevalent, though. Inspired by the wrapped remains of Peruvian mummies tucked away into niches, the bones became fully realized figures. In 1984, the first mixed media painting was executed. *Bad Ugly Proud Disconcerned* (p. 13) marks a move to three-dimensionality that has defined her work since. It was subsequently chosen for "Fresh Paint: The Houston School." Peter Marzio had recently taken over as Director of the Museum of Fine Arts, Houston, heralding a new period of expansive vision for that institution. Curated by Susie Kalil and Barbara Rose, "Fresh Paint" attempted to define a new movement of imagist painters in Houston, and in hindsight, possibly defined one of the most original and productive periods in the Houston art scene. It most certainly helped to forward the careers of the artists involved.

Sculpture

Around 1985, the first fully sculptural work appeared. *Female Figure* (1985) was an attempt to create a figure directly inspired by the Peruvian mummies, using papier-mâché. Other works followed, and they quickly began taking on a more animated appearance. Through the humble medium of papier-mâché, she was able to coax nuance, emotion and humor from her mummified sculptural figures. In *The Couple* (p. 16), after an eternity, the married couple still gazes at each other. Of *Eternal Bliss* (p. 17), Kopriva says, "This couple has taken the idea a step further."

Kopriva's Catholic faith began to appear in her sculptural work in 1986. *Penitent Woman* (p. 27) marks a transitional phase where the Christian cross is combined with the mummy form. It marks an attempt to merge her interest in pre-Christian beliefs with her deeply held faith. It leads directly to some of the most powerful sculptures of her career, *The Martyrs* (pgs. 29-33). These works are reverent and infused with an ecstatic belief in the power of Christian symbolism.

Ed and Nancy Reddin Kienholz

One of the most transformative influences on the work of Sharon Kopriva was the friendship she forged, beginning in 1987, with Ed and Nancy Kienholz. Kopriva had a deep respect for their work. "In graduate school, we were exposed to all this minimalist sculpture. Then I saw the work of Ed and Nancy, artists who tackled hard social issues. I respected the chances they took, really putting their careers on the line to make this really powerful work."

Ed Kienholz first reacted to Kopriva's work at the home of a mutual friend, Marilyn Oshman. Oshman had carefully built a strong collection of Modern and contemporary art, with a healthy representation of Texans. Walking through this collection containing works ranging from Diego Rivera and Frida Kahlo to James Surls and Jim Roche, he suddenly came upon *The Couple*. Mistaking it for an ethnographic object, he became intrigued when he discovered that the work had been created recently by Kopriva. As a result, Ed and Nancy offered Kopriva a residency in their program at a converted schoolhouse in Hope, Idaho. Eventually trading art for land, Kopriva and her husband, Gus, have spent every summer in Hope, Idaho, since 1989.

Ed and Nancy Kienholz encouraged Kopriva to expand her sculptural work into larger, more intricately crafted tableaus. With *The Confessional* (pgs. 50-51) – a narrative tableau with multiple figures, complete with a light element – the Kienholz influence is dramatically illustrated. Ed, especially, became an important mentor, not only conceptually, but in the craft of actually building these works. Kopriva recounts, "We were driving one day, and found this old piano on the side of the road. Ed said, 'You want that to work with?' I asked him how I was supposed to get it home. He had a few assistants, who took the piece to the studio. That became the first piano piece, *In Excelsis Deo* (p. 56)."

Transition

In 2001, two events occurred that would shake the deeply held beliefs of Kopriva to the core, the terrorist attacks of 9/11 and first rumblings of a storm of child sexual abuse cases against the clergy of the Catholic Church. In the works, *From Without* and *From Within* (pgs. 70-71), she gives these events equal treatment. The towering structures of American invulnerability and Catholic righteousness are depicted in ruins. Once again, Kopriva was faced with a re-examining of her core beliefs.

With *Prey for Us* (p. 102), Kopriva executed a sculptural tableau that is perhaps one of the most powerful statements of her career. A child stands with his back turned to the viewer in the phallic shadow of a Cardinal. The child's posture is vulnerable, and the figure is somehow, without ever seeing his face, infused with a deep sorrow. His crayons have fallen to the floor. Facing the cross, the symbol of the promise of salvation, he has written "Prey for us."

"Post-9/11, I began an investigation of yet another way of viewing God and a culture that we have been spiritually at odds with since long before the Great Crusades. Like many others I found myself re-visiting history and architecture, like pyramids, ziggurats and Babel, with its architectural gardens. It was the beginning of a return to landscape, digging into soil that, unlike Peru, I had never stepped upon."

Verde

Every summer, Kopriva packs up her studio and her beloved Peruvian Hairless dogs, and moves into the house that she and Gus built on land in Hope, Idaho. Brought initially by the schoolhouse residency offered by Ed and Nancy Kienholz, the Koprivas fell in love with the environment. The land borders one of the deepest lakes in North America. The peninsula on which it is situated is designated as a Wildlife Protection Area, and deer are more plentiful than anywhere I have experienced in the world. Her friends Marilyn Oshman and Nancy Kienholz are her neighbors and mahjongg partners there (and in Houston). The surrounding forests are majestic in a way that can inspire awe in the most hardened urban dweller. As I have heard several people say, "This is God's country."

Almost daily during the summer months, Kopriva hikes the mountain forests of Northern Idaho. Her dogs – Luna, Pluto and Thor – make the journey with her, as protectors and companions. I had the honor, in the summer of 2012, of joining them on one of these hikes. It was immediately clear that her most recent work is about that land, about those forests, and her involvement – both spiritually and physically – with that place.

In works like *Hallowed Hall* (pg. 86), *Alchemist's Tree* (pg. 85) and the monumental *Cathedral Green* (pgs. 82-83), Kopriva has used images of Gothic European Cathedrals as a background for her depictions of this landscape. "*Hallowed Hall* depicts the merger of earth and religion," she explains. "It sees the spirit of the earth as a powerful, positive influence on mankind. The forest entwines itself with formal religion, creating new light and spirituality. Nature encroaches on a place of formal worship and redefines how we as individuals connect with universal spirituality."

The sculptural tableau, *Matrimony* (pg. 80), depicts the ritual of marriage between bride and man-tree. The egg form has returned as a symbol of fertility. Vines are overtaking the bride. "The bride and groom and nature are one," says Kopriva. "They emphasize the importance of our natural environment and the role it plays in defining spirituality. This is a marriage of religion and nature. The decaying groom fertilizes new life, held in the bride's hands. It is the circle of life – death, decay and rebirth."

Walking down a mountain trail, we stop at a small stream to let the dogs drink. Kopriva sits on a moss-covered log under a spider web glowing in the afternoon sun. "What does this forest mean to you?" I ask.
"It means life. It represents a spirituality that will be here forever. The green has become very important to me. I am entering a new period in my work that I call Verde. Sometimes I see the trees bending together, and it reminds me of cathedrals. I just have a very personal, private relationship with these woods."

"Do you find that this is your cathedral, your sacred place?" I ask.

"God is here. God is in a lot of places, but God talks to me here, and I talk to God here. It is fine to have the formal buildings for religion," she says with a smile, "but I prefer this one."

Bradley Sumrall
Chief Curator
Ogden Museum of Southern Art

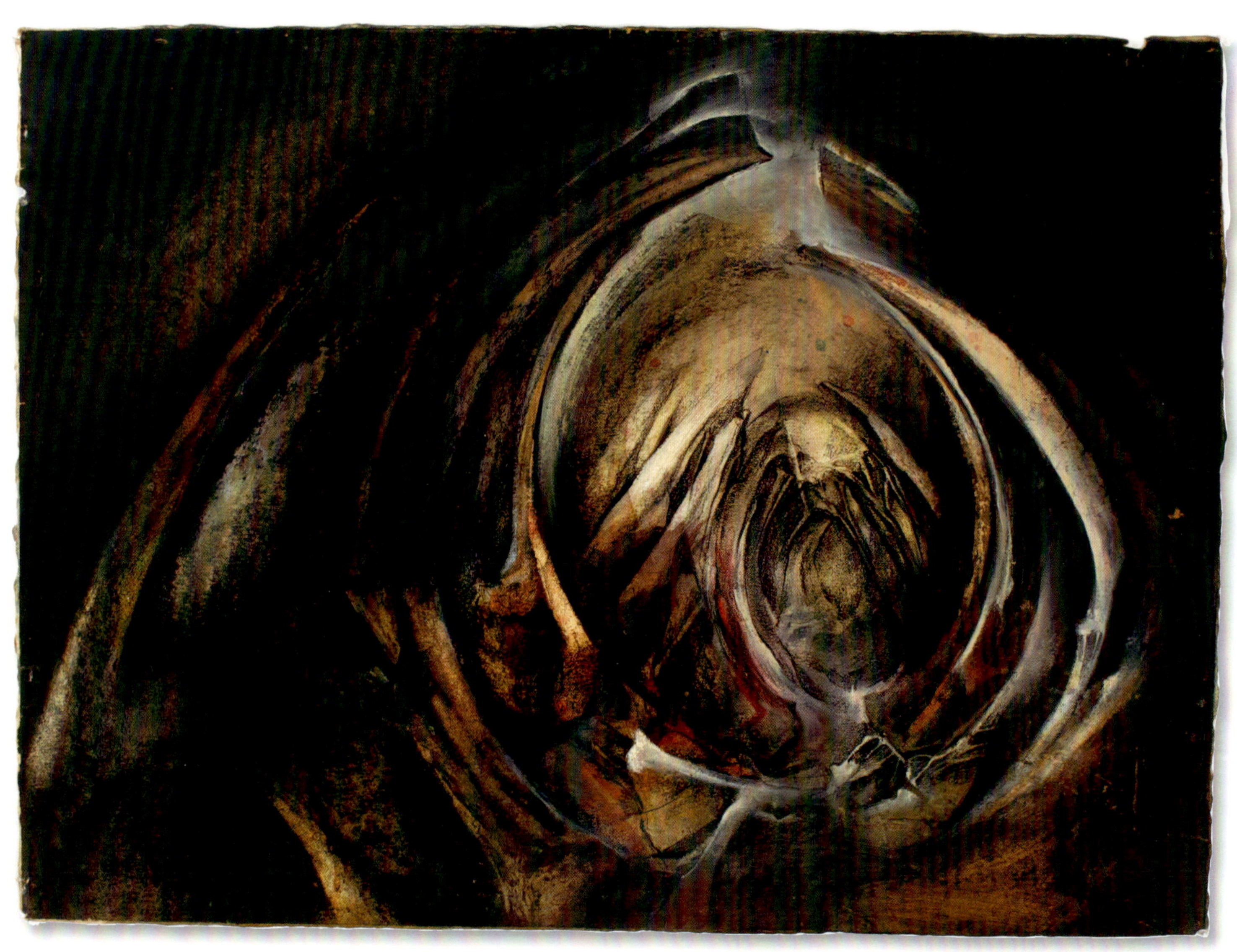

Cavity, circa 1981,
Oil and graphite on paper, 16 x 28 inches.
Collection of the artist.

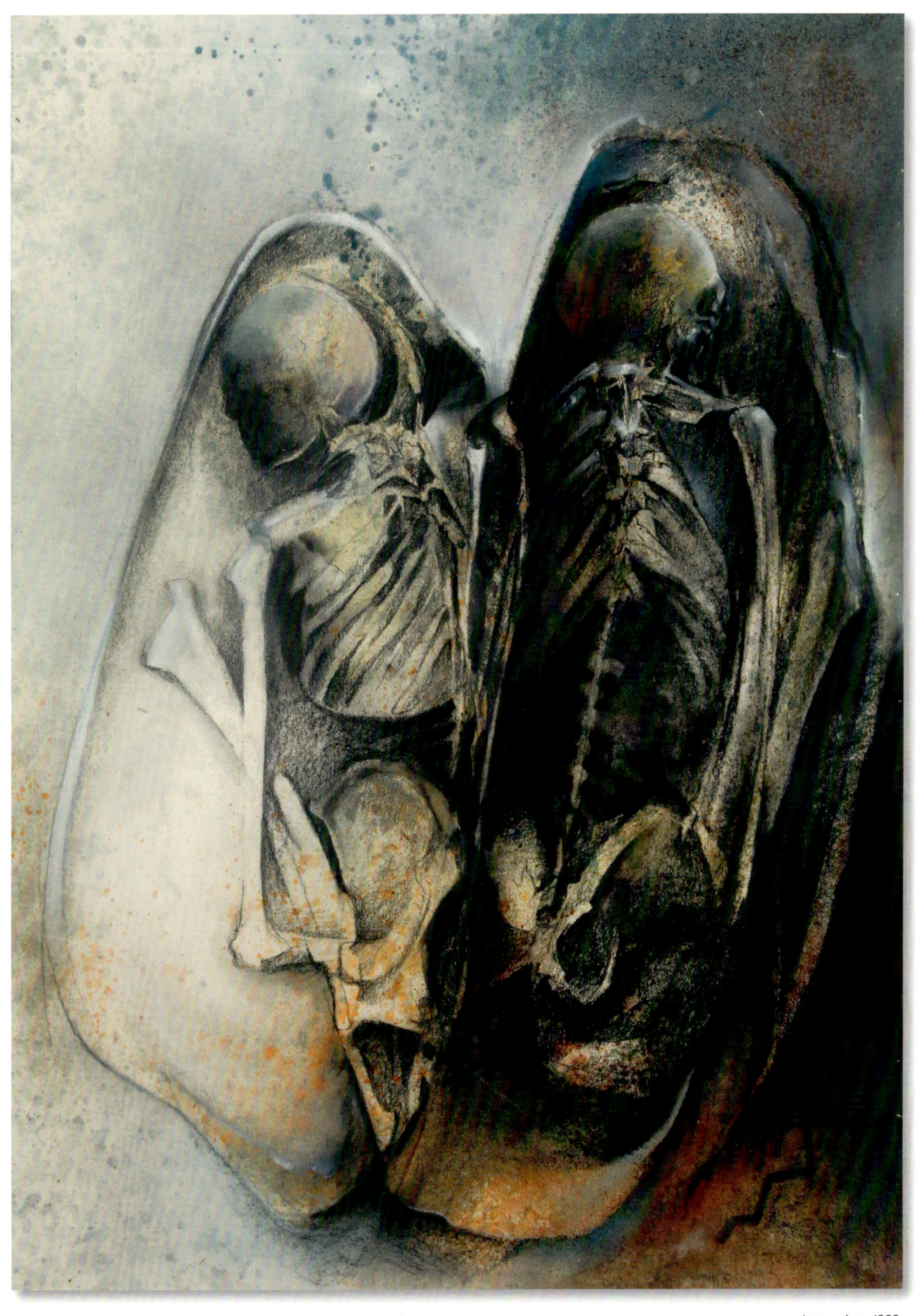

Impressions, 1982,
Oil and graphite on paper, 28 x 20 inches.
Collection of Marilyn Oshman.

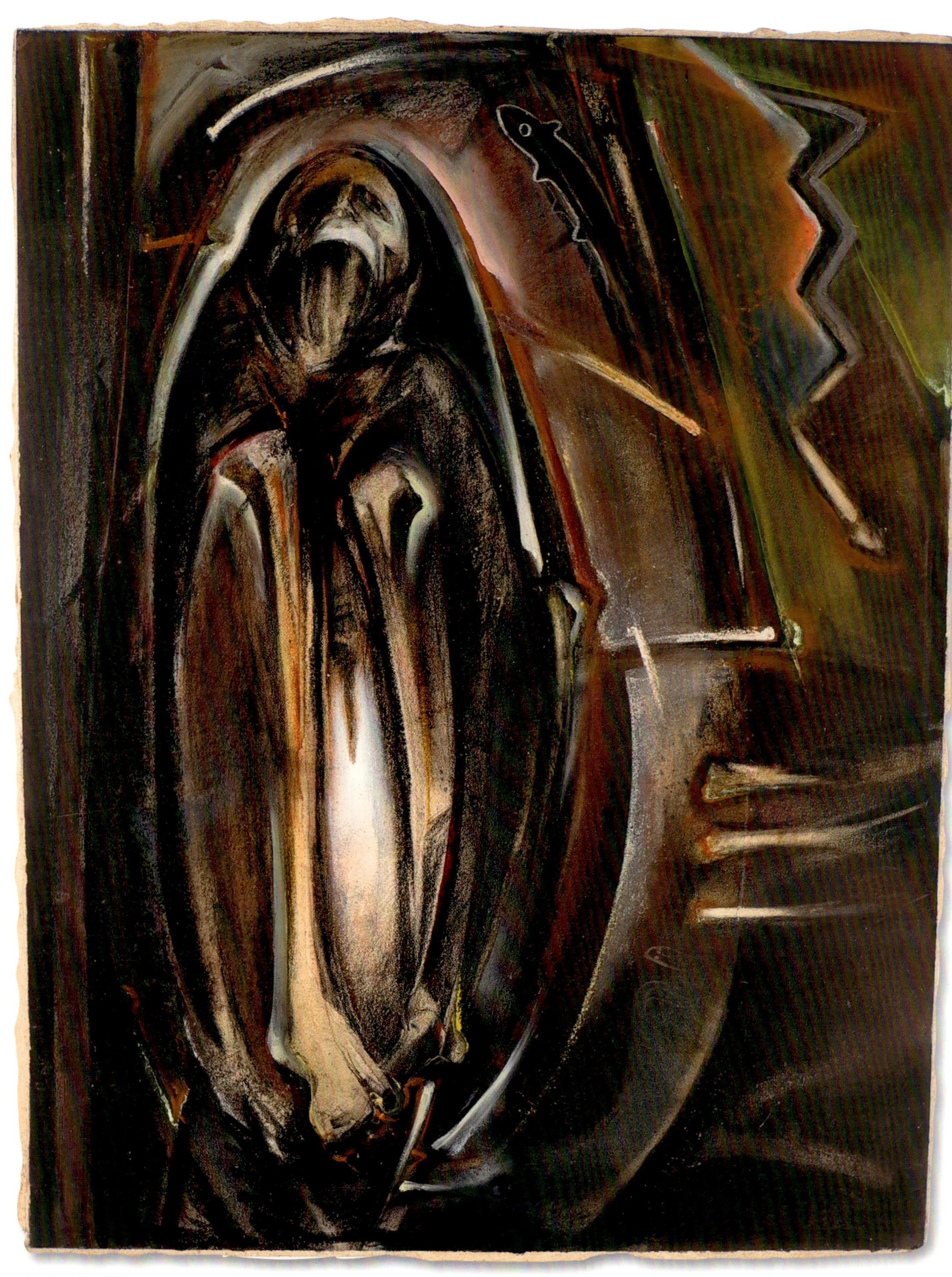

Inca Drawing, 1983,
Oil and graphite on paper, 27.5 x 21 inches.
Collection of the artist.

To see the works of Sharon Kopriva is to encounter a modern sensibility capable of evoking the primordial feelings of a primitive society. Sharon's sculpture vibrates mysteriously and creates the same authentic visceral response as do many of the great tribal fetishes from disappearing cultures.
- Allan Stone

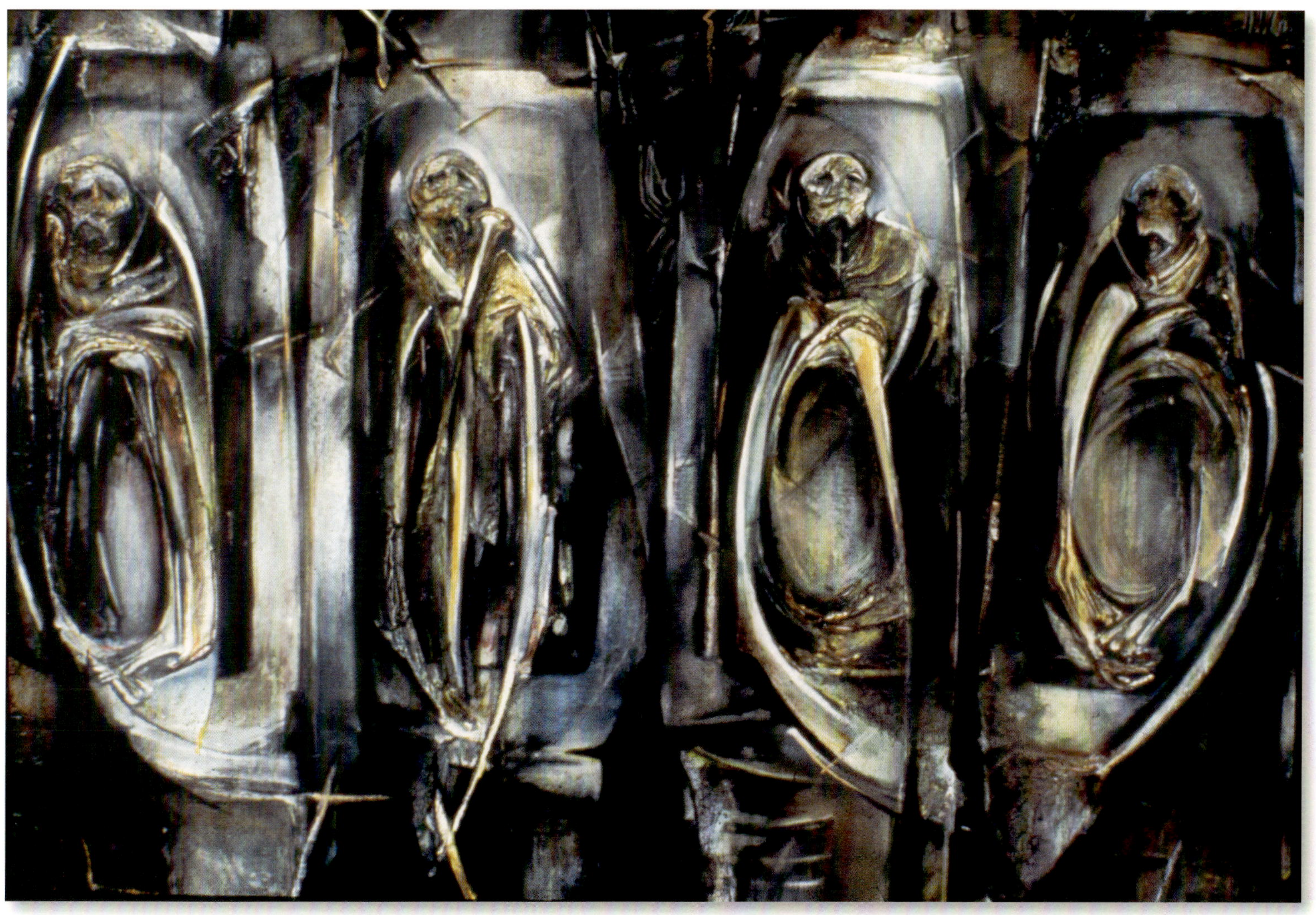

Bad Ugly Proud Disconcerned, 1984,
Oil and mixed media on canvas, 72 x 98 inches.
Collection of Allan Stone.

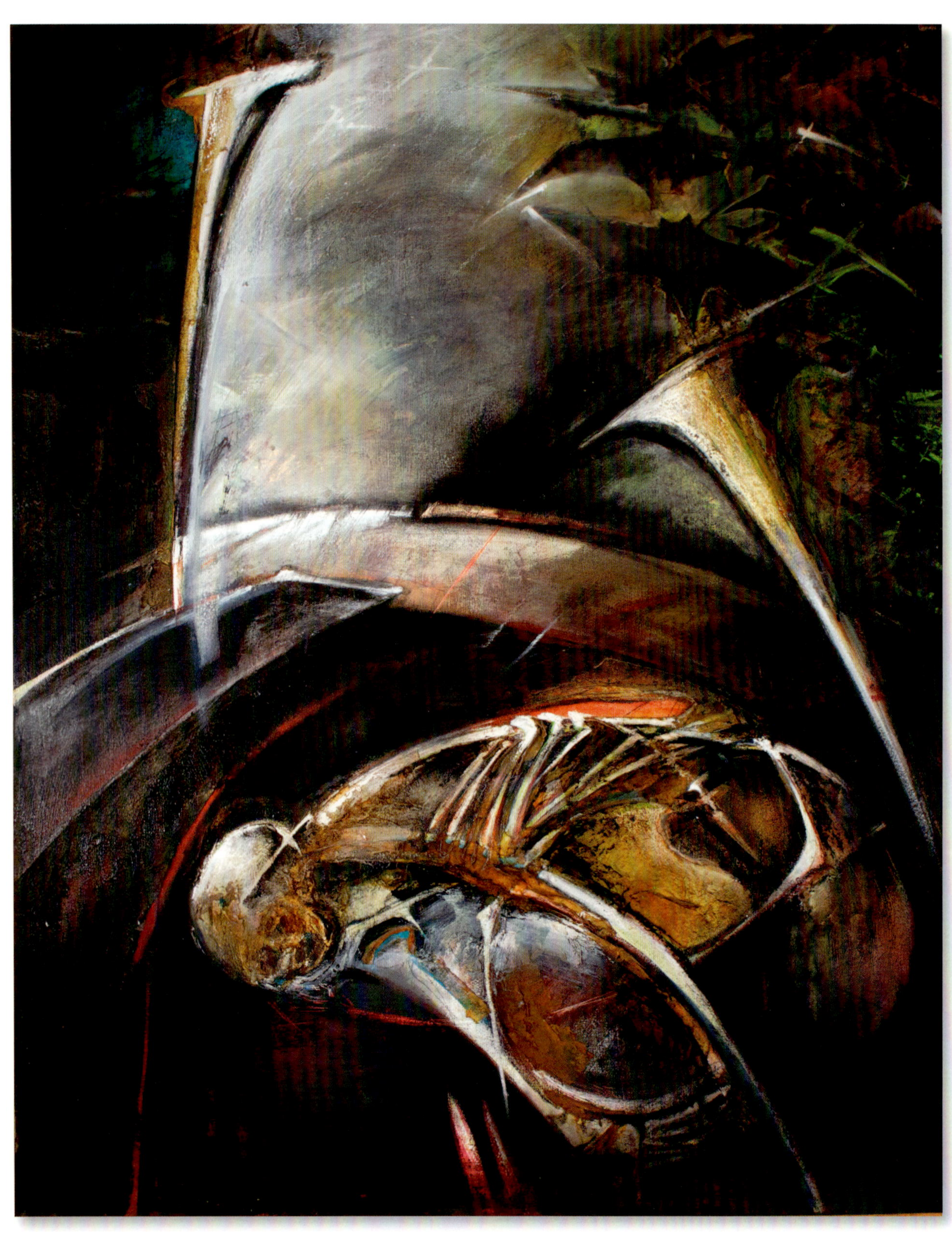

Surveillance, 1986,
Oil and mixed media on canvas, 61 x 49 inches.
Collection of the artist.

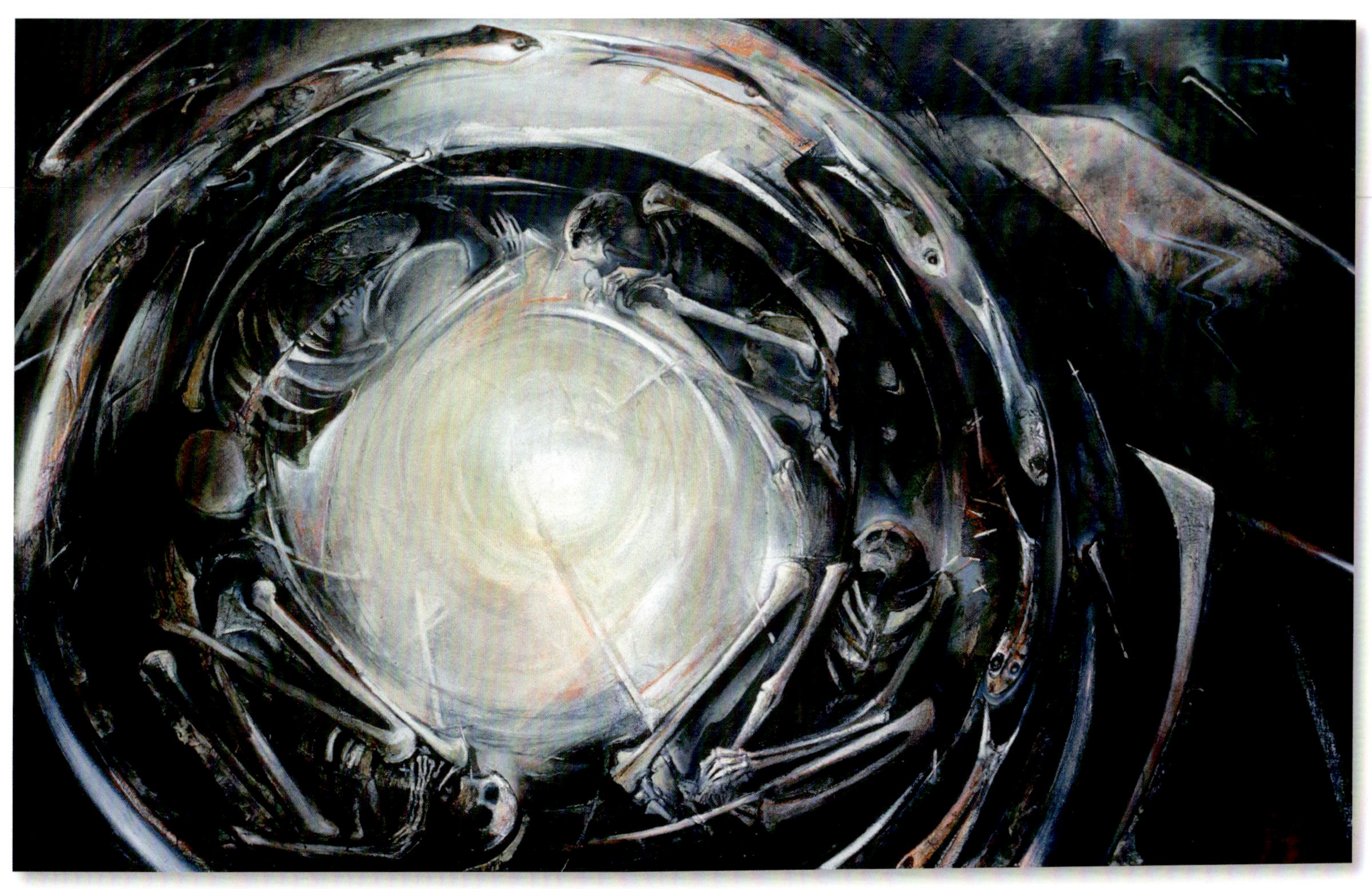

Cosmic Fish, 1985,
Oil and mixed media on canvas, 72 x 120 inches.
The Menil Collection.

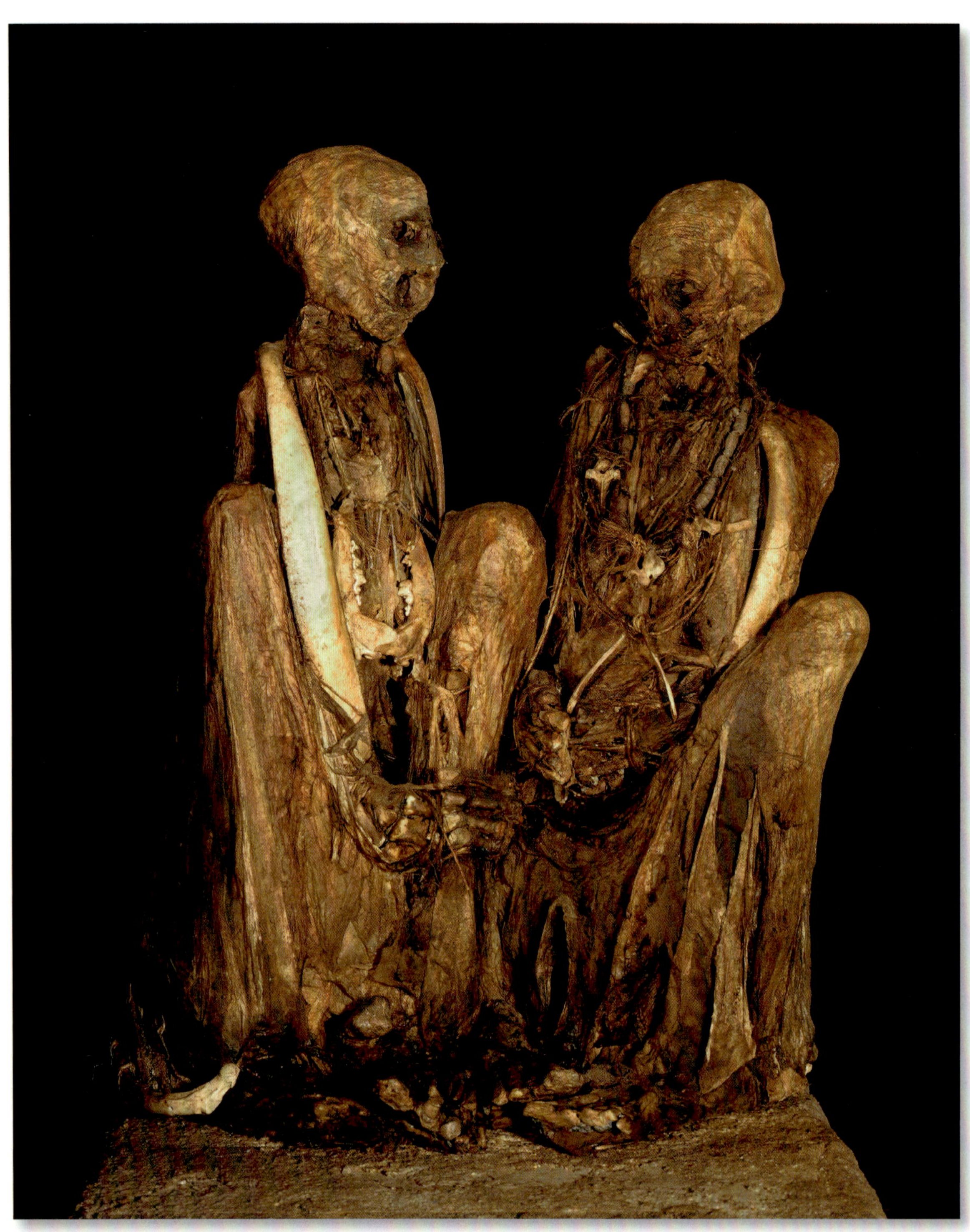

The Couple, 1986,
Papier-mâché and mixed media, 36 x 35 x 24 inches.
Collection of Marilyn Oshman.

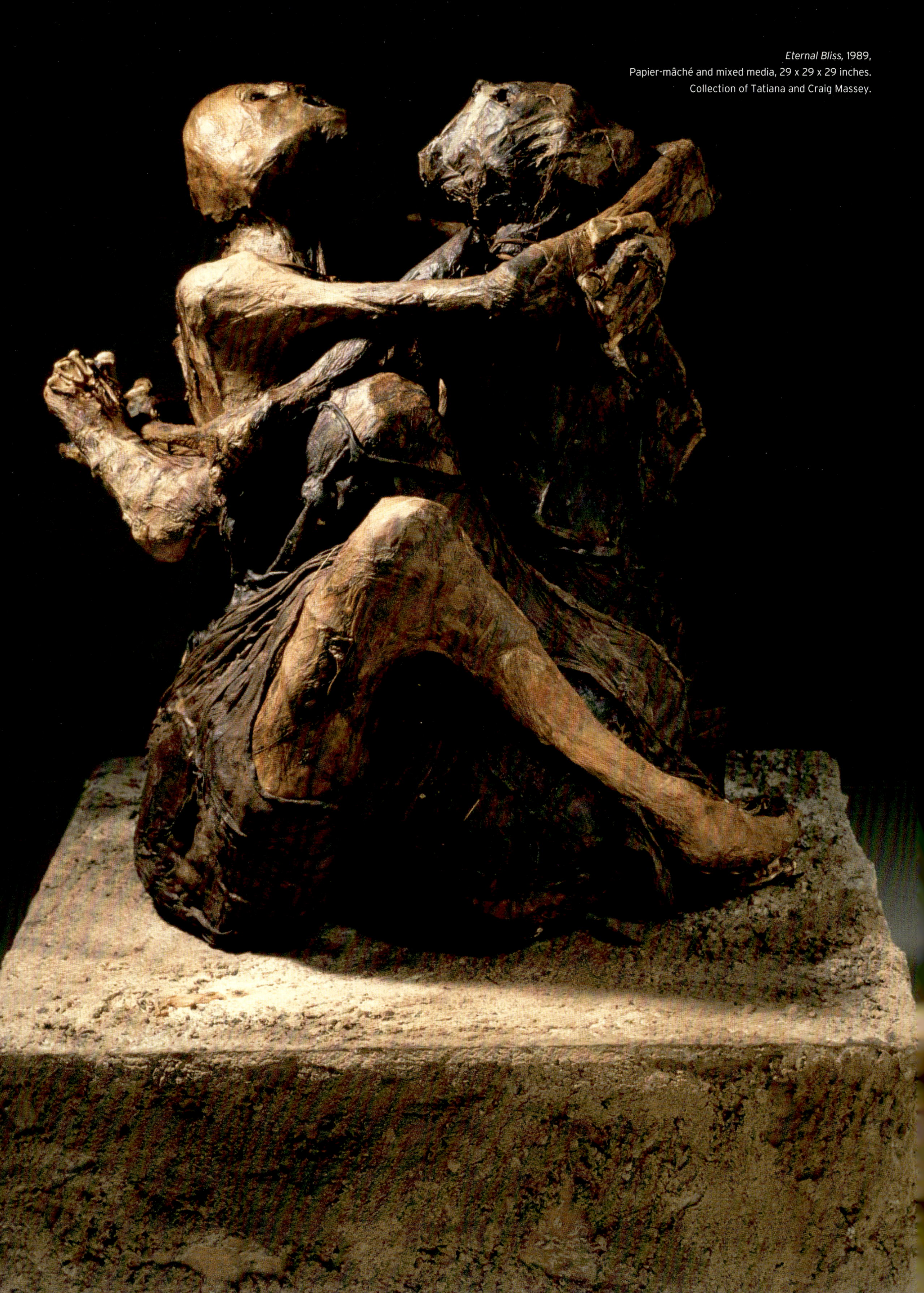

Eternal Bliss, 1989,
Papier-mâché and mixed media, 29 x 29 x 29 inches.
Collection of Tatiana and Craig Massey.

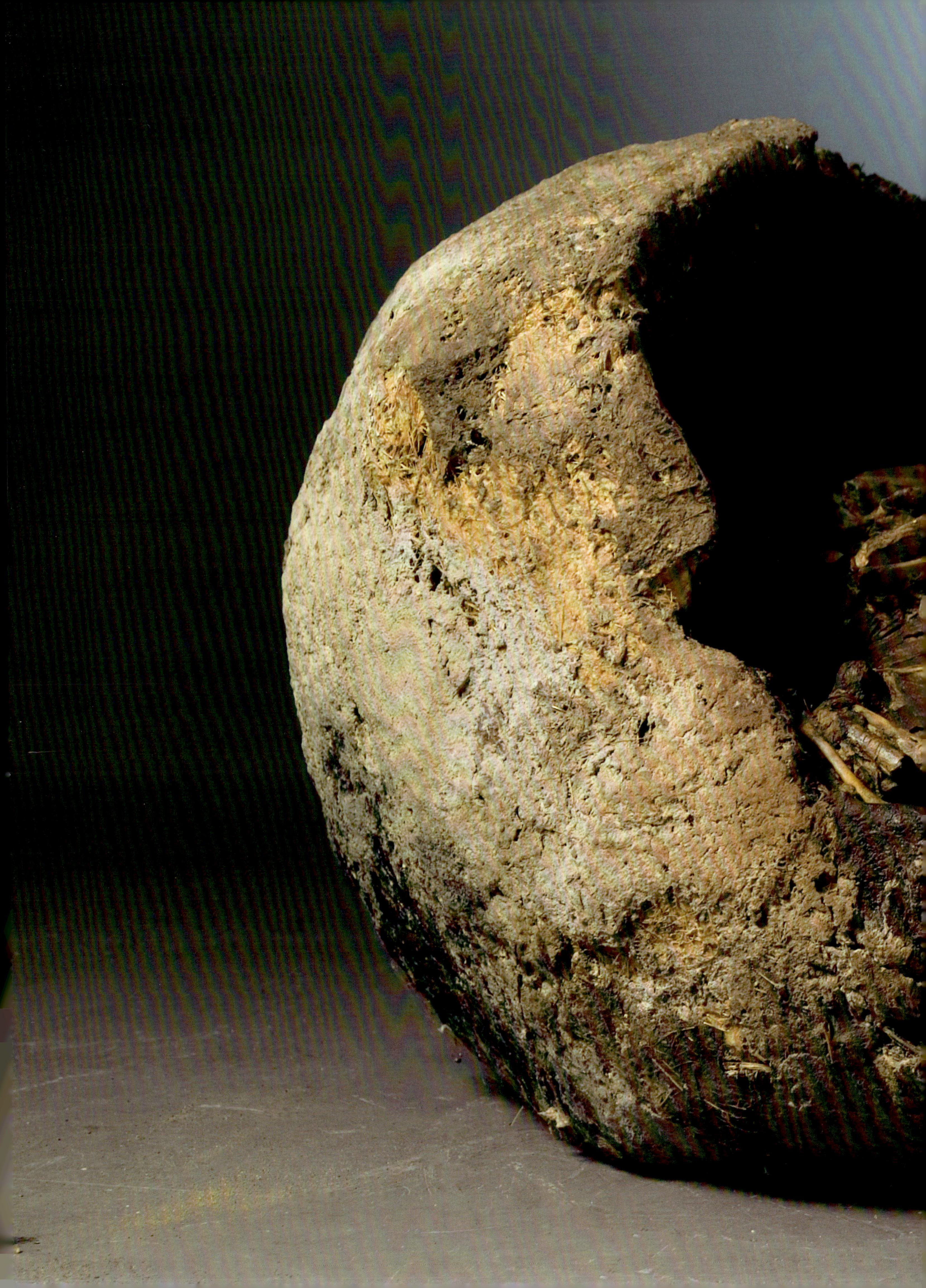

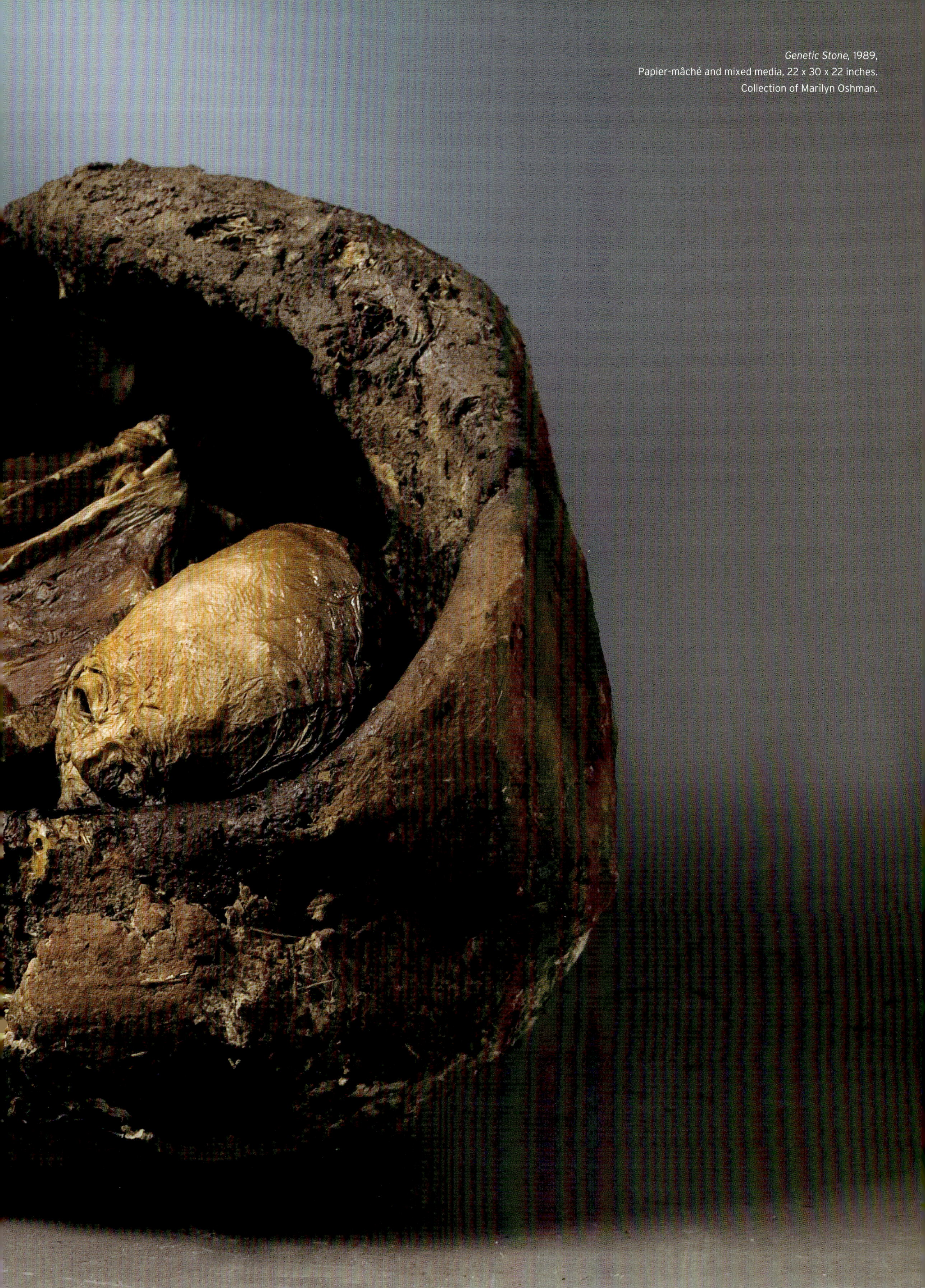

Genetic Stone, 1989,
Papier-mâché and mixed media, 22 x 30 x 22 inches.
Collection of Marilyn Oshman.

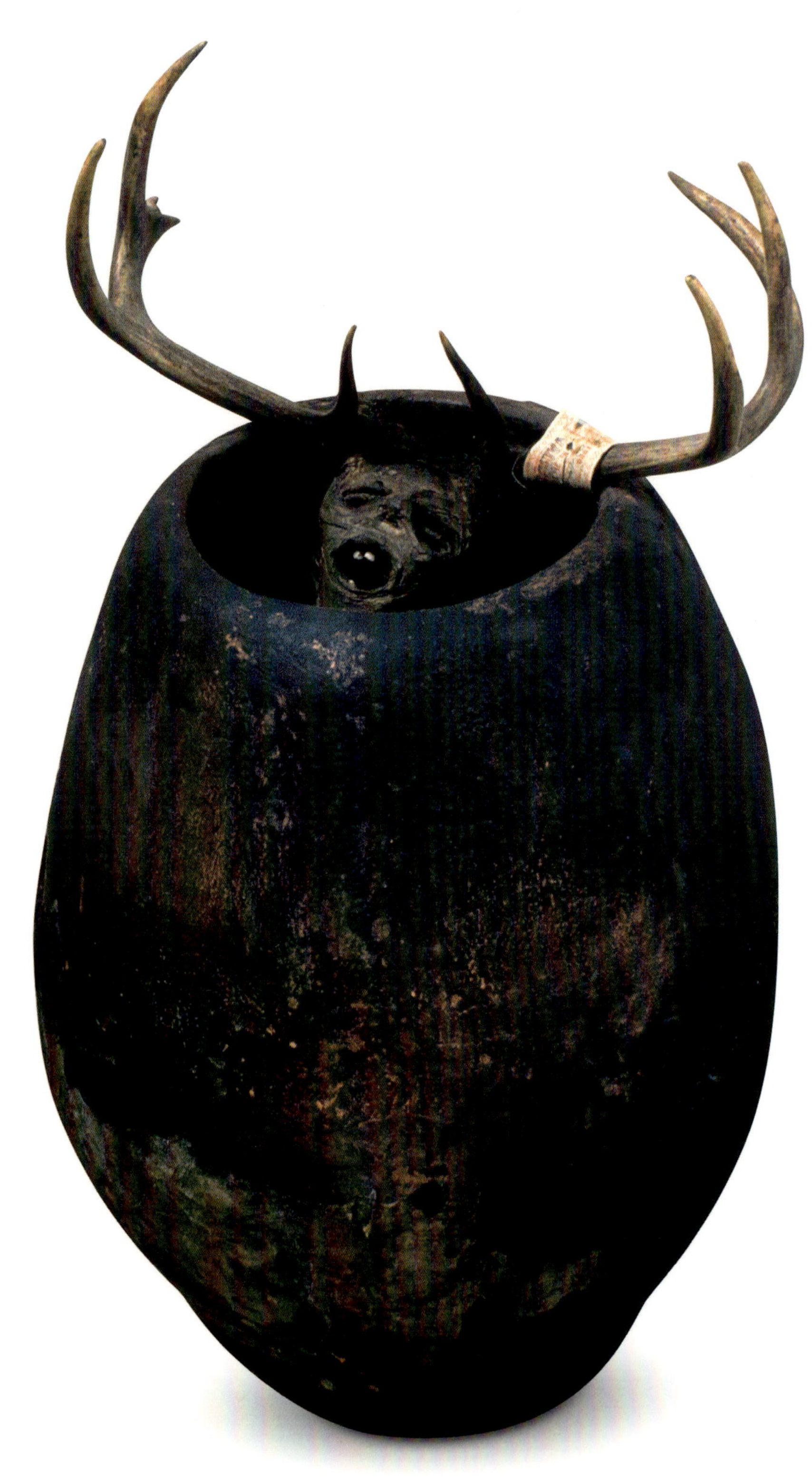

Deerborne, 1989,
Papier-mâché, horn and clay, 33 x 22 x 18 inches.
Collection of the artist.

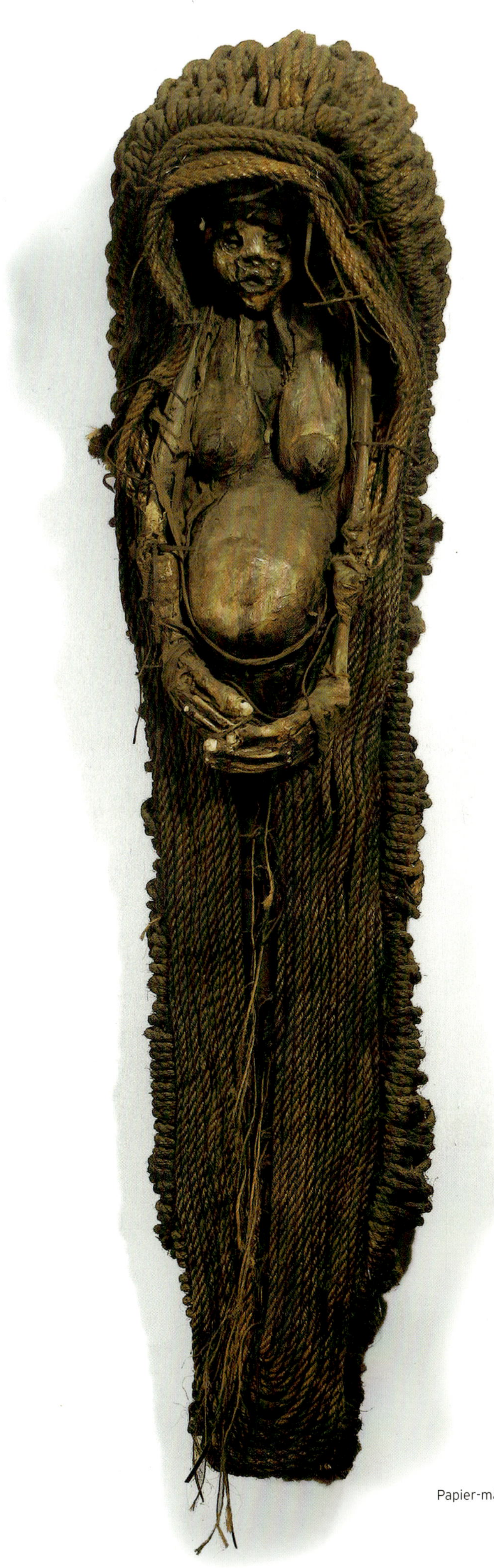

Linea Negra, 1989,
Papier-mâché, mixed media and rope, 70 x 18 x 18 inches.
Collection of Tony Markey.

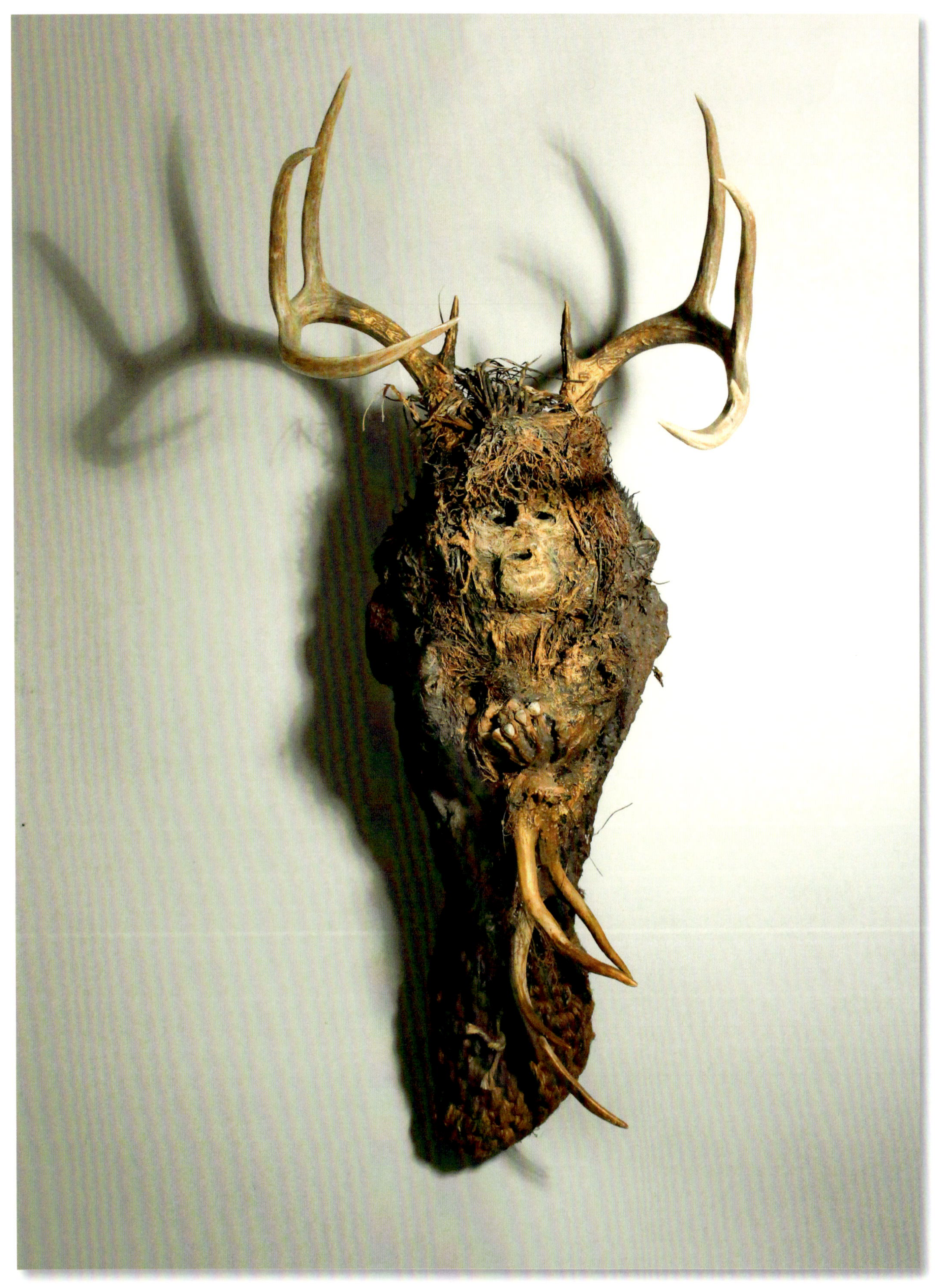

Woodrow, 1996,
Papier-mâché, horn and mixed media, 34 x 15 x 12 inches.
Collection of the artist.

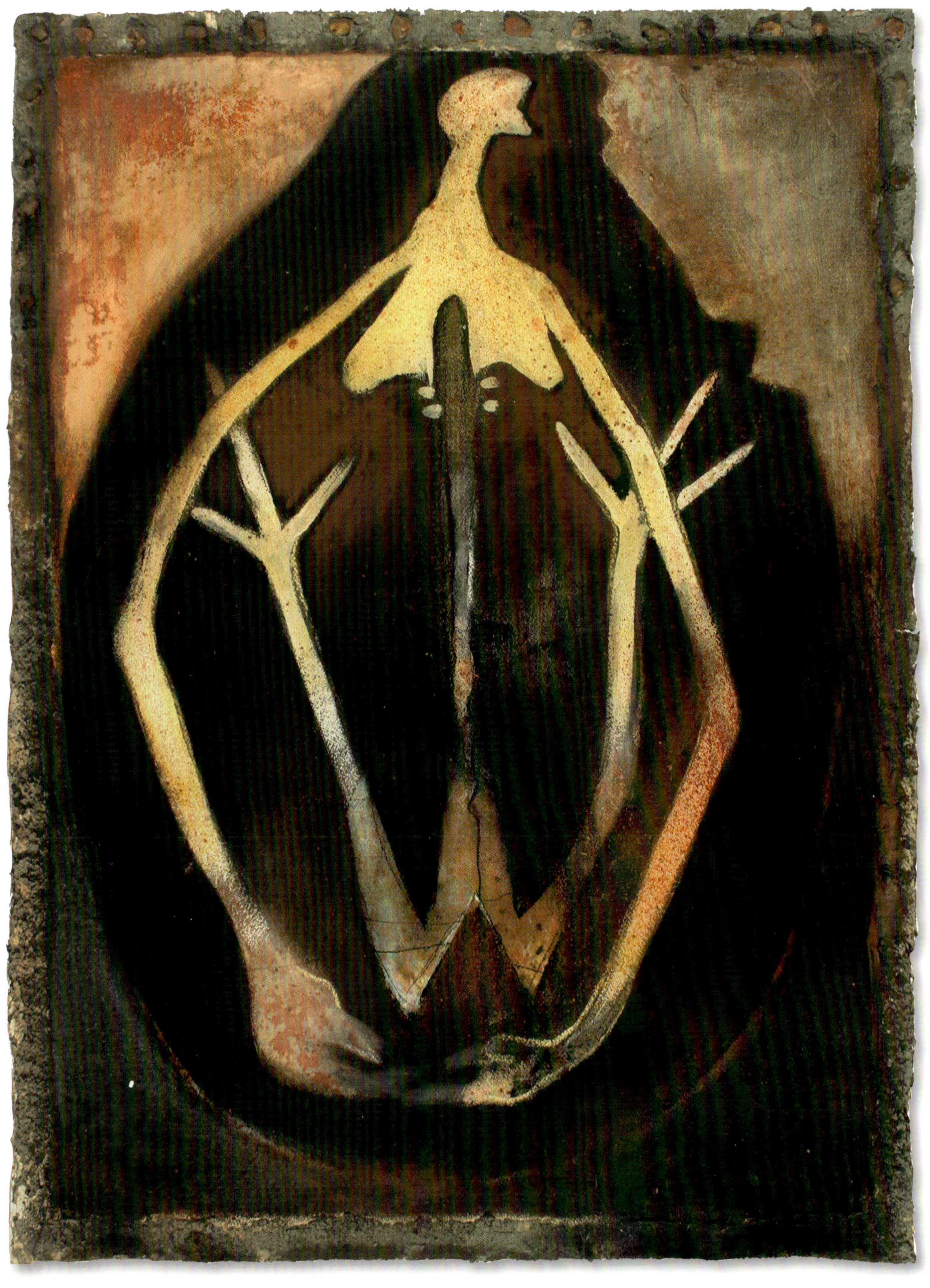

Birthing, 1993,
Oil and mixed media on paper, 28 x 21 inches.
Collection of the artist.

In 1993, I had the opportunity to take advantage of a residency in Australia, and to step onto another, different, sacred soil. This experience resulted in a series of aboriginal-based images inspires by the religion and mythology of the Northern Territory. Shades of red, yellow and brown ochre filled the space of these small works-on-paper which were a tribute to the Arnhem Land and its unique cultural history.

– Sharon Kopriva

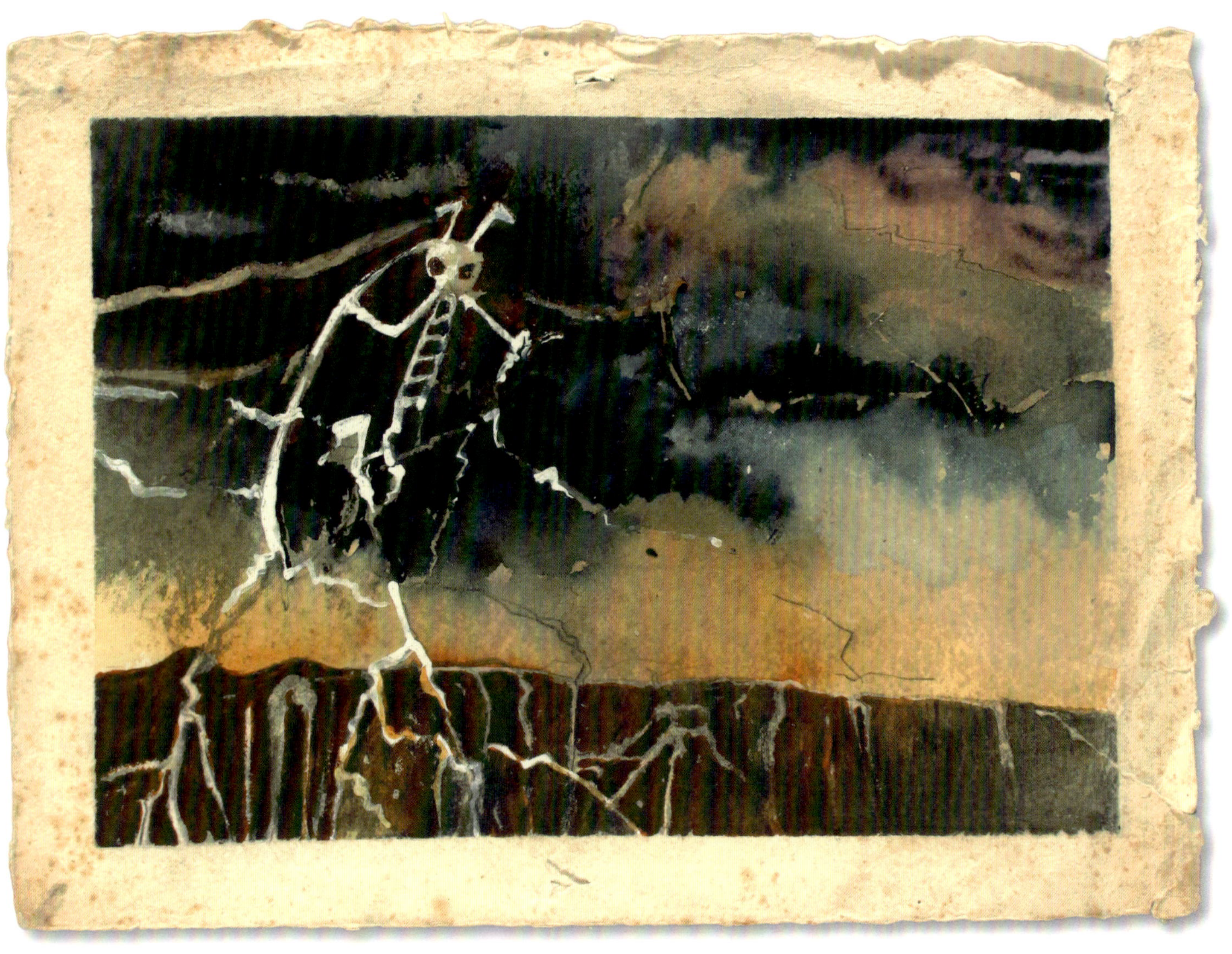

Lightning Man, 1993,
Oil and mixed media on paper, 9.5 x 13 inches.
Collection of the artist.

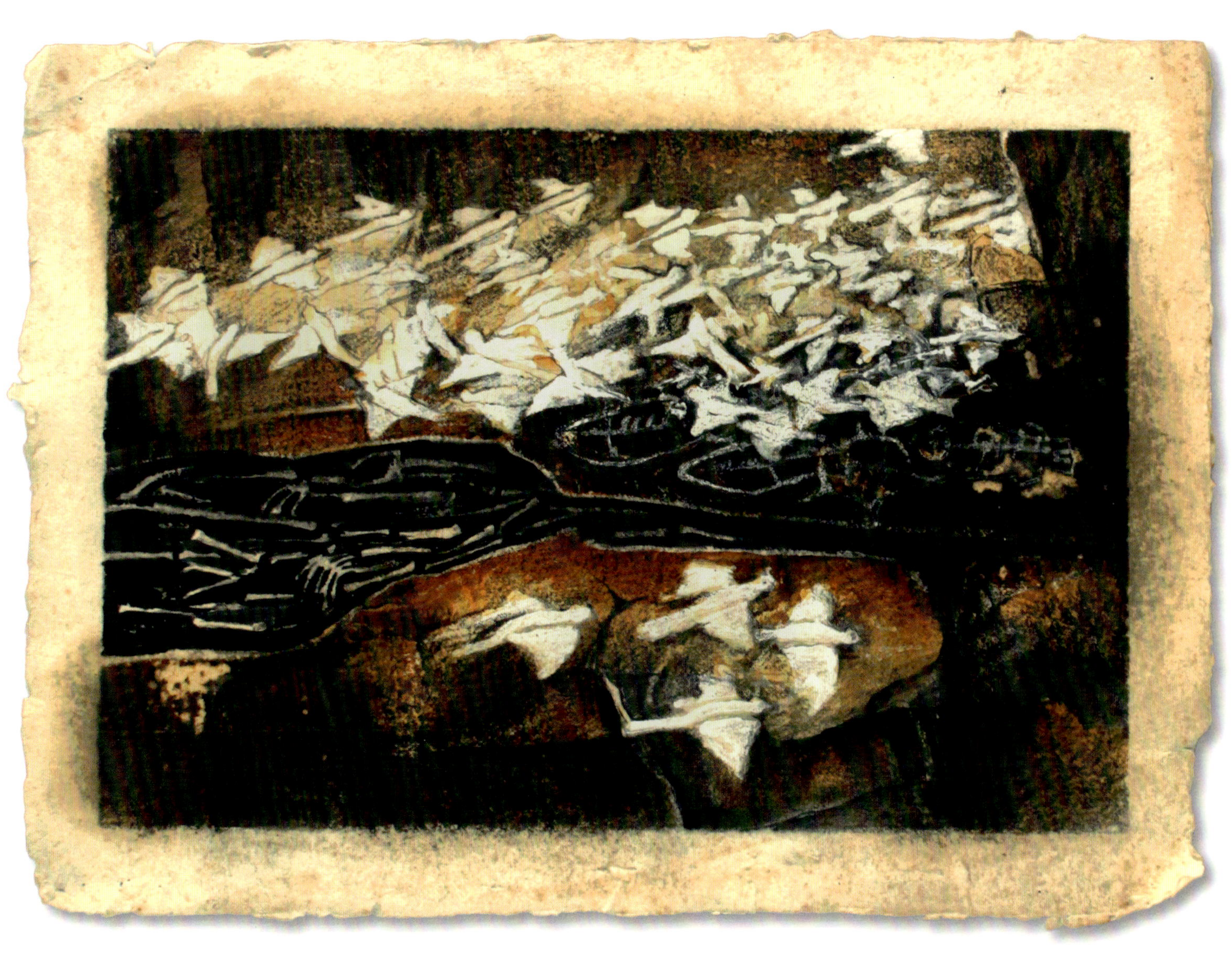

Cockatiels, 1993,
Oil and mixed media on paper, 9.5 x 13 inches.
Collection of the artist.

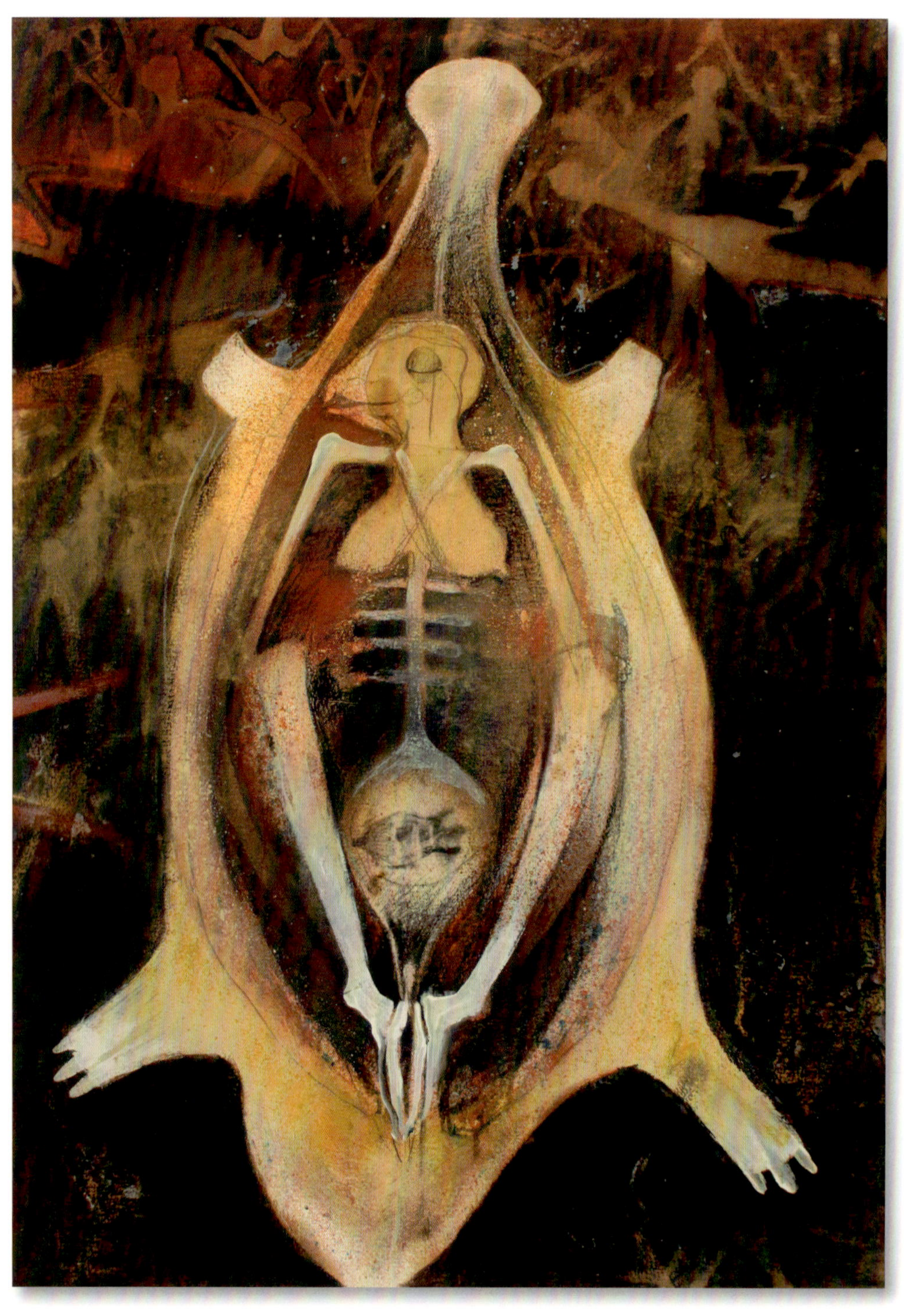

Turtle Dreaming, 1993,
Oil and mixed media on paper, 28 x 21 inches.
Collection of the artist.

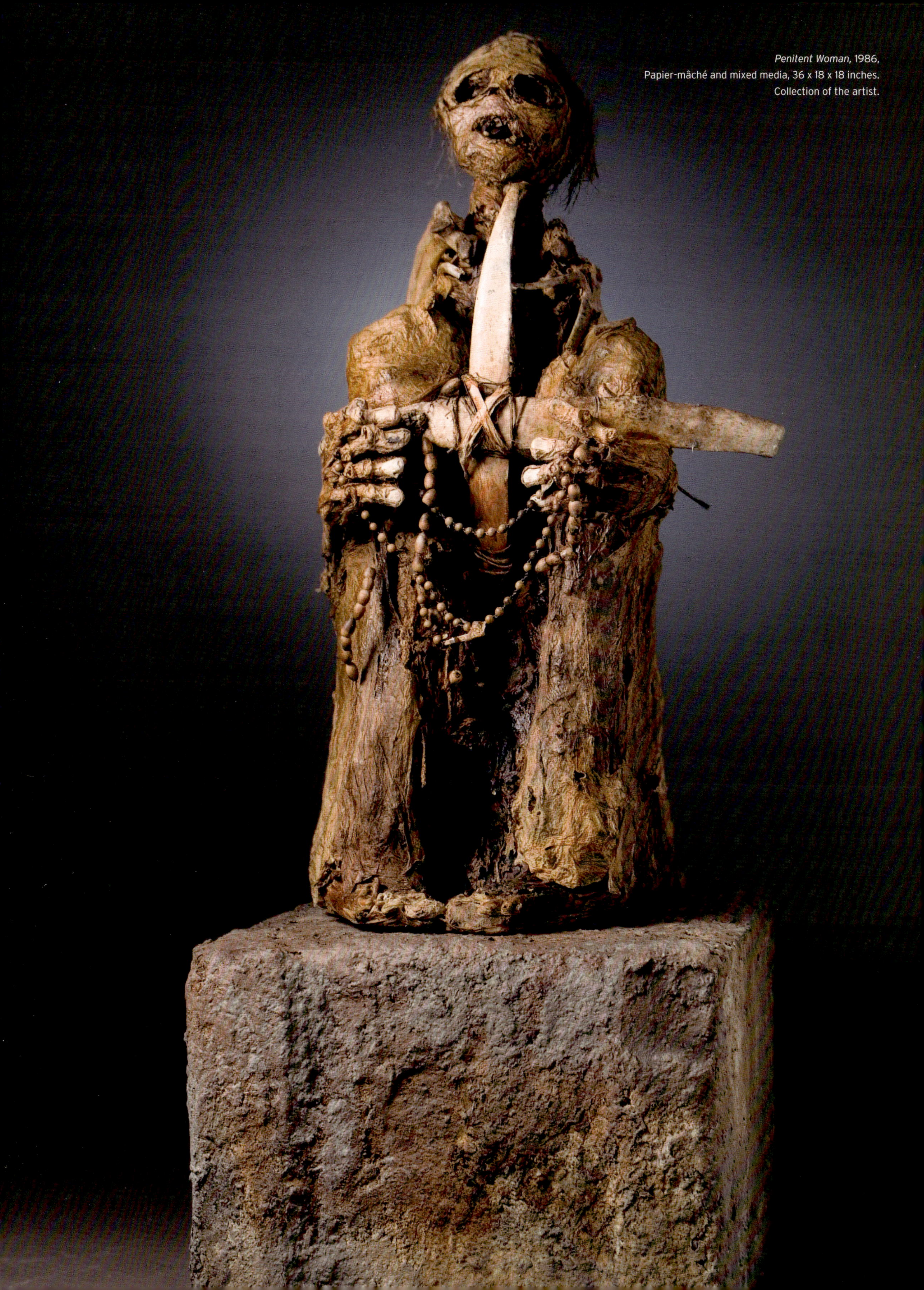

Penitent Woman, 1986,
Papier-mâché and mixed media, 36 x 18 x 18 inches.
Collection of the artist.

Sebastian's Shield, 2000.
Oil, graphite, tin and photo collage, 31 x 13 x 2 inches.
Collection of Nancy Allen.

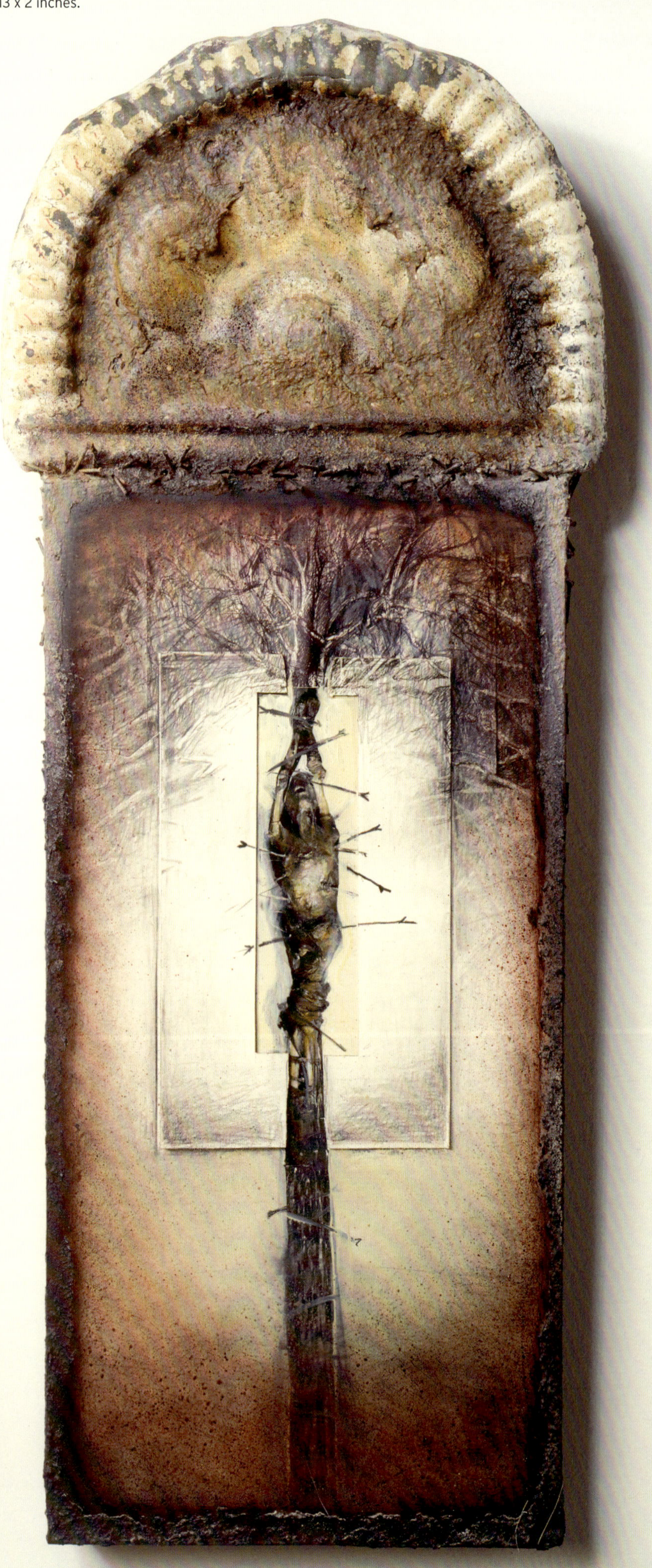

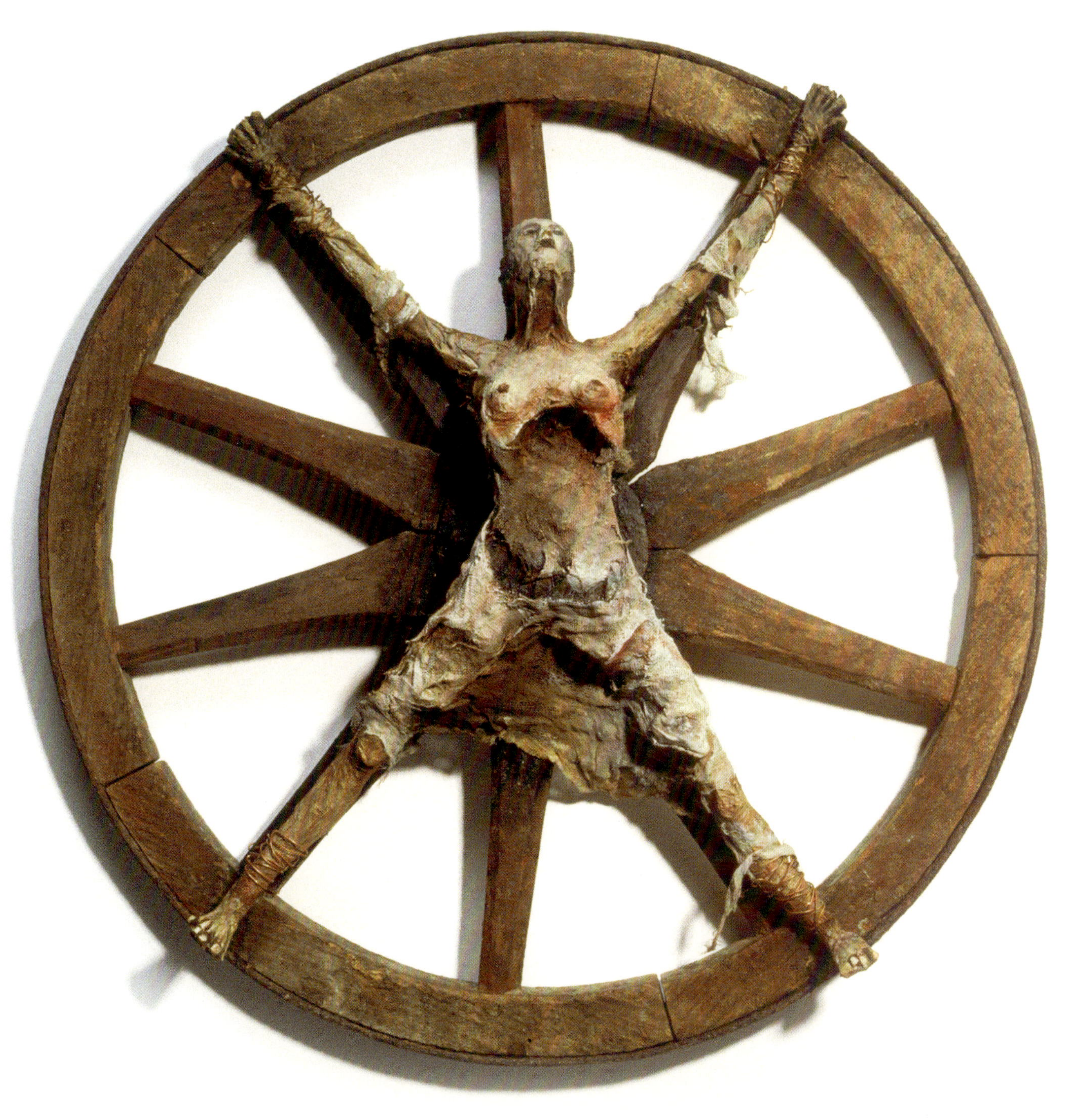

Catherine's Wheel, 1996,
Papier-mâché, wood, iron, fabric and paint, 14 x 14 x 2 inches.
The Menil Collection.

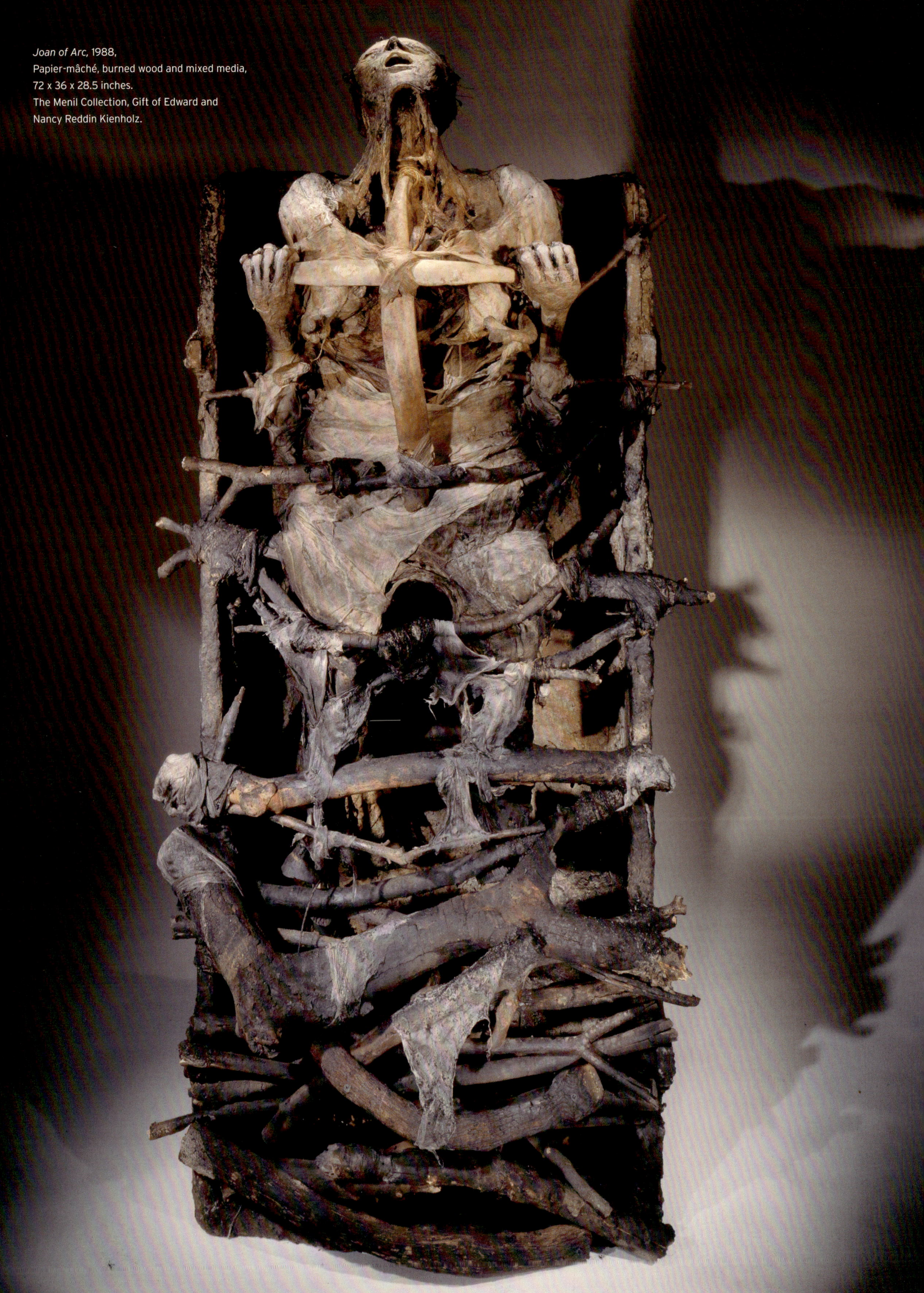

Joan of Arc, 1988,
Papier-mâché, burned wood and mixed media,
72 x 36 x 28.5 inches.
The Menil Collection, Gift of Edward and
Nancy Reddin Kienholz.

Of Kopriva's works from The Menil Collection, *Joan of Arc* reflects her admiration for the 17-year-old girl burned at the stake, whom the Church waited five hundred years to declare a saint. A gift of the Kienholzes, *Joan of Arc* was a work Dominique de Menil greatly admired. She also acquired *Catherine's Wheel*, thus personally placing Kopriva in the select group of Texas artists found in the museum's collection. Clearly both the Christian and spiritual qualities in Sharon Kopriva's art touched Dominique de Menil.

– Walter Hopps

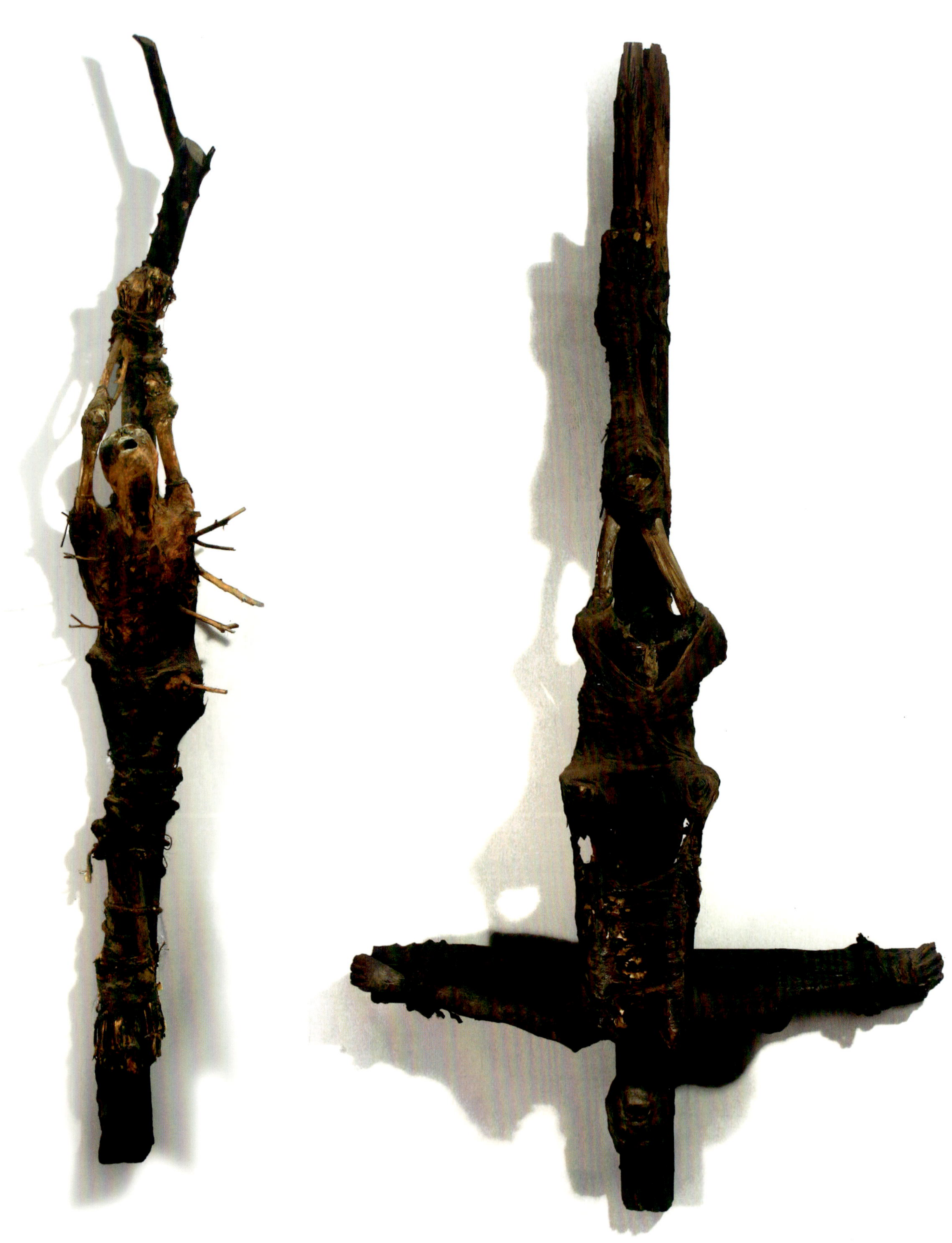

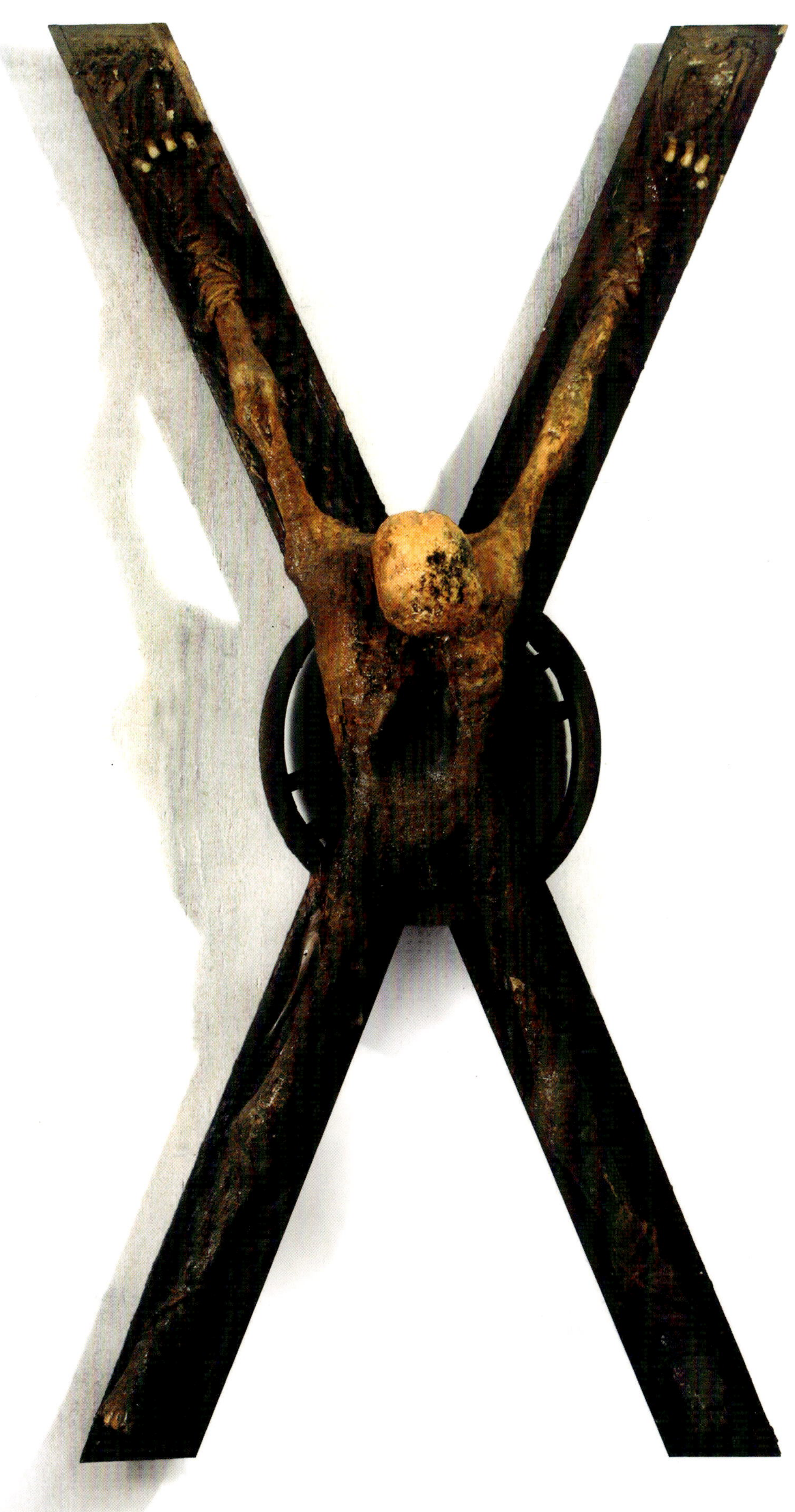

Opposite page left:
Sebastion, 1989,
Papier-mâché and mixed media,
94 x 20 x 13 inches.
Collection of Cindy and
Andrew Lubetkin.

Opposite page right:
Peter, 1989,
Papier-mâché and mixed media,
96 x 53 x 18 inches.
Collection of the artist.

Andrew, 2000,
Papier-mâché and mixed media,
94 x 47 x 21 inches.
Collection of Michele and Joe Carte.

Boats were an integral part of my early life. My father sold fishing boats and repaired outboard motors. I began drawing boats from early on. In the early '80s as I turned to three-dimensional works, the boat and vessel shape became a recurring theme. *The Pair* was the first vessel I made, one housing a mummified couple and their effects. From there, I developed a 12-foot-long canoe, *Rite of Passage*, complete with three passengers and a blind guide to lead them into a new existence. Boats represent transition and transformation, physical, psychological and spiritual. *Resurrection* was about recovery and healing from Hurricane Katrina, supplicating the Virgin Mary's assistance.

Boats hold, secure and protect their travelers from imminent harm, taking them to many forms of higher ground.

– Sharon Kopriva

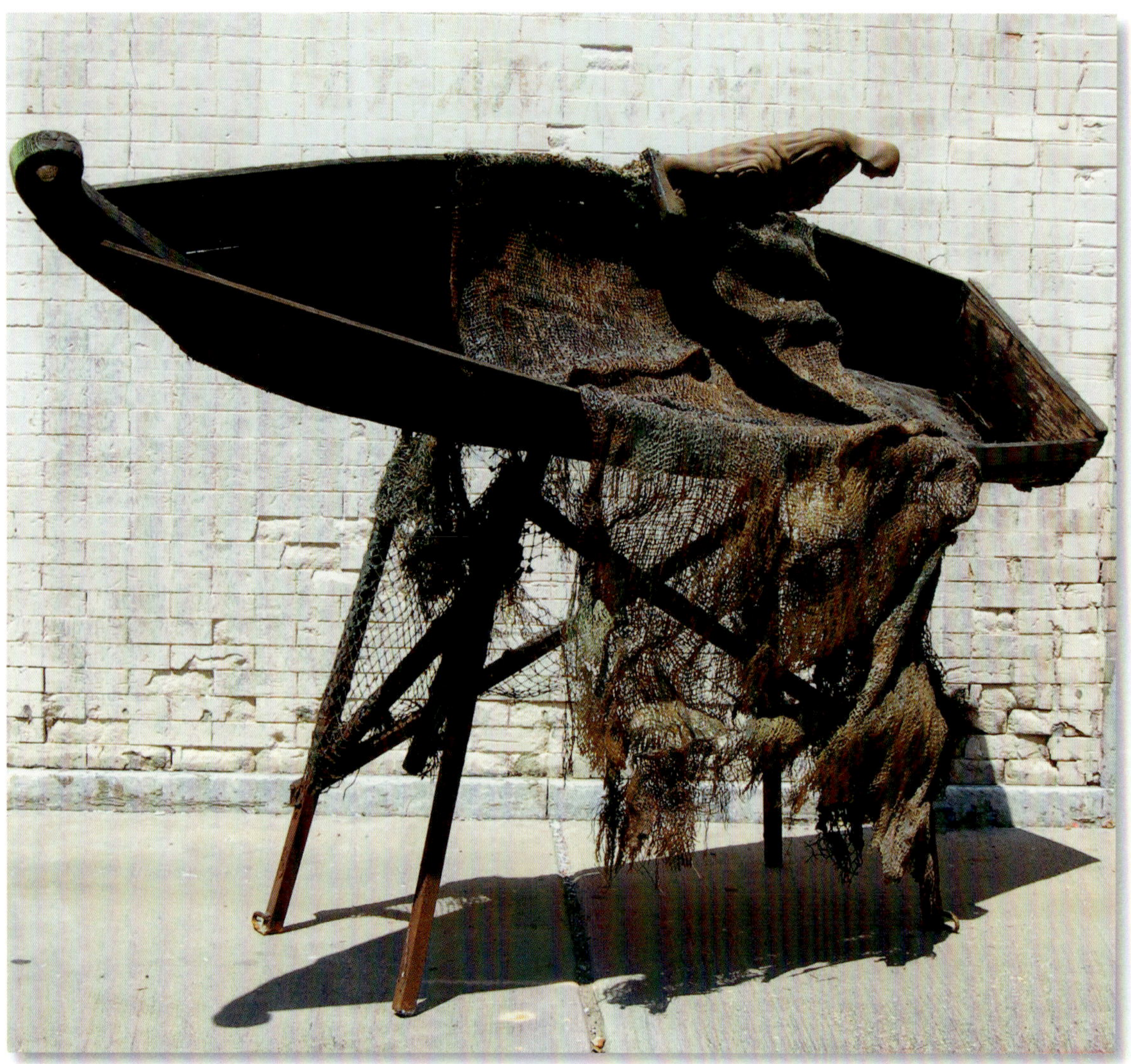

Resurrection, 2008,
Wood, fabric and found objects,
61 x 99 x 33 inches.
Collection of the Ogden Museum of
Southern Art, New Orleans.

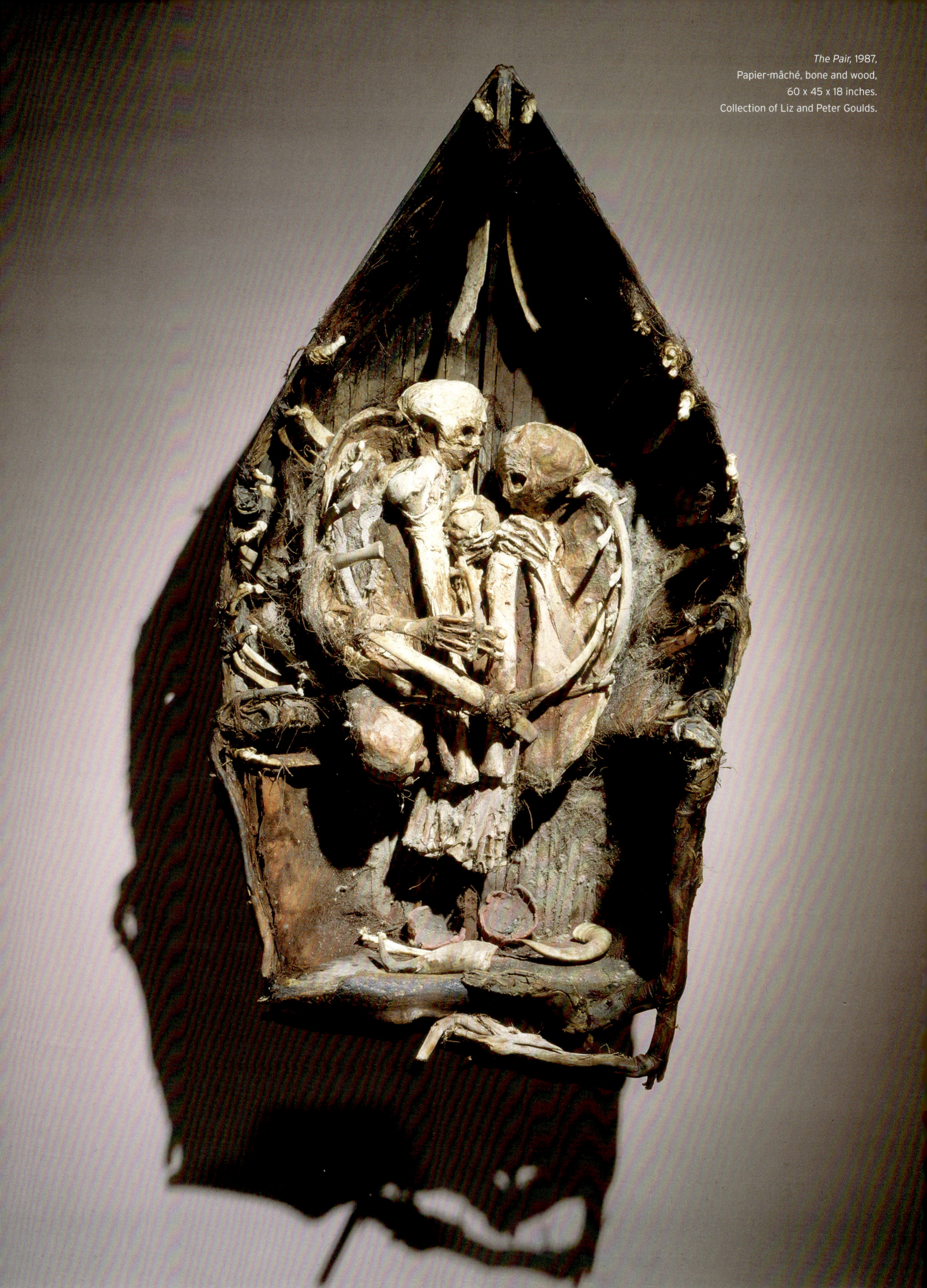

The Pair, 1987,
Papier-mâché, bone and wood,
60 x 45 x 18 inches.
Collection of Liz and Peter Goulds.

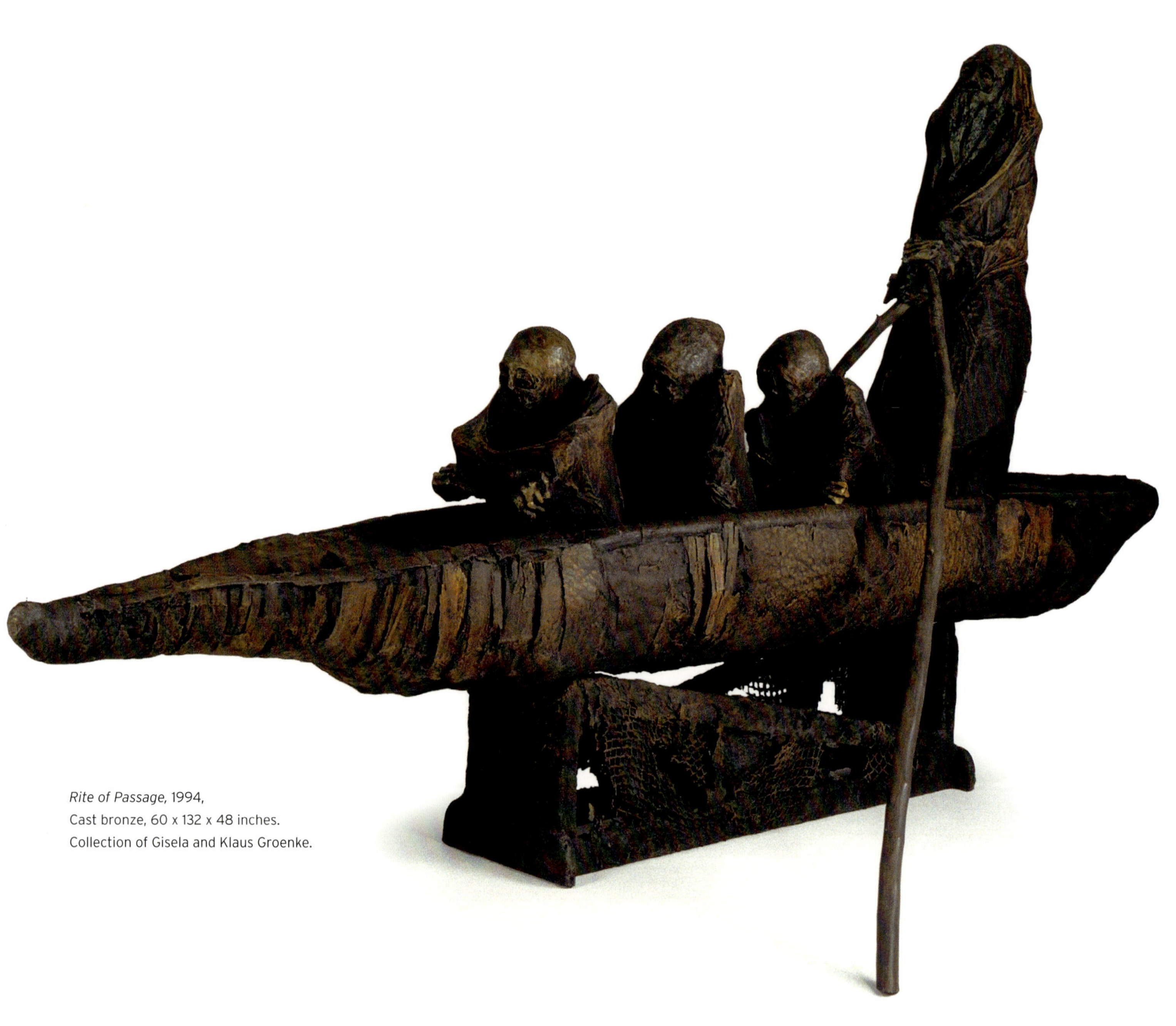

Rite of Passage, 1994,
Cast bronze, 60 x 132 x 48 inches.
Collection of Gisela and Klaus Groenke.

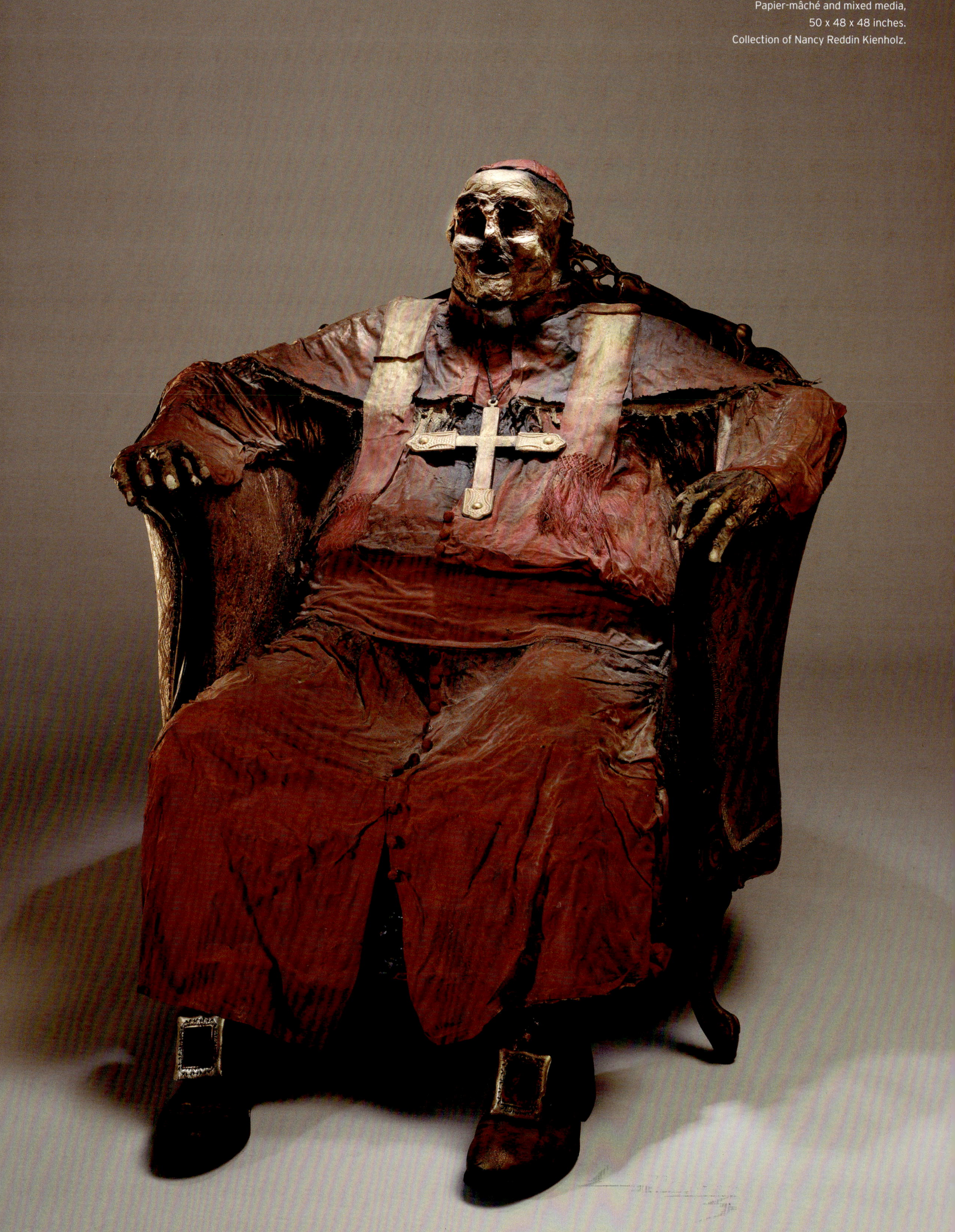

The Cardinal, 1994,
Papier-mâché and mixed media,
50 x 48 x 48 inches.
Collection of Nancy Reddin Kienholz.

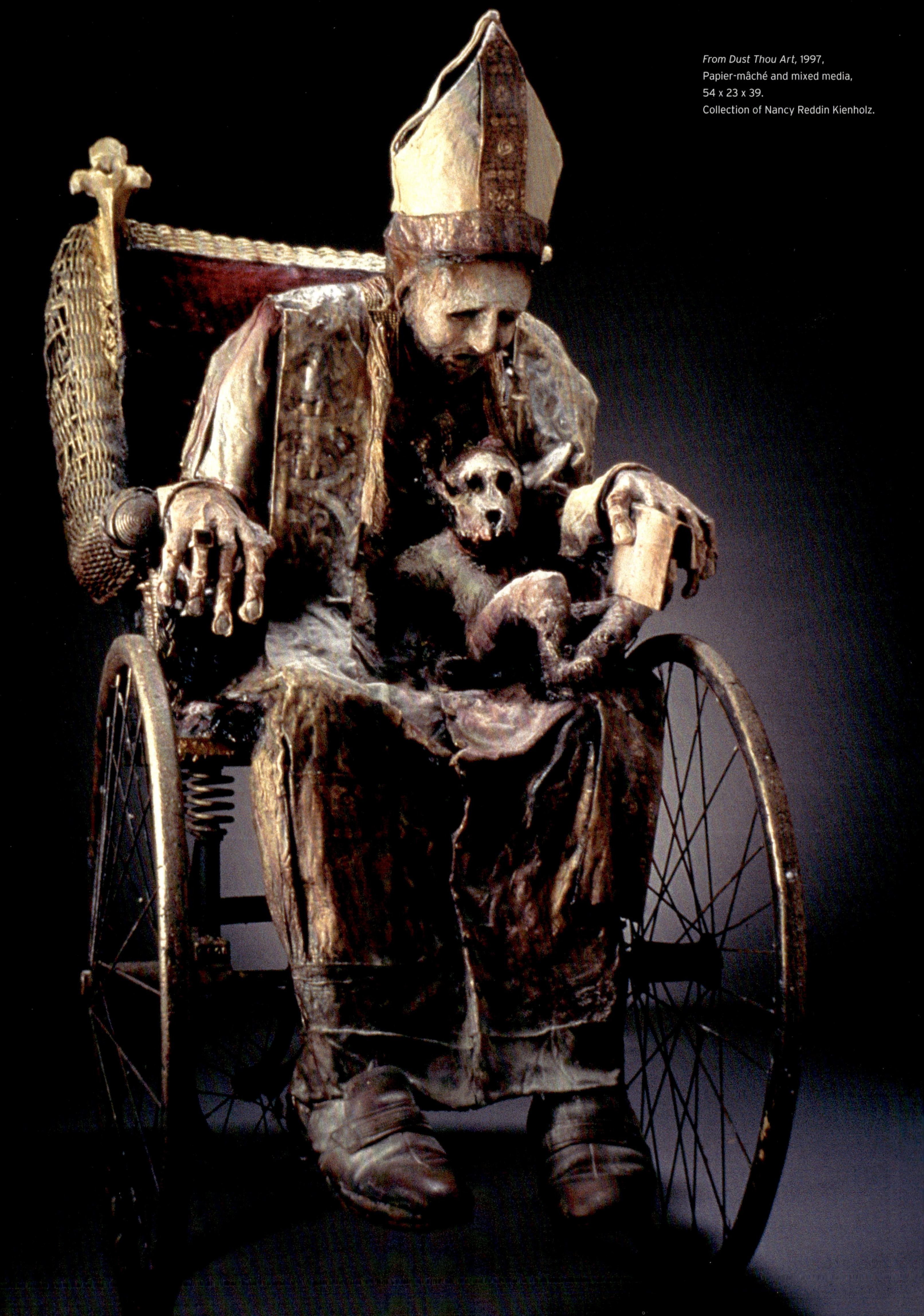

From Dust Thou Art, 1997,
Papier-mâché and mixed media,
54 x 23 x 39.
Collection of Nancy Reddin Kienholz.

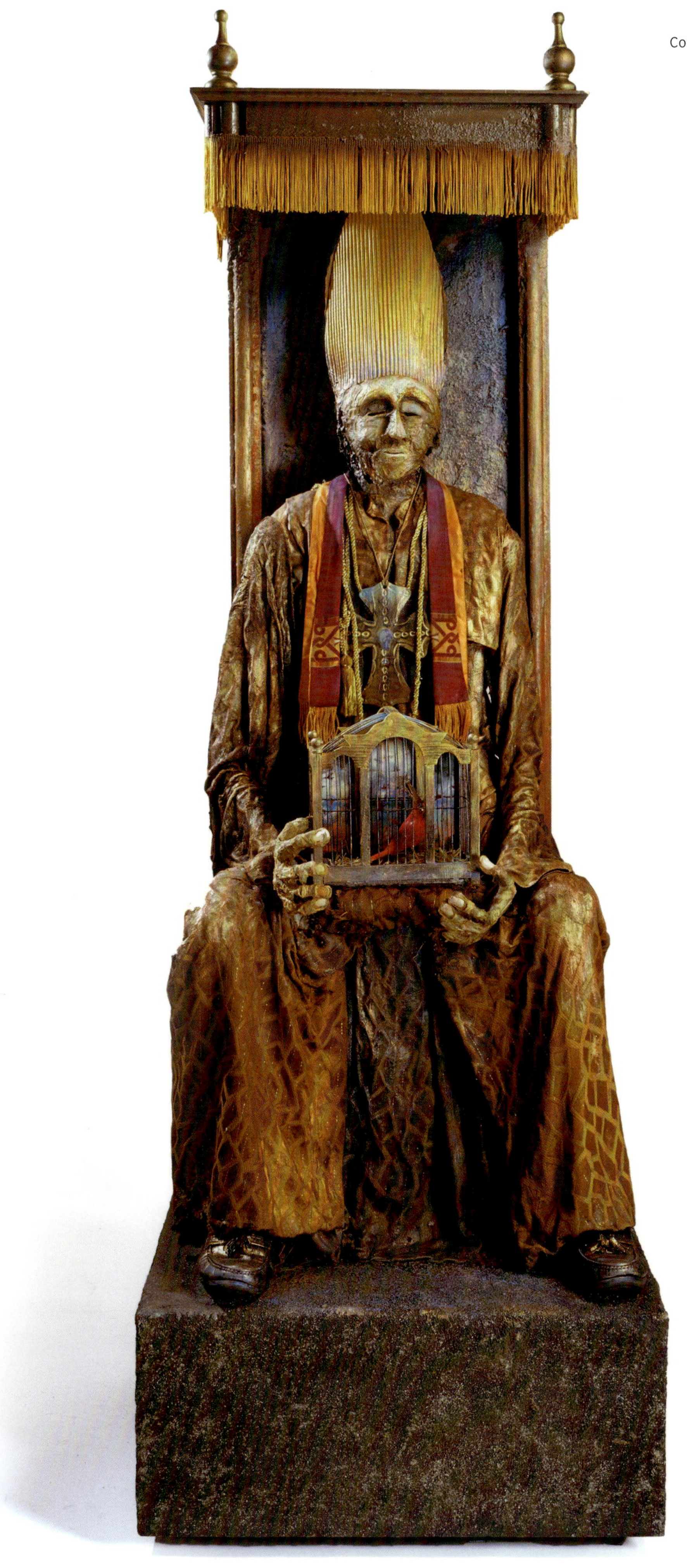

Bird in Hand, 2001,
Mixed media, 79 x 27 x 27 inches.
Collection of Bill Bowman and Adriene Parks.

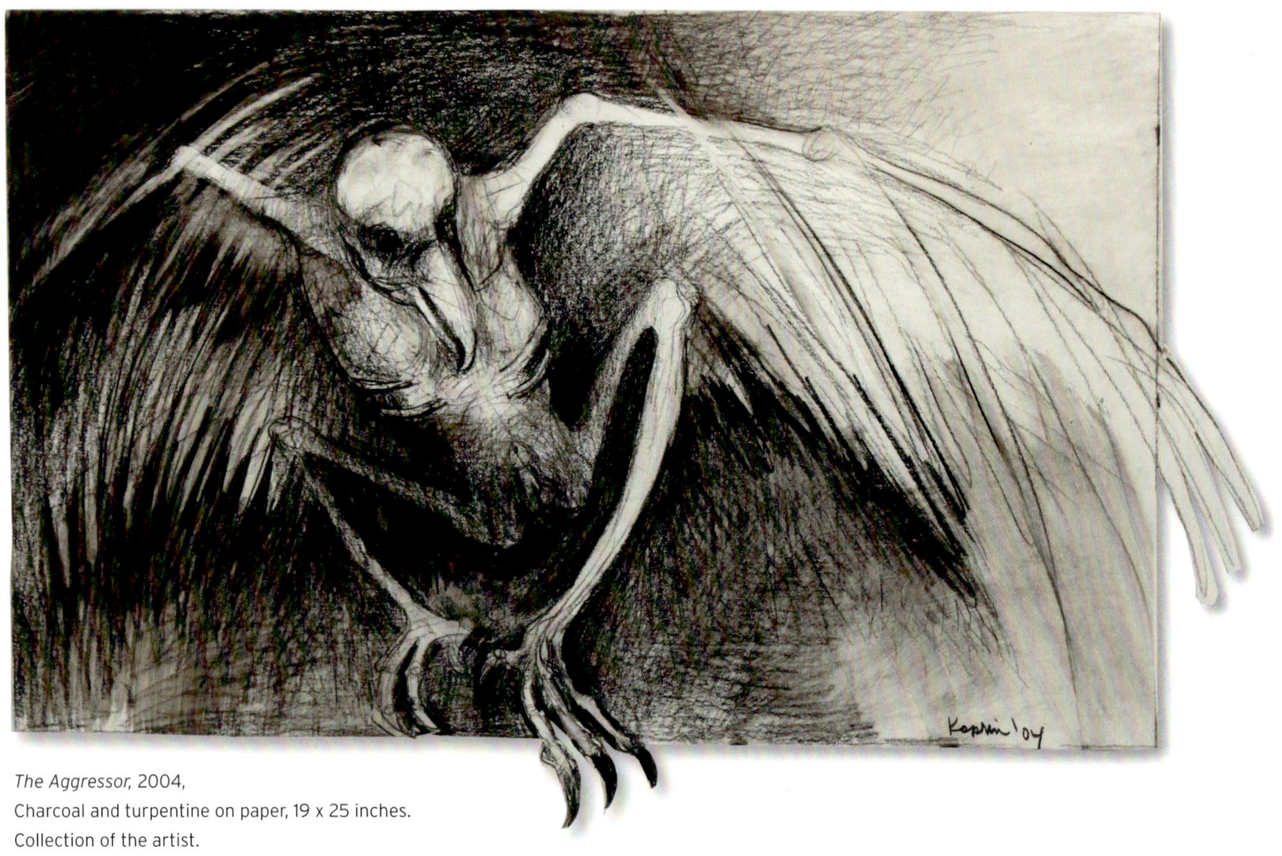

The Aggressor, 2004,
Charcoal and turpentine on paper, 19 x 25 inches.
Collection of the artist.

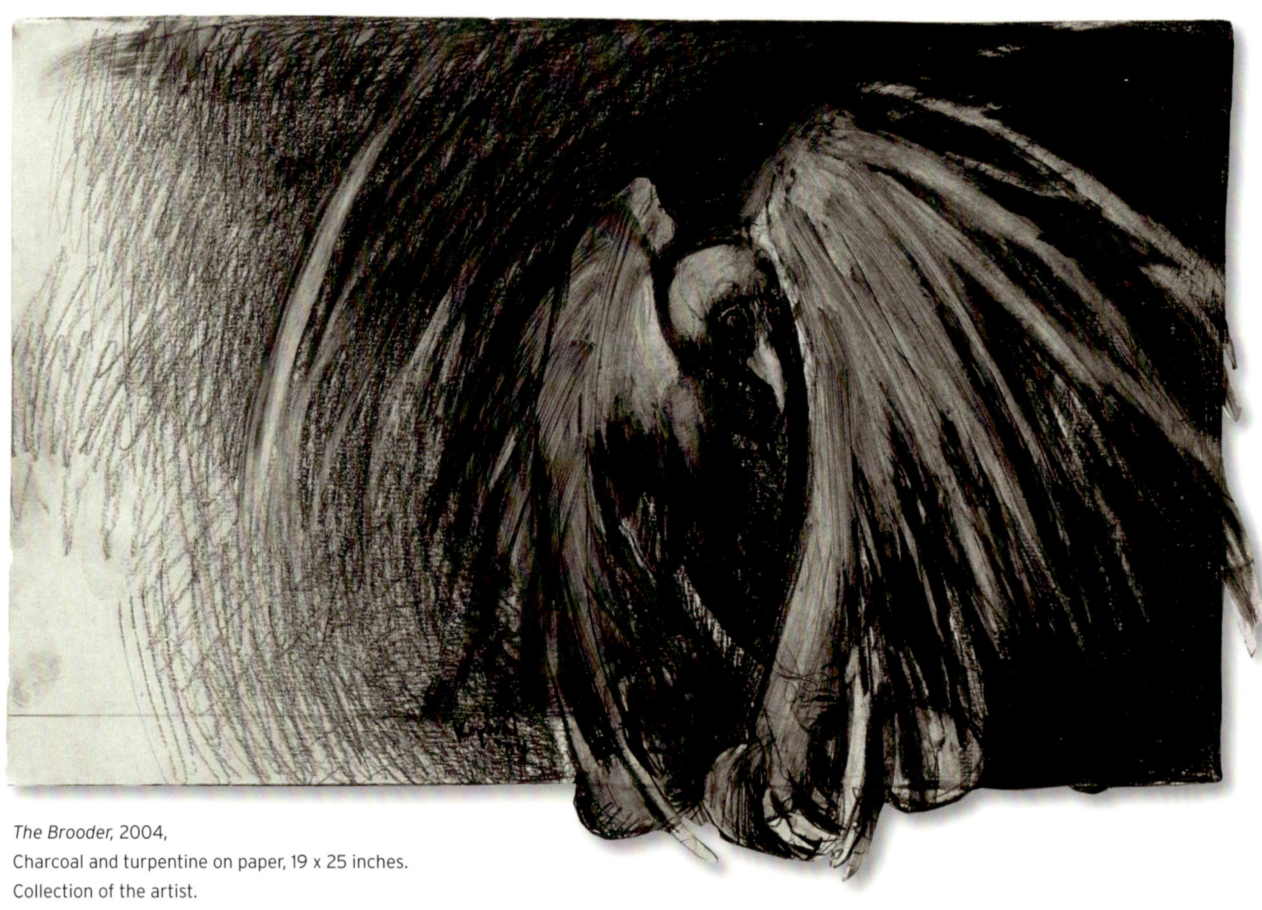

The Brooder, 2004,
Charcoal and turpentine on paper, 19 x 25 inches.
Collection of the artist.

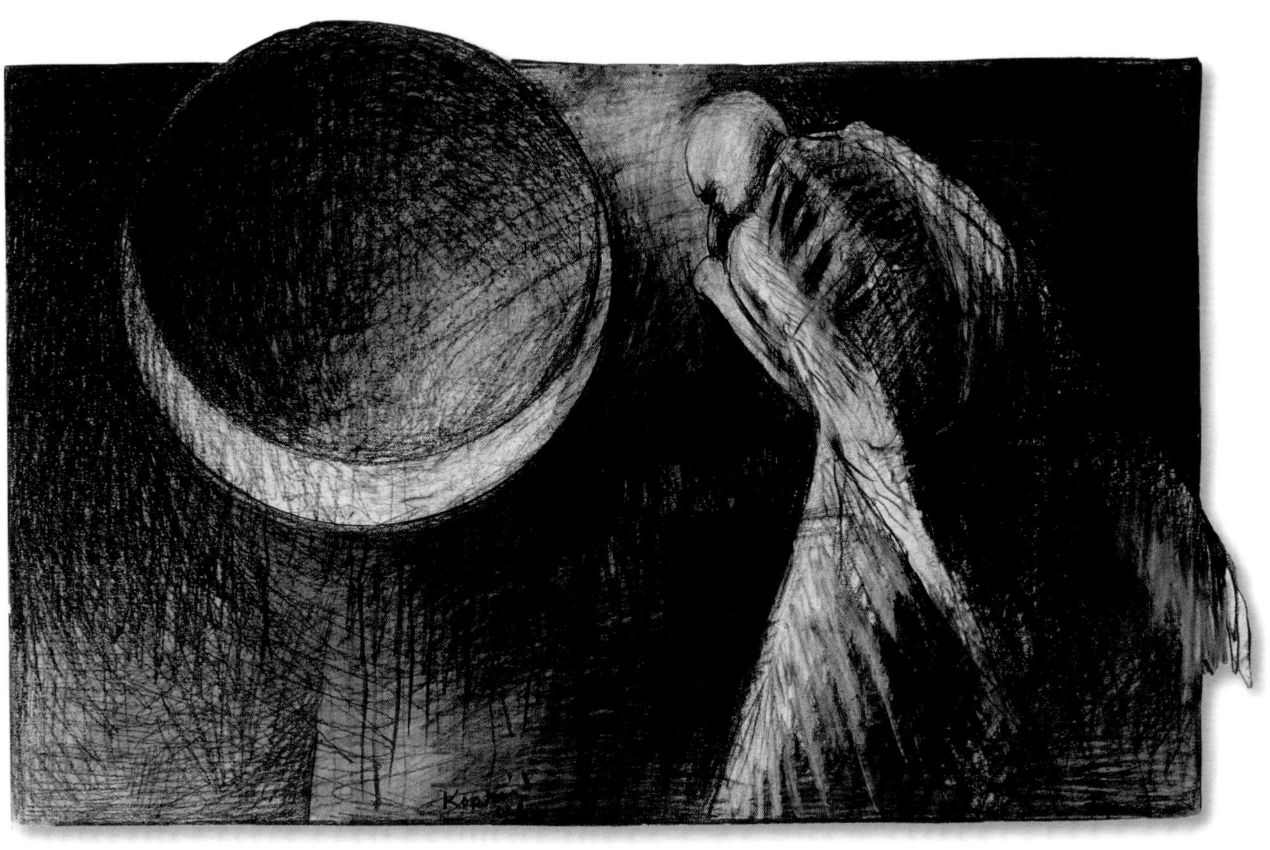

The Observer, 2004,
Charcoal and turpentine on paper, 19 x 25 inches.
Collection of the artist.

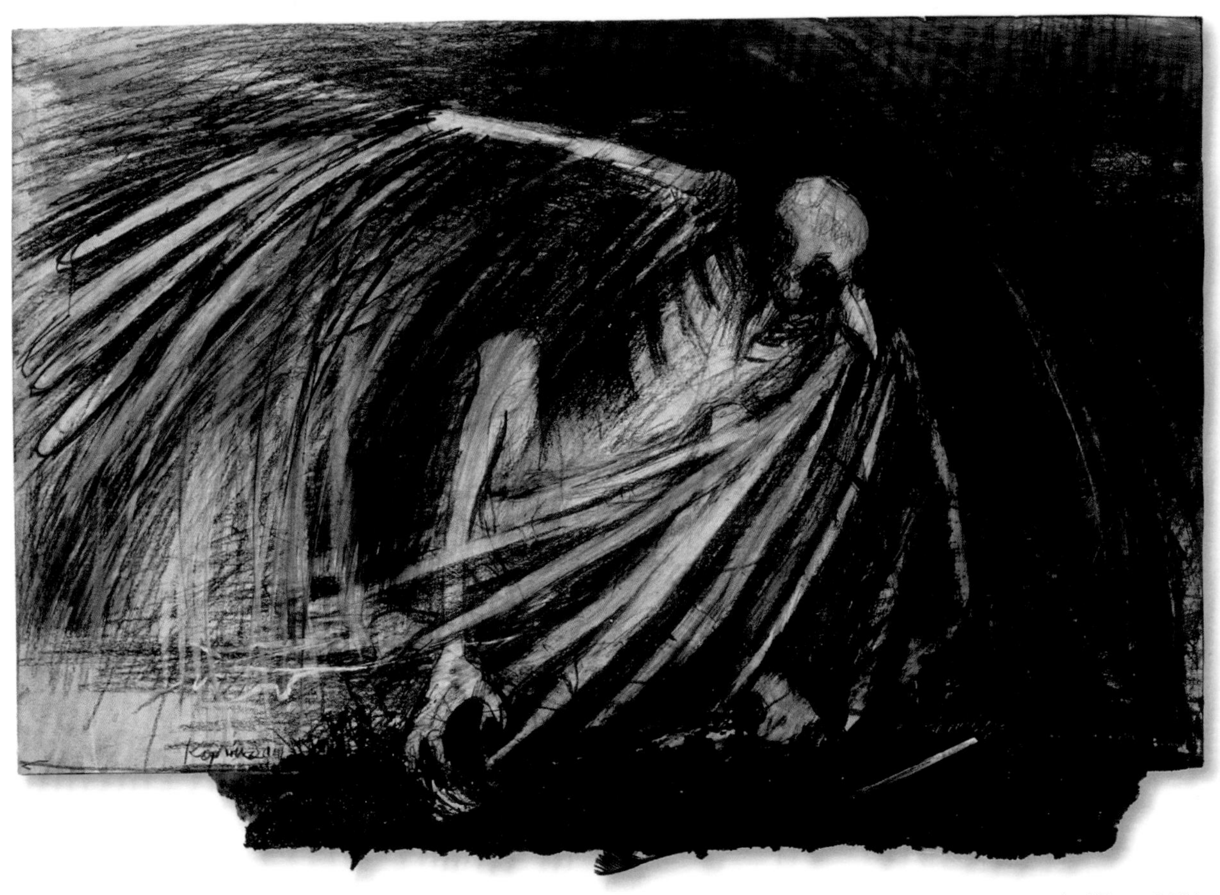

Last Tango, 2004,
Charcoal and turpentine on paper, 19 x 25 inches.
Collection of Michele and Joe Carte.

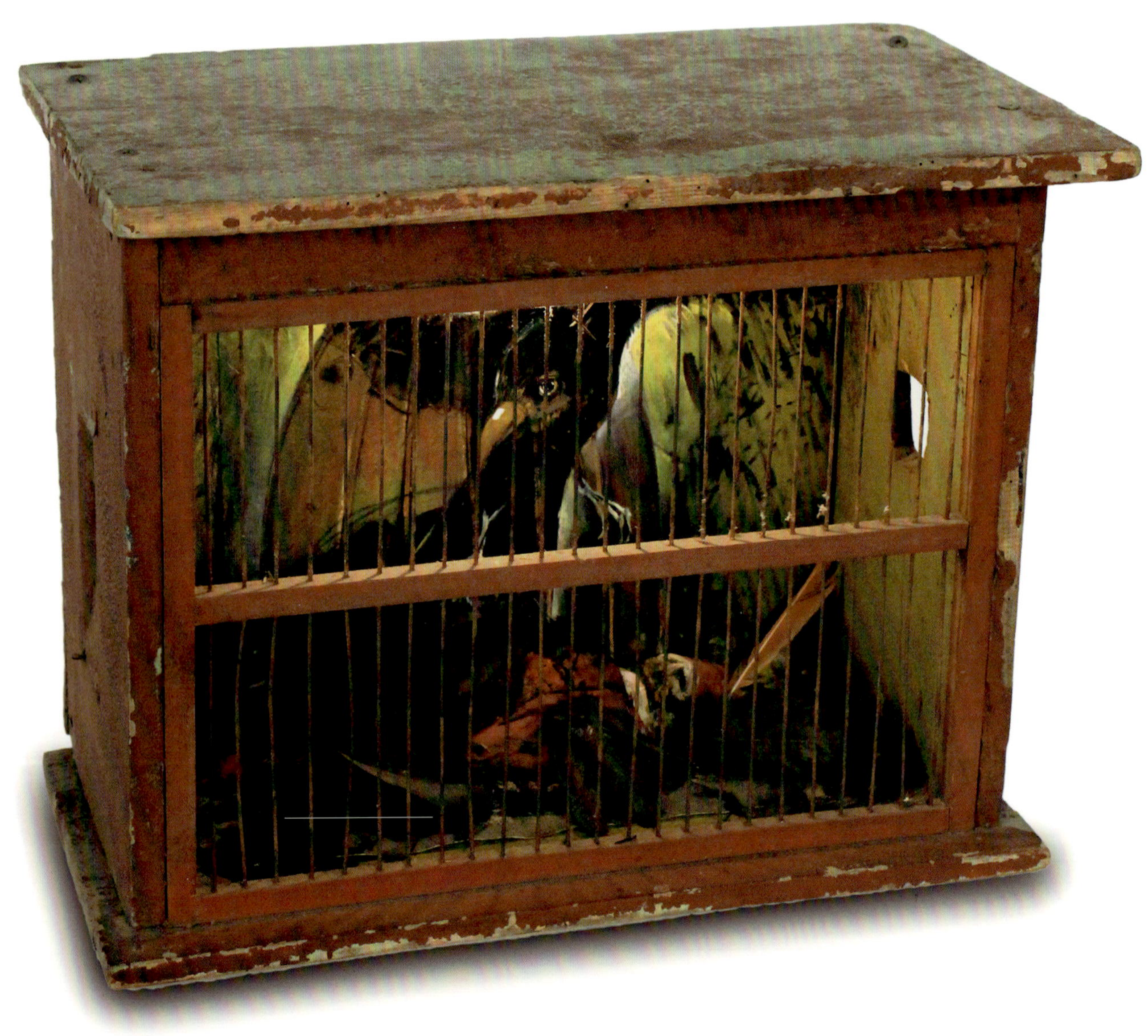

Cardinal Luciani's Nightmare, 2000,
Mixed media, 11 x 15 x 8 inches.
Collection of David Waller and Kirk Baxter.

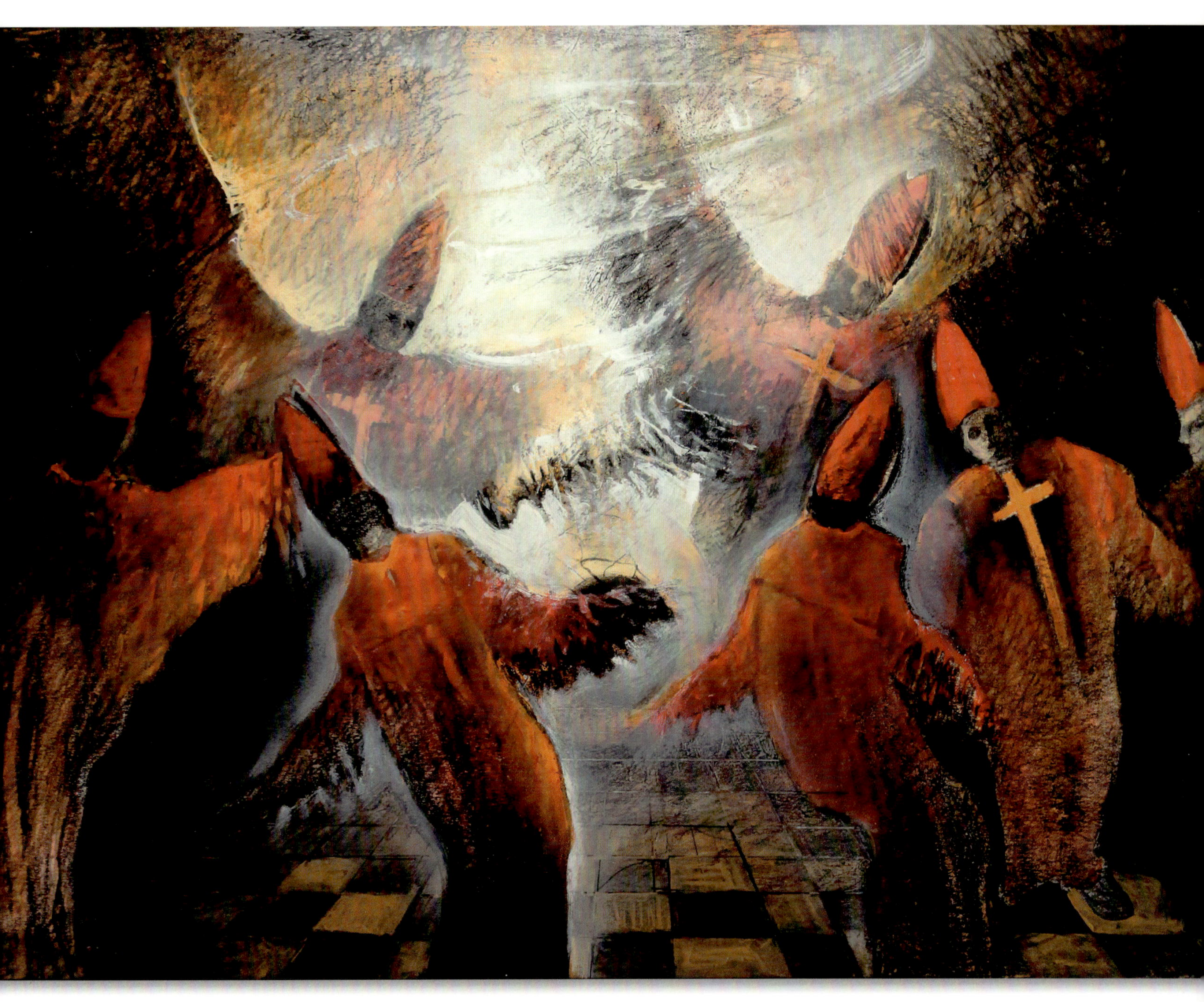

Red Dance / White Smoke, 1998,
Oil and mixed media on paper, 21 x 26 inches.
Collection of Renee Wallace.

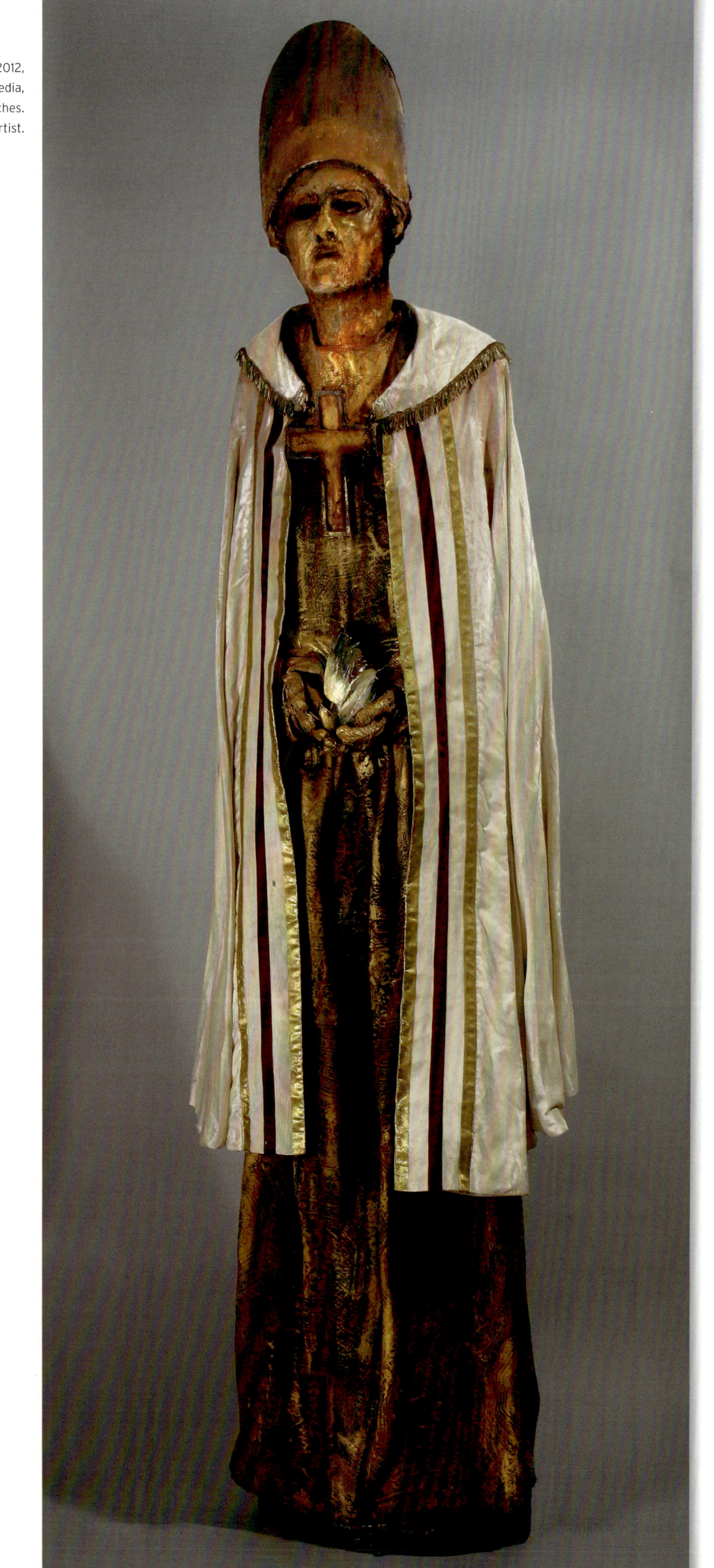

Basalt Bishop, 2012,
Papier-mâché and mixed media,
98 x 23 x 18 inches.
Collection of the artist.

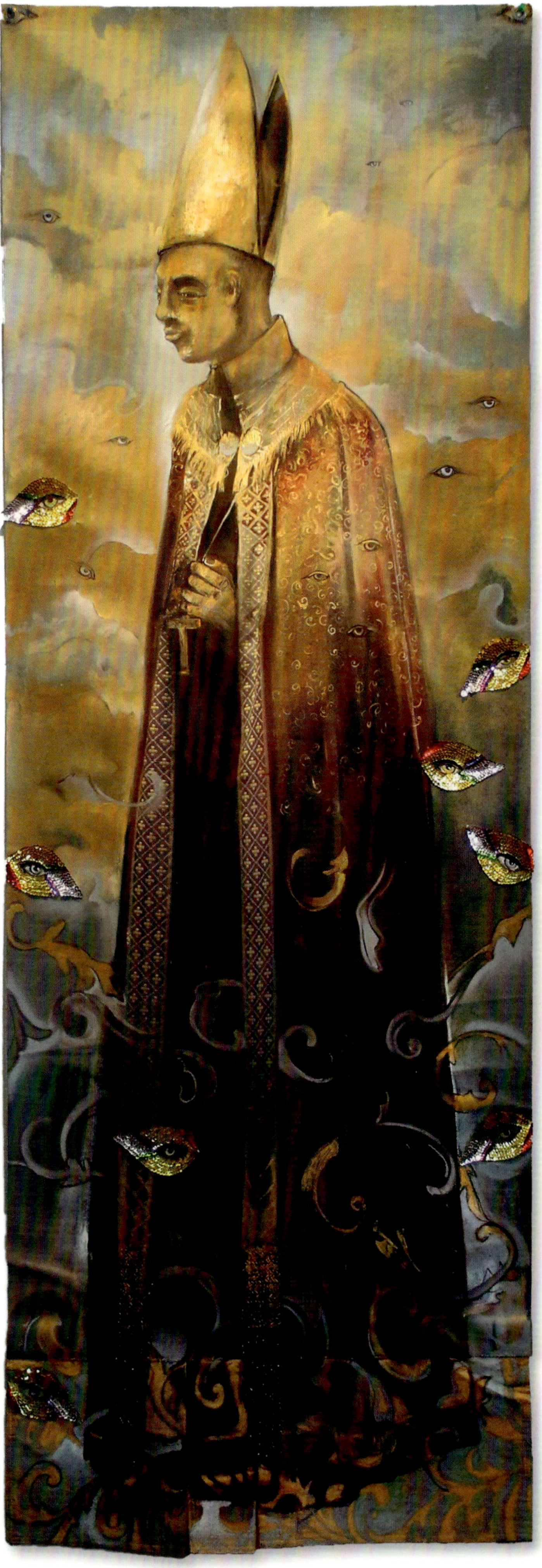

The Bishop's Conscience, 2011,
Oil and mixed media on photo canvas,
83 x 30 inches.
Collection of the artist.

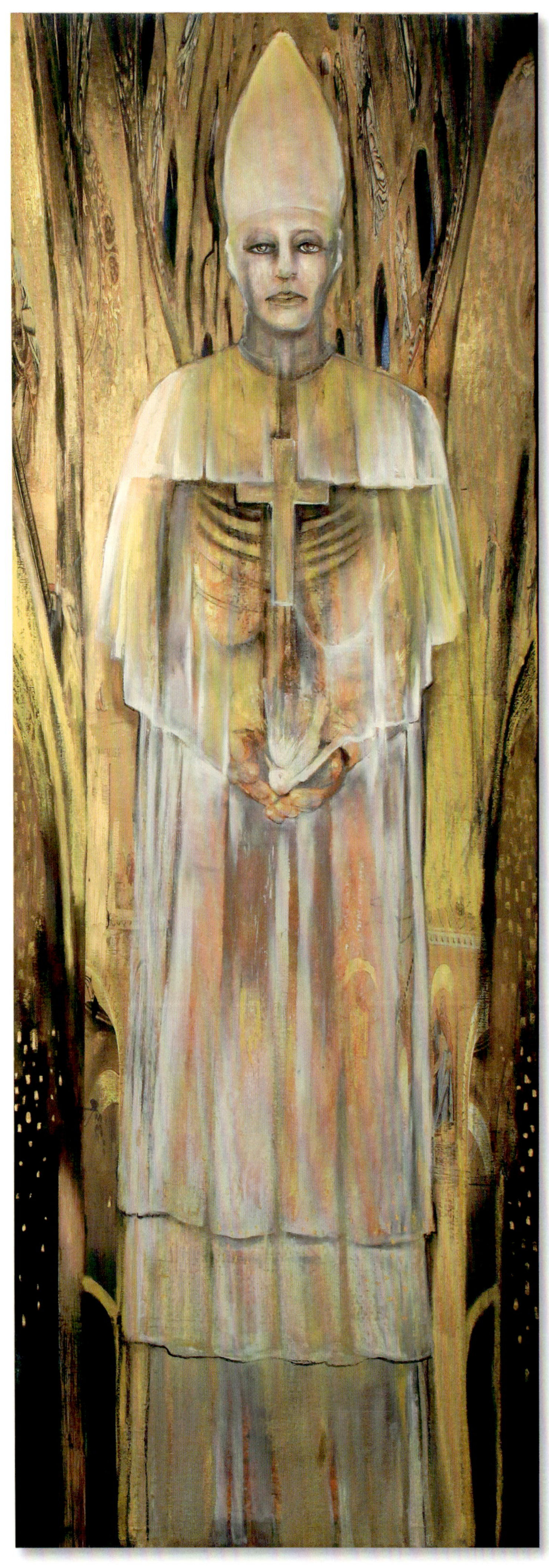

Phantom Bishop, 2011,
Oil and mixed media on photo canvas,
83 x 30 inches.
Collection of the artist.

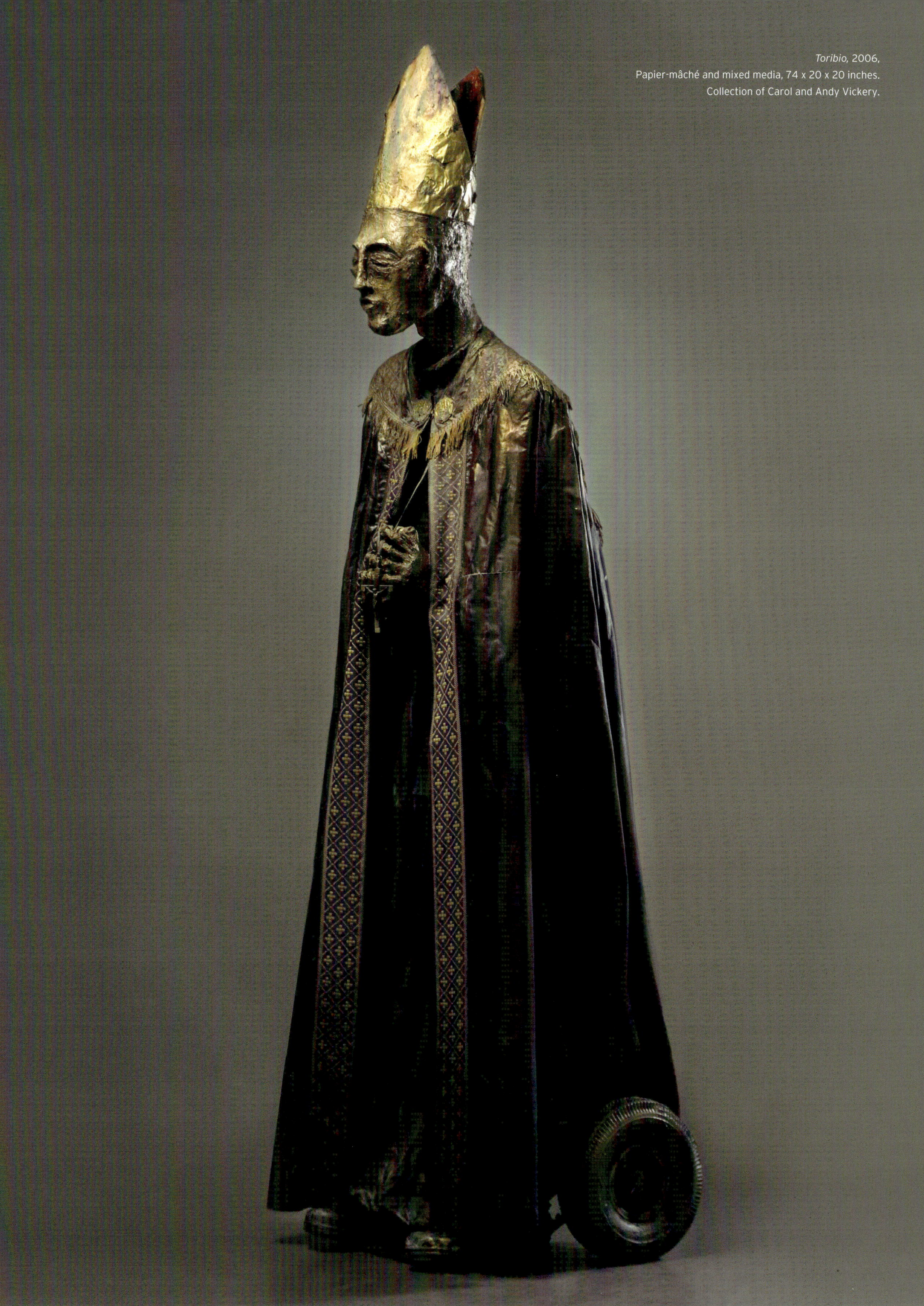

Toribio, 2006,
Papier-mâché and mixed media, 74 x 20 x 20 inches.
Collection of Carol and Andy Vickery.

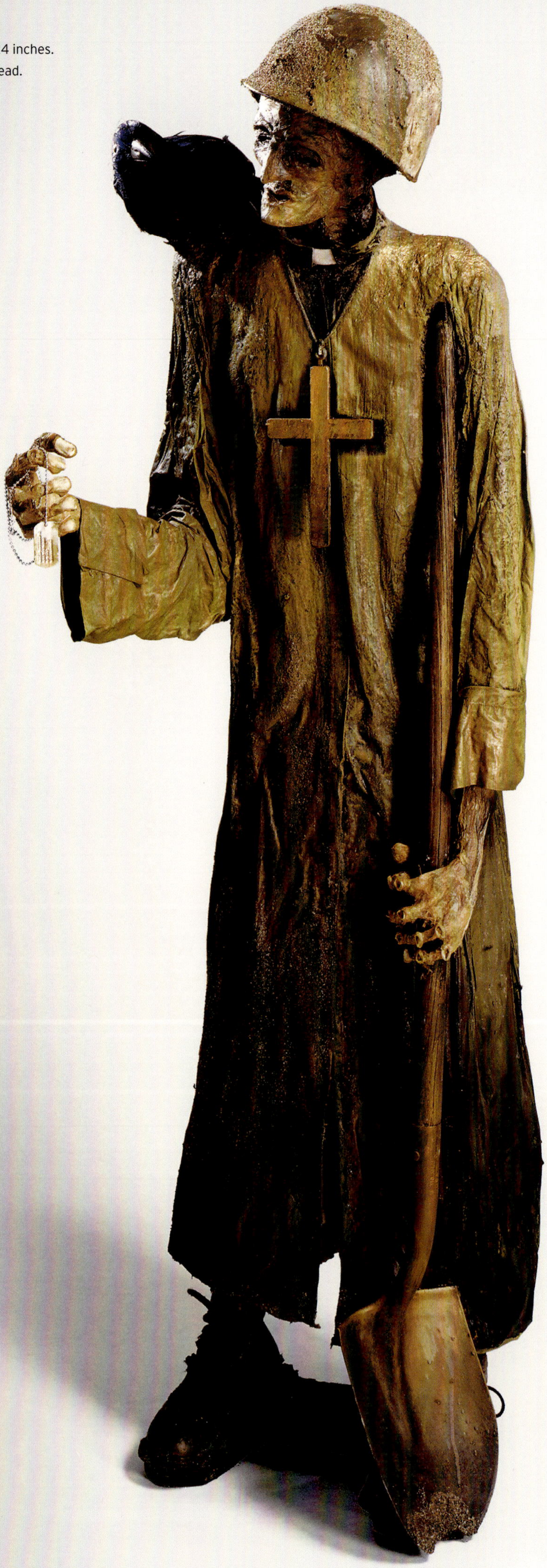

The Chaplain, 2001,
Papier-mâché and mixed media, 69 x 21 x 24 inches.
Collection of Laura Morris and Gary Bankhead.

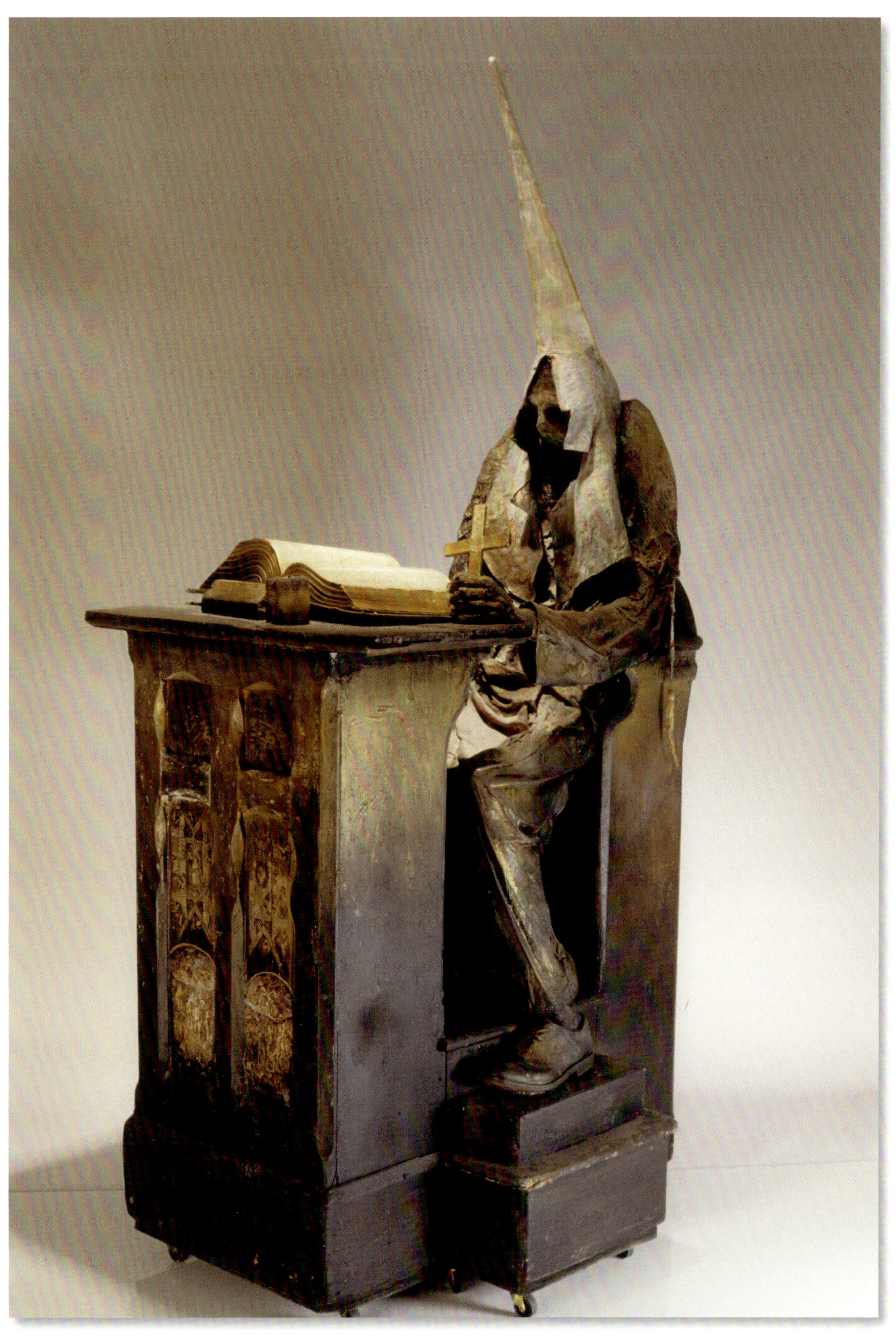

The Raven, 1998,
Papier-mâché and mixed media, 86 x 40 x 43 inches.
Private collection.

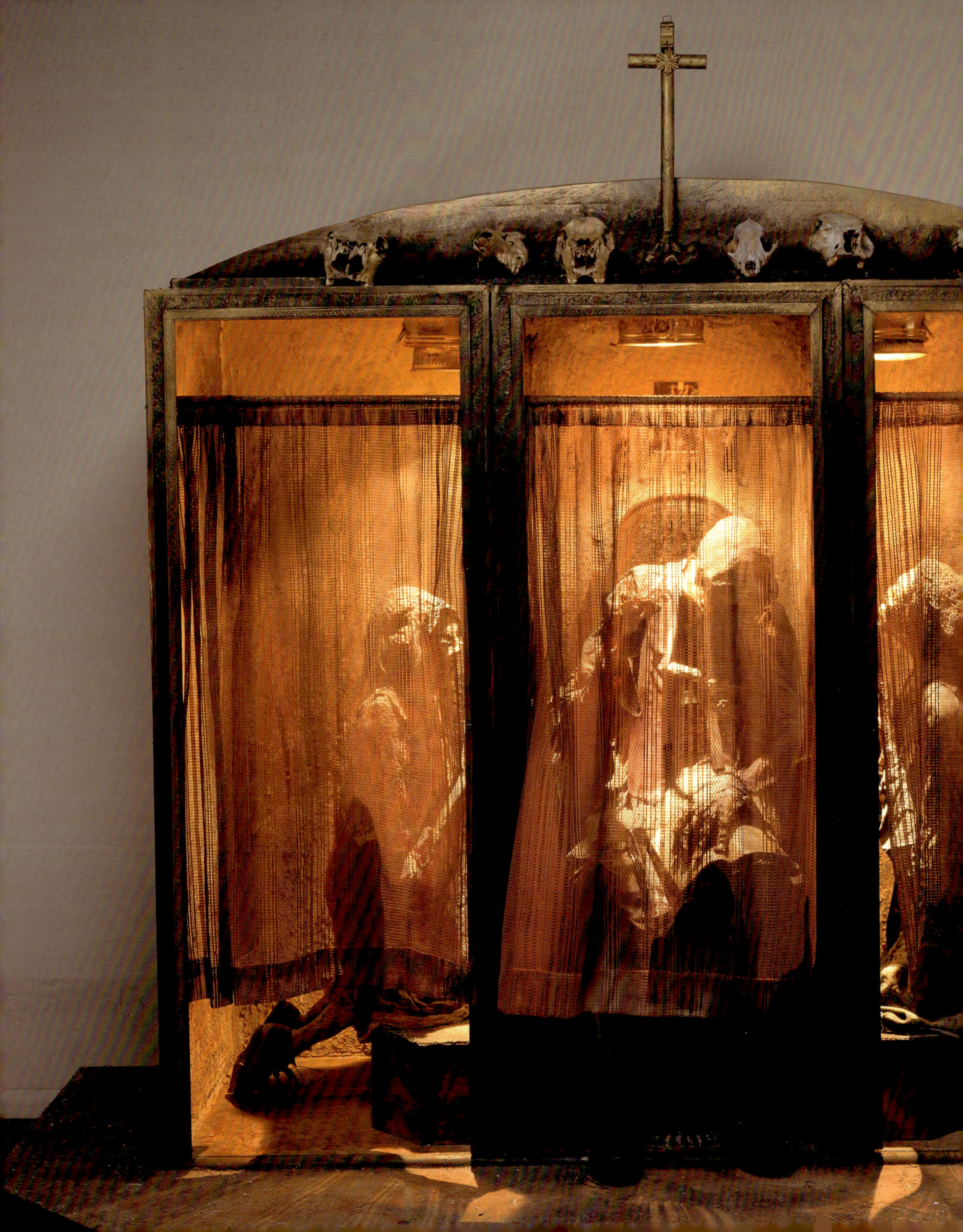

The Confessional, 1992,
Papier-mâché, wood and mixed media, 84 x 96 x 36 inches.
Collection of the artist.

The art of Sharon Kopriva provides a refreshing antidote to the preoccupations of many artists today. While issues of gender, race, ecology, pop culture, and even pure aesthetics are latent, her concerns are devoid of polemics. By assembling figures from animal bones and skeletons wrapped in thickly encrusted layers of linen and papier-mâché and presenting them in life-like settings with suitable furniture and symbolic attributes, she makes us think about life itself. More importantly, she forces us to consider how we deal with the inevitability of death. Yet she does so with a gentleness and sensitivity that leaves us reassured about the goodness of humanity. Her cardinals gesticulate in mock seriousness, as if they were real people acting a part. Her nuns play the piano or engage in animated conversation, as if they enjoyed life. There is nothing sad or macabre about the rituals her figures perform, and no effort to disguise figures as real people.

– Ted Pillsbury

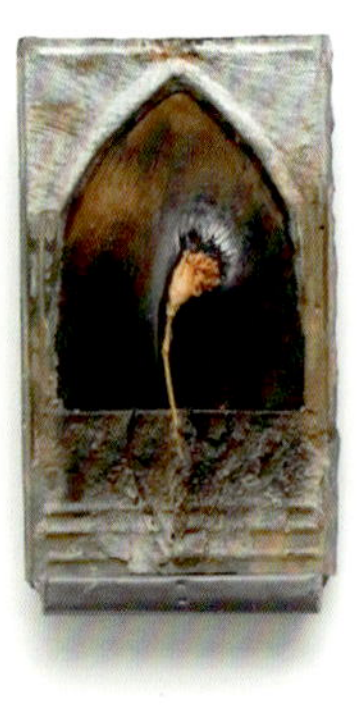 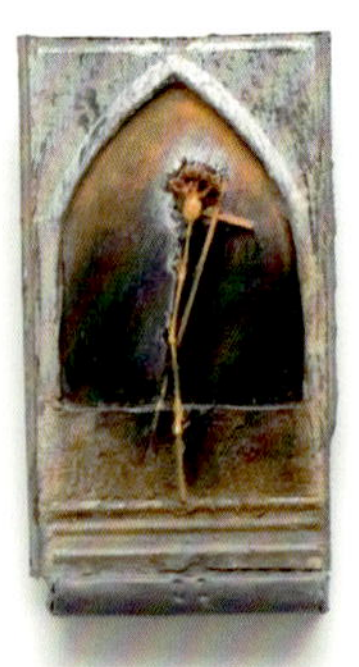 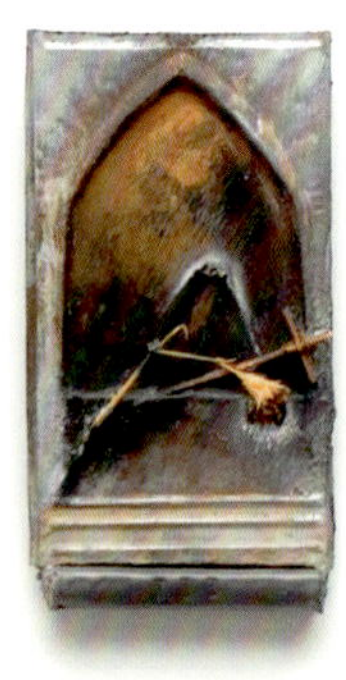 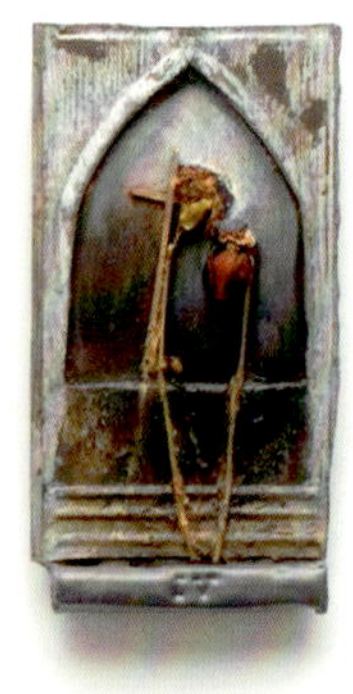 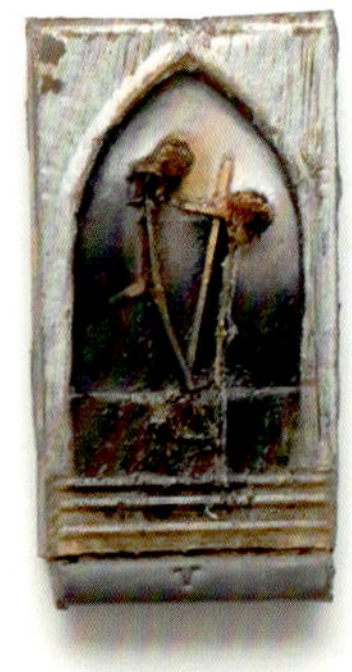 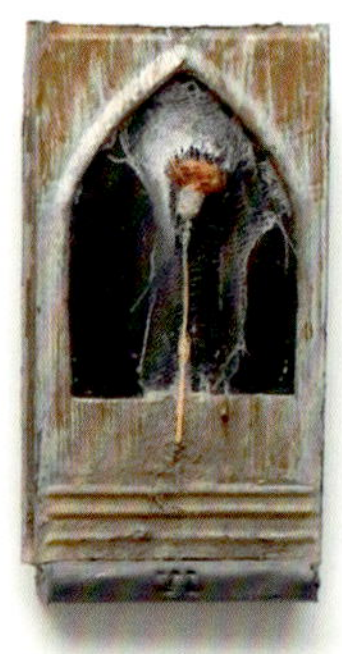 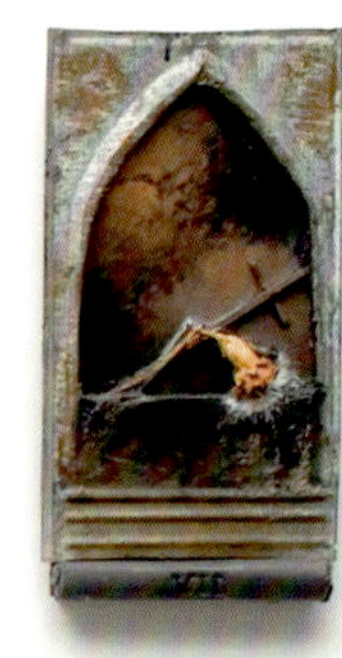

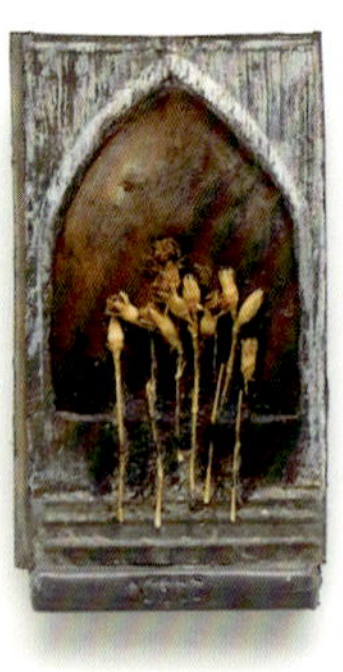 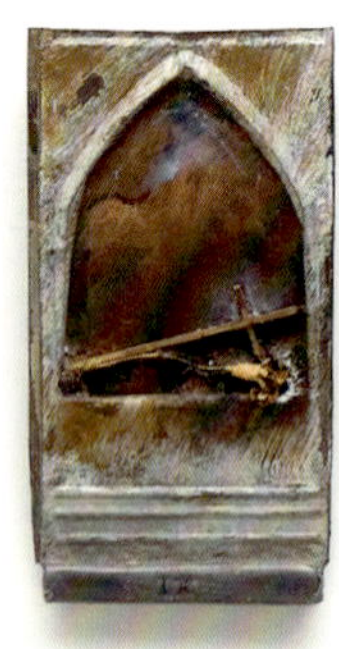 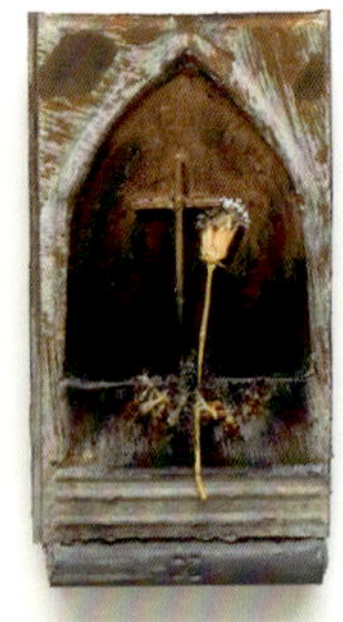 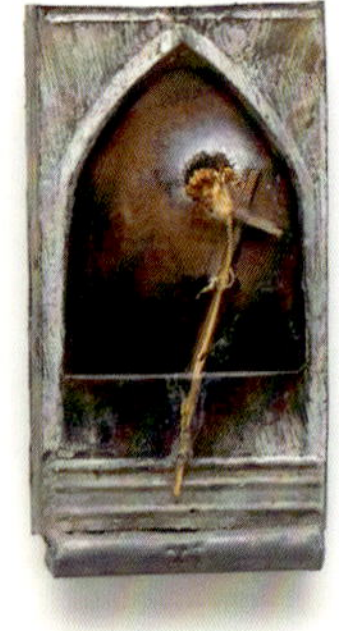 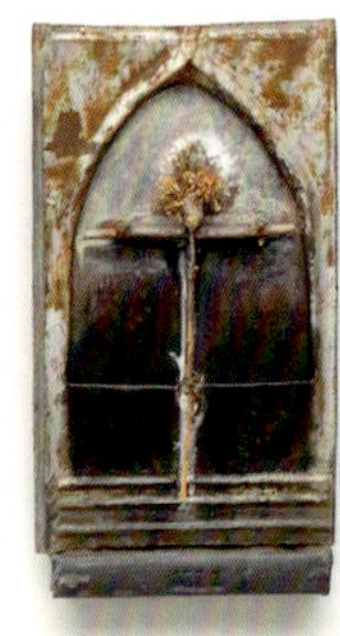 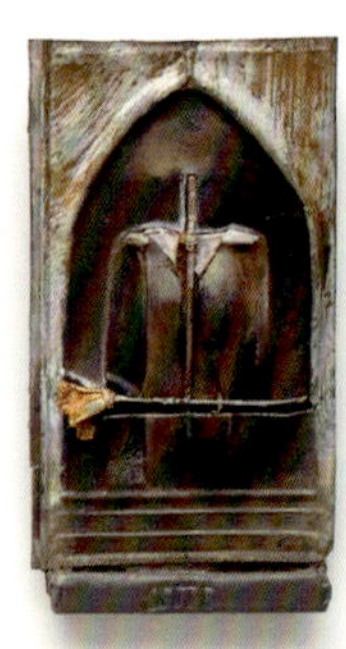 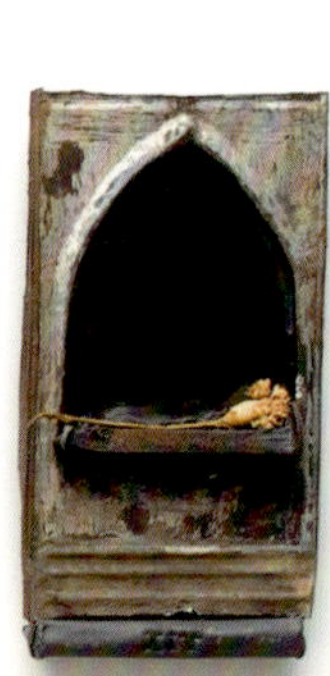

Stations of the Cross, 2002,
Clayboard, tin, dried flowers, paint
and mixed media, 15 x 150 x 1 inches.
Collection of the artist.

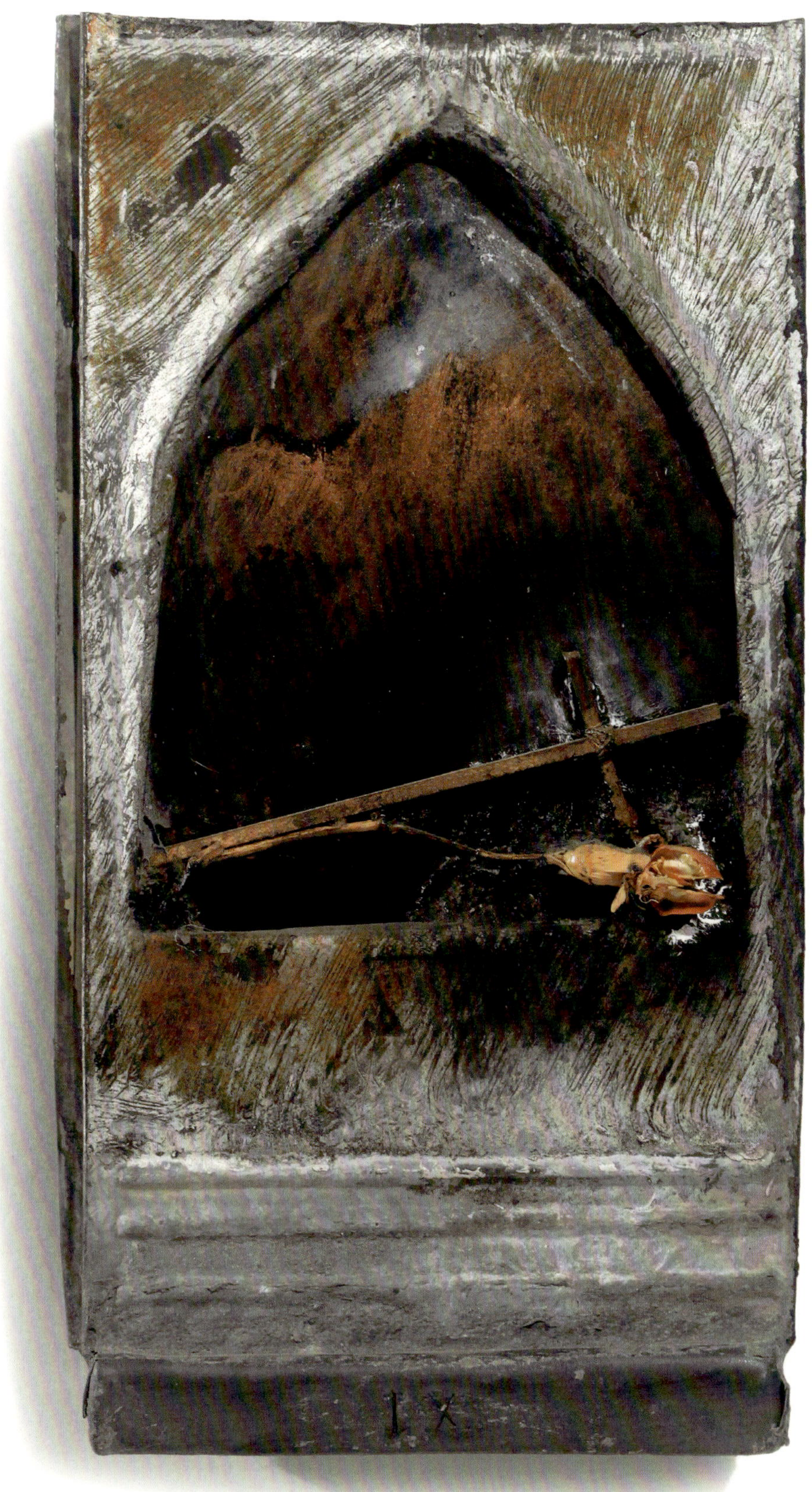

Since their inception, the Stations of the Cross have been rendered in a wide array of pictorial styles. Narrative in their intent, they very closely follow the Biblical script of Jesus Christ's execution, including his falling with his cross at stations number 3, 7 and 9. What is totally unique about Kopriva's *Stations of the Cross* is her incorporation of a carnation to signify the body of Christ – his head represented by the flower, his body by the stem. In Sharon Kopriva's *Stations of the Cross*, there is a wondrous simplicity and sense of the fragility of human life, just as there is the illuminated sense of the transcendental in her "Forest Cathedrals" [exhibition].

– Jim Edwards

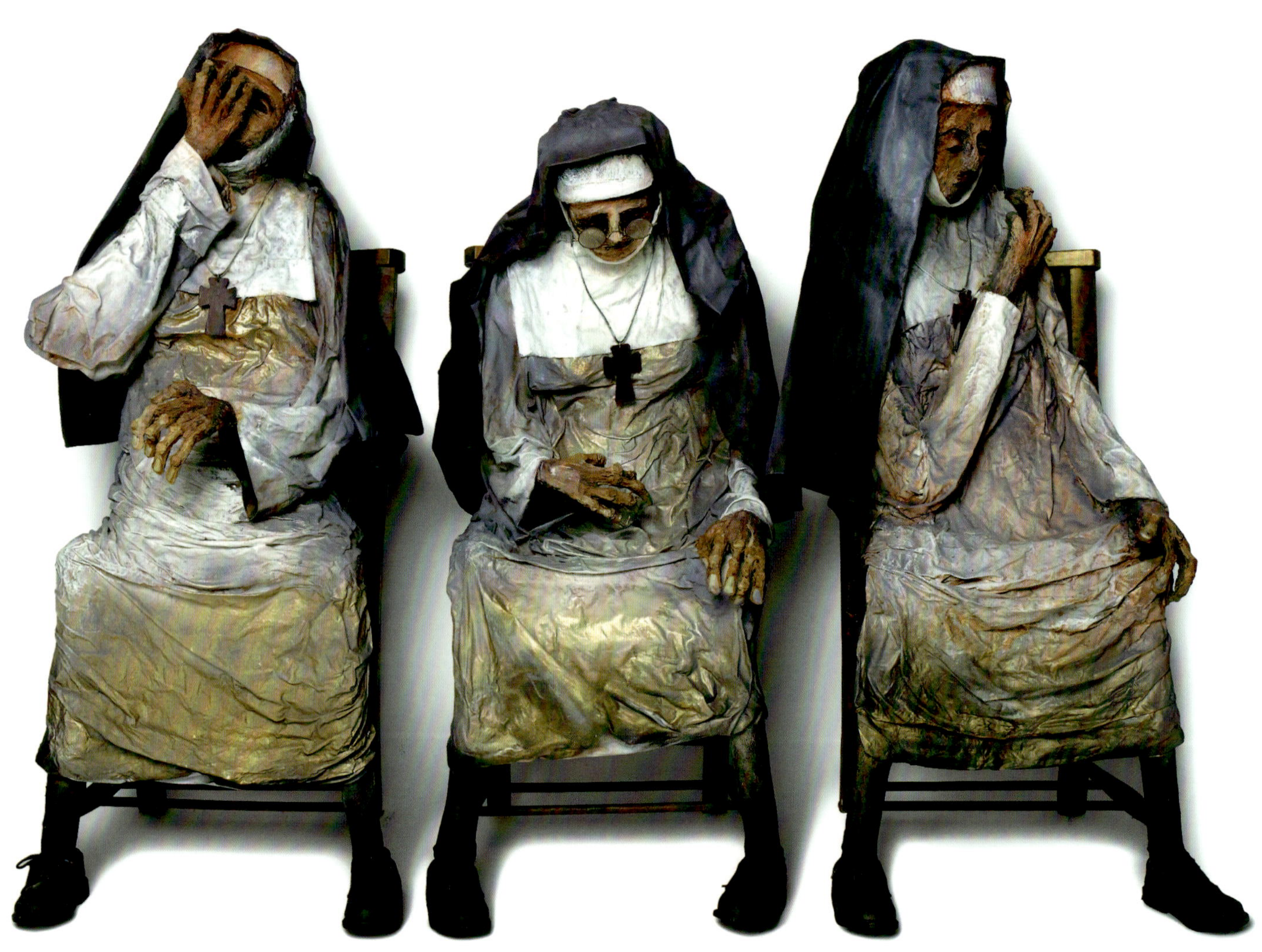

In the Name of the Father, and of the Son, and of the Holy…, 2003,
Papier-mâché and mixed media, 38 x 80 x 24 inches.
Collection of the artist.

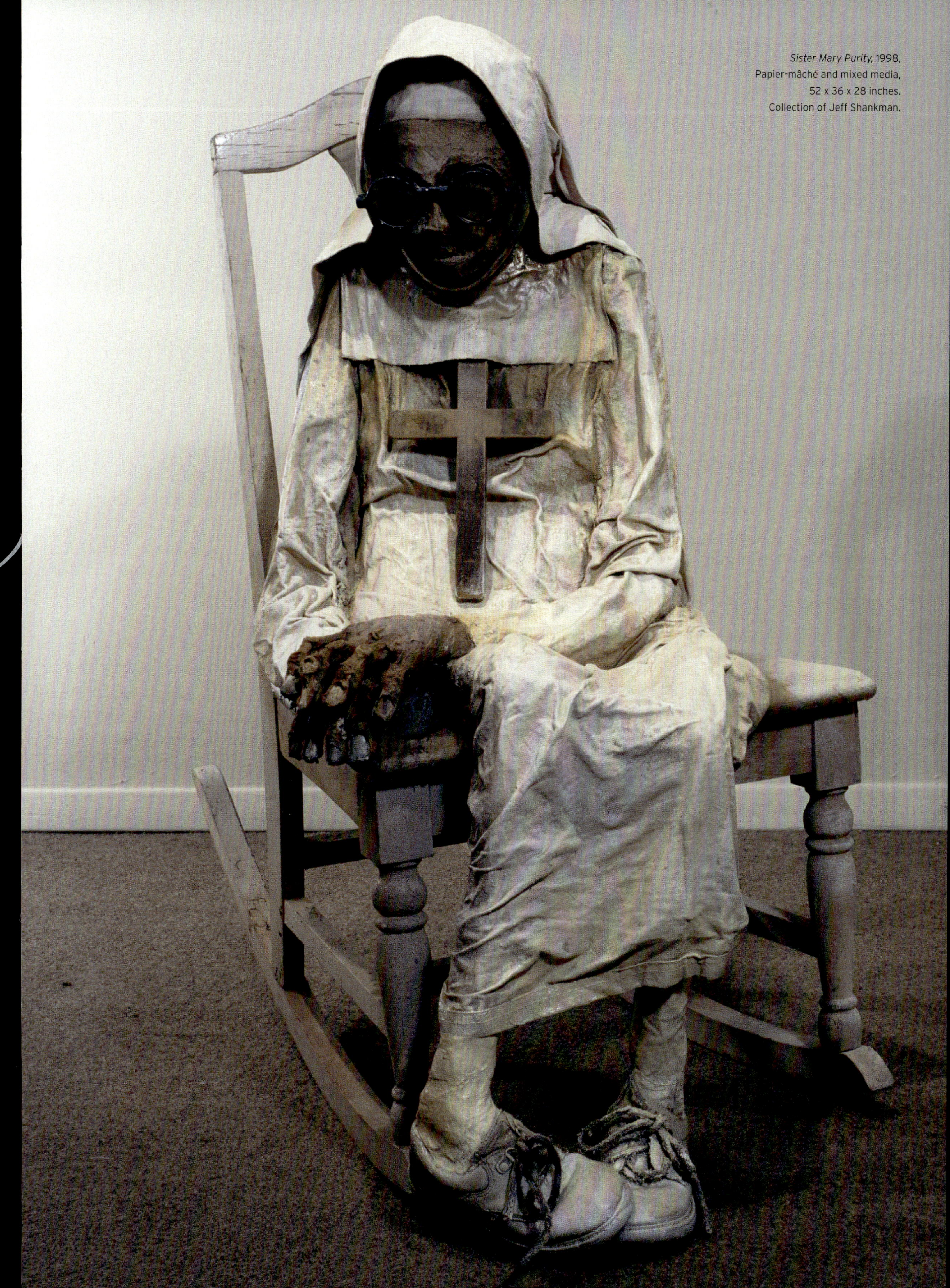

Sister Mary Purity, 1998,
Papier-mâché and mixed media,
52 x 36 x 28 inches.
Collection of Jeff Shankman.

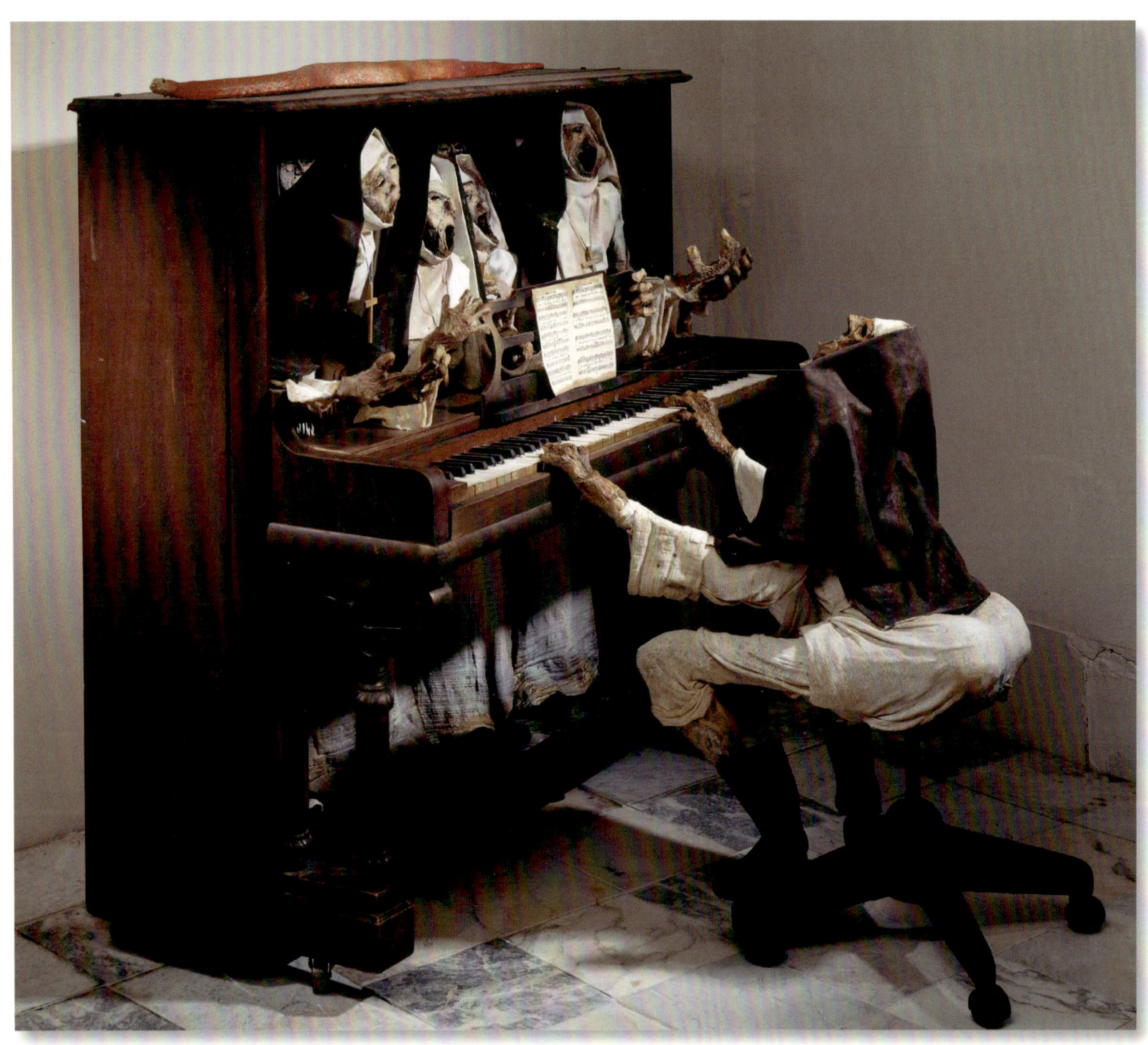

In Exelsis Deo, 1996,
Piano, papier-mâché and mixed media, 58 x 60 x 61.
Collection of Renee Wallace.

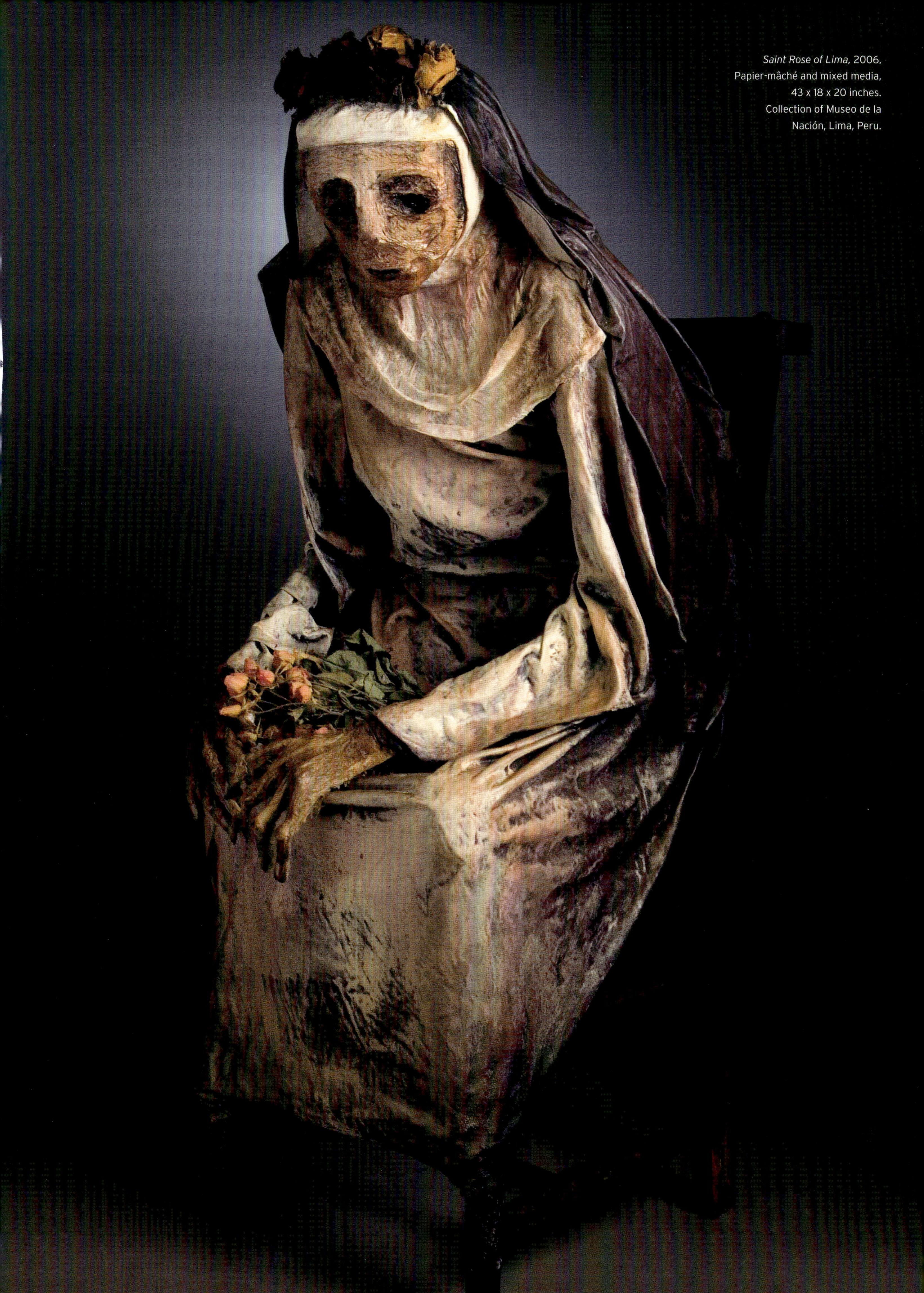

Saint Rose of Lima, 2006,
Papier-mâché and mixed media,
43 x 18 x 20 inches.
Collection of Museo de la
Nación, Lima, Peru.

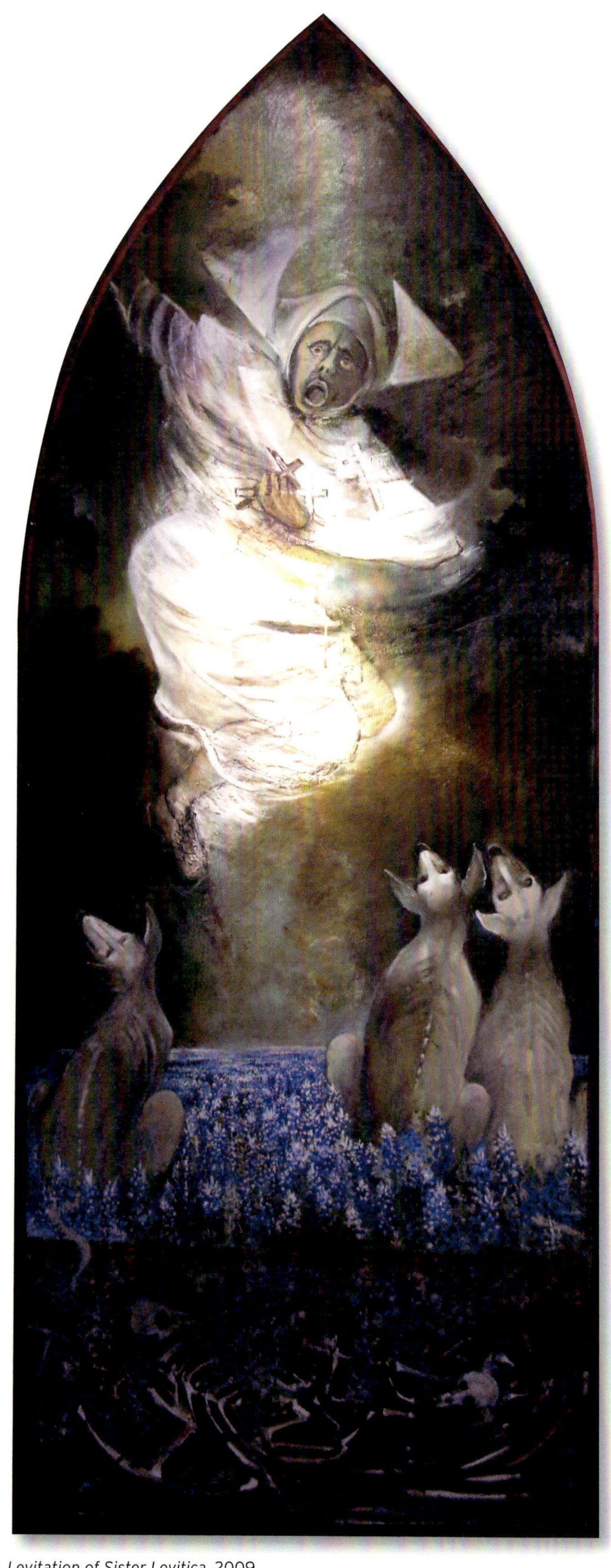

Levitation of Sister Levitica, 2009,
Oil on wood, 80 x 33 inches.
Collection of the artist.

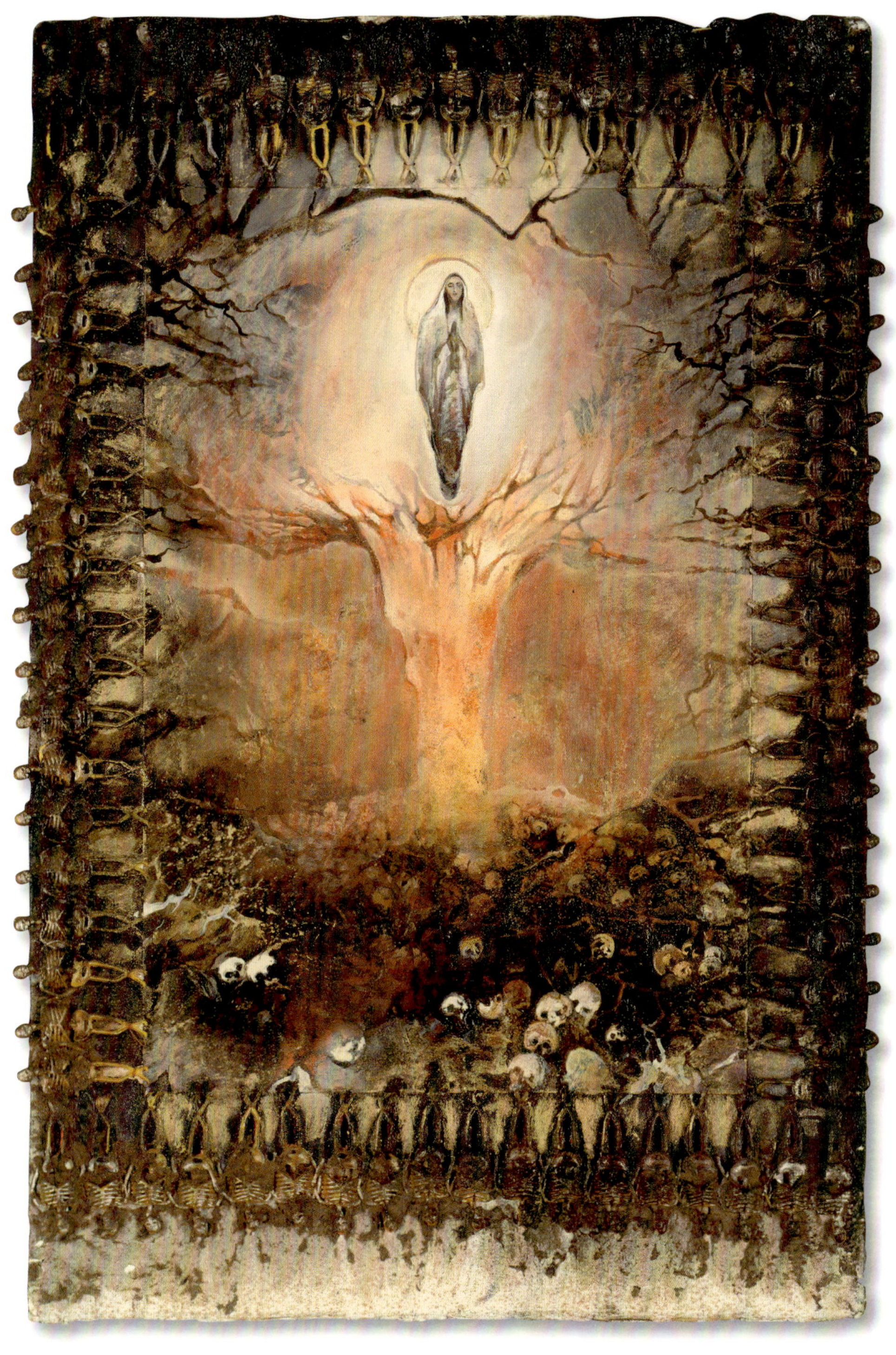

Fatima - Apparition, 1990,
Photograph, oil, papier-mâché and mixed media on paper,
22.5 x 16 inches.
Collection of Nancy Reddin Kienholz.

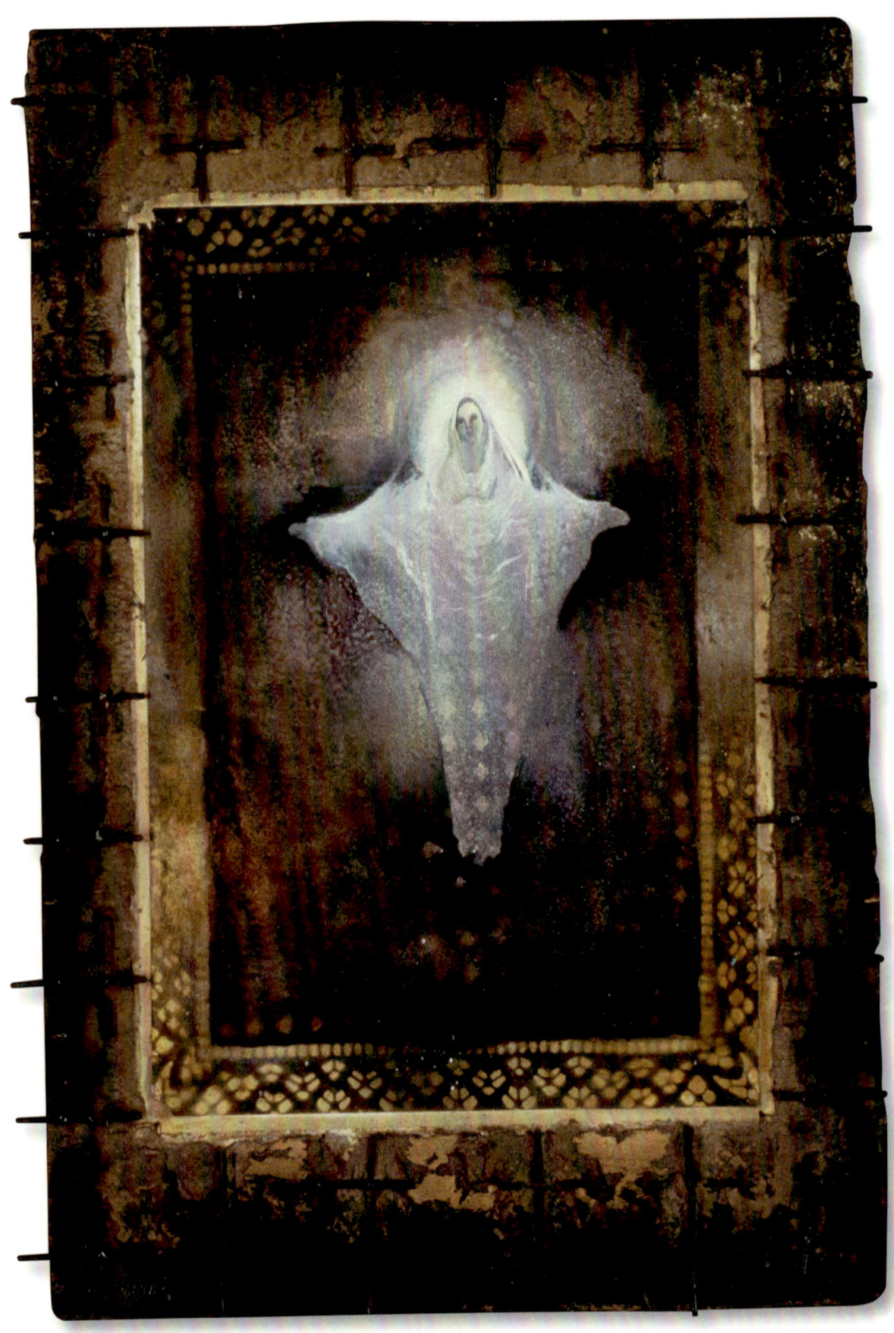

Medjugorje - Apparition, 1990,
Photograph, oil, thread and wire on paper, 22.5 x 16 inches.
Collection of Jennifer and Scott Palermo.

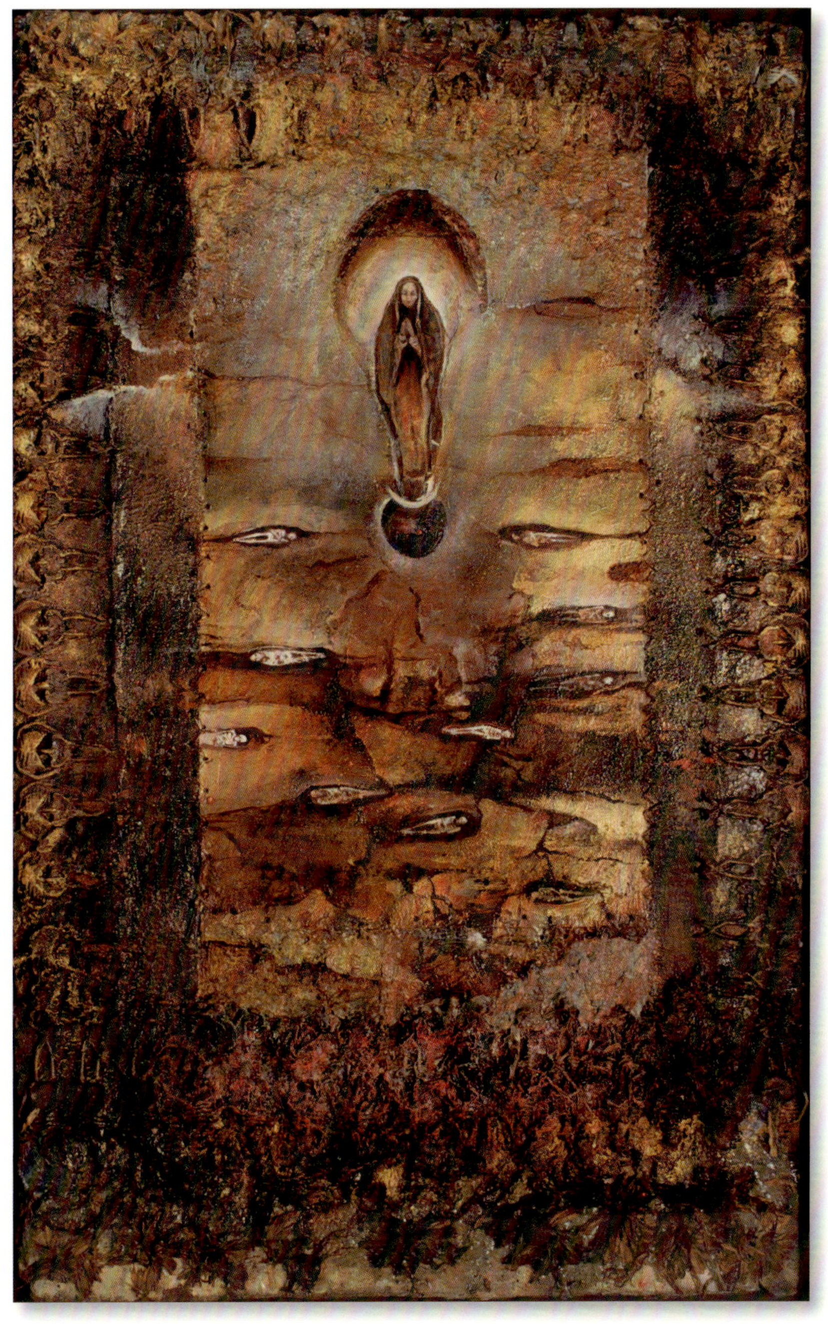

Guadalupe - Apparition, 1991,
Photograph, oil, and mixed media on paper, 22.5 x 16 inches.
Collection of Ron Garcia.

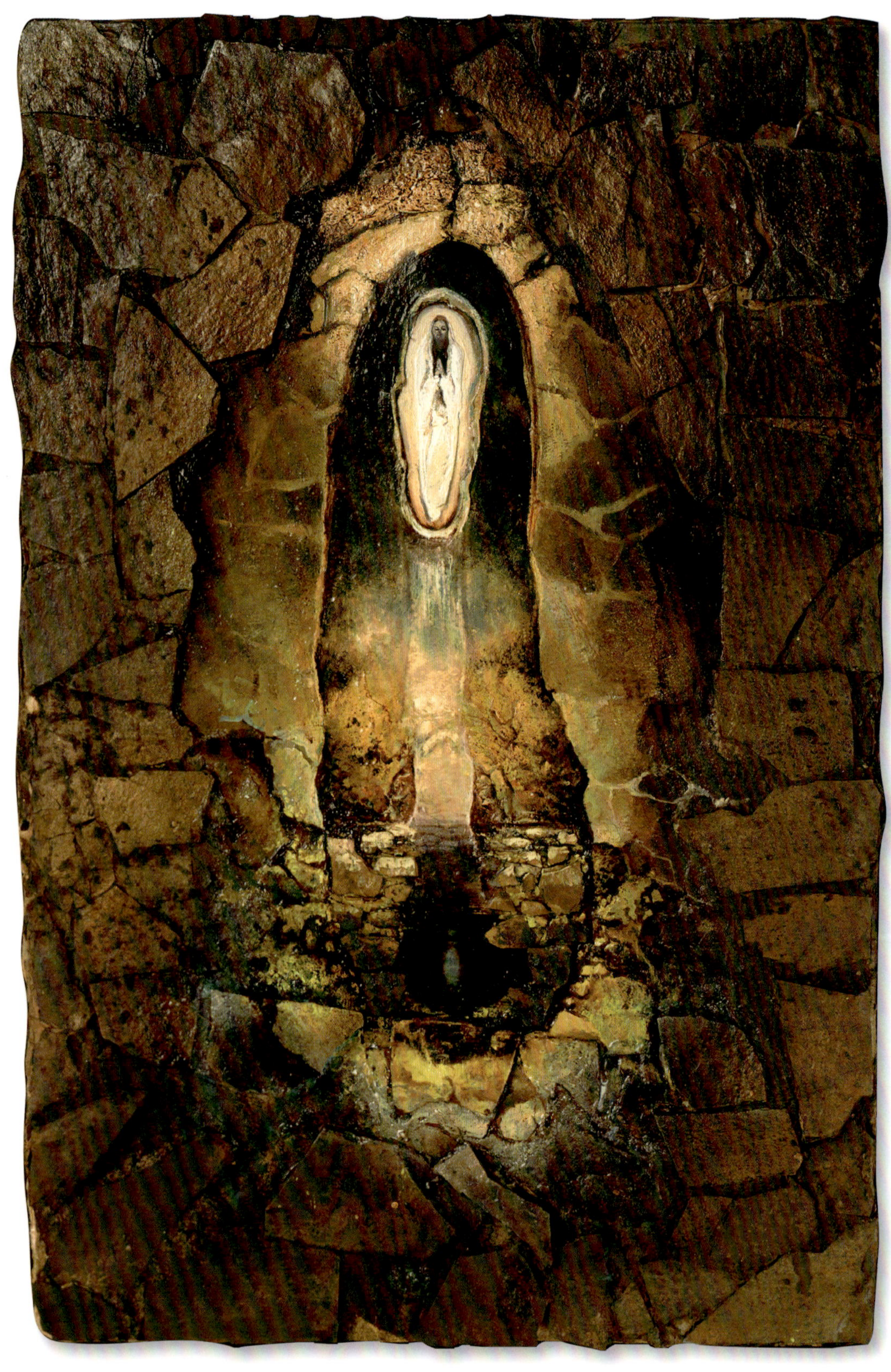

Lourdes – Apparition, 1991,
Photograph, oil and mixed media on paper, 22.5 x 16 inches.
Private collection.

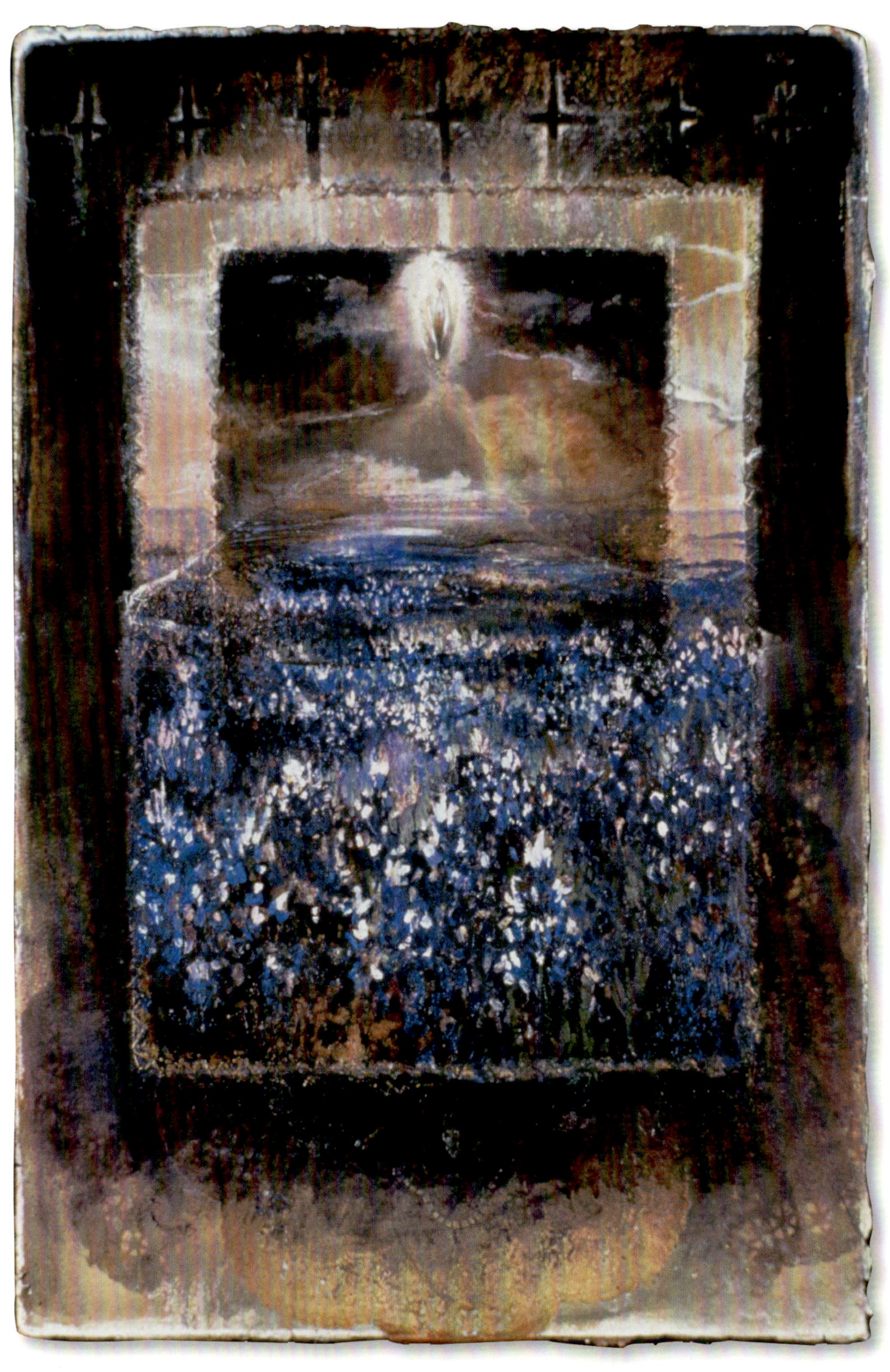

Madonna of the Bluebonnets – Apparition, 1991,
Photograph, oil and mixed media on paper, 22.5 x 16 inches.
Collection of Mary and Roy Cullen.

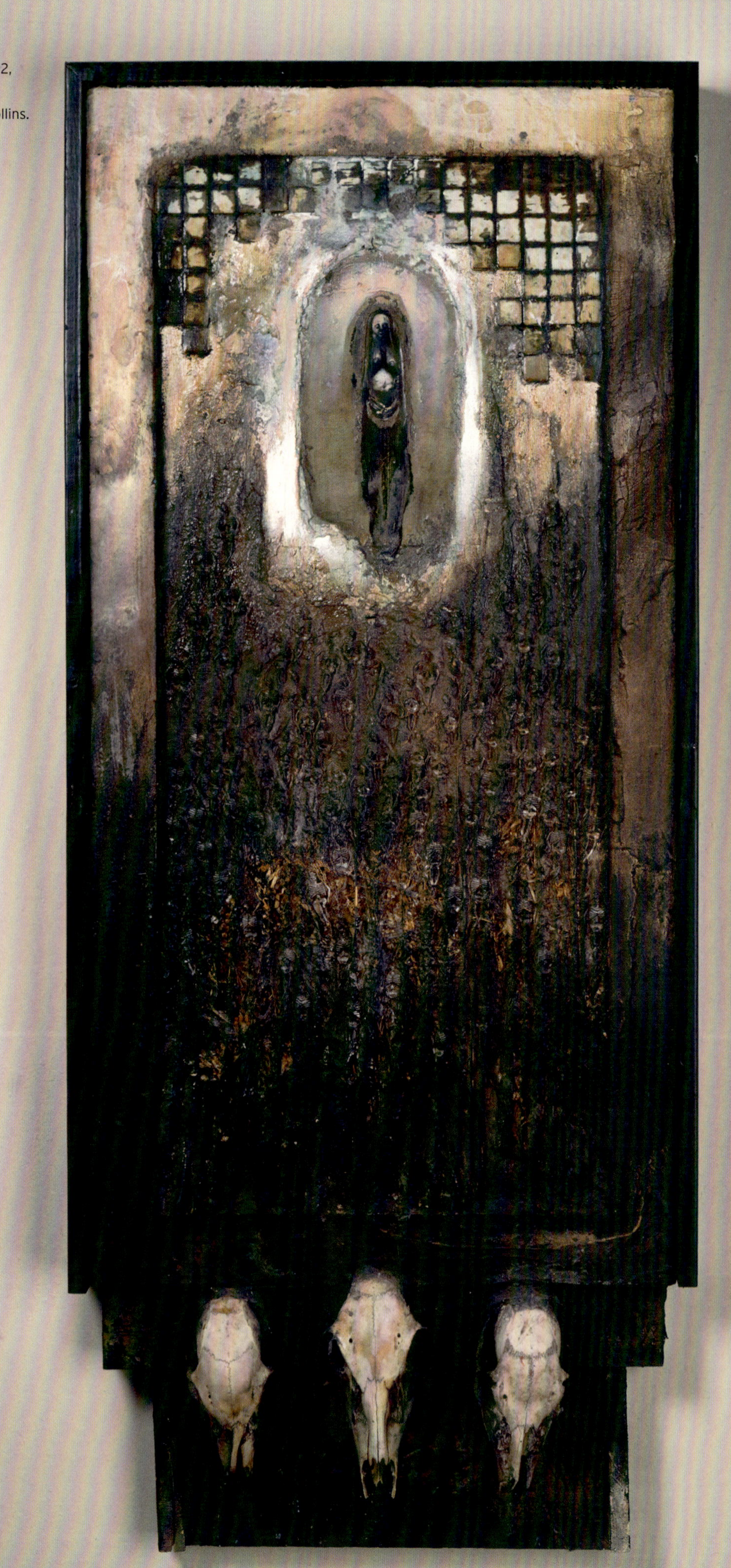

Madonna of Heaven and Earth, 1992,
Mixed media relief, 59 x 25 x 3.5.
Collection of Gayle and Michael Collins.

AN INTERVIEW WITH JOHN ALEXANDER

John Alexander was Sharon Kopriva's painting teacher from 1976 through 1979 at the University of Houston. She intentionally sought him as teacher after seeing his work at Meredith Long Gallery. What began as an academic relationship quickly evolved into one of mutual respect and has developed into a life-long friendship.

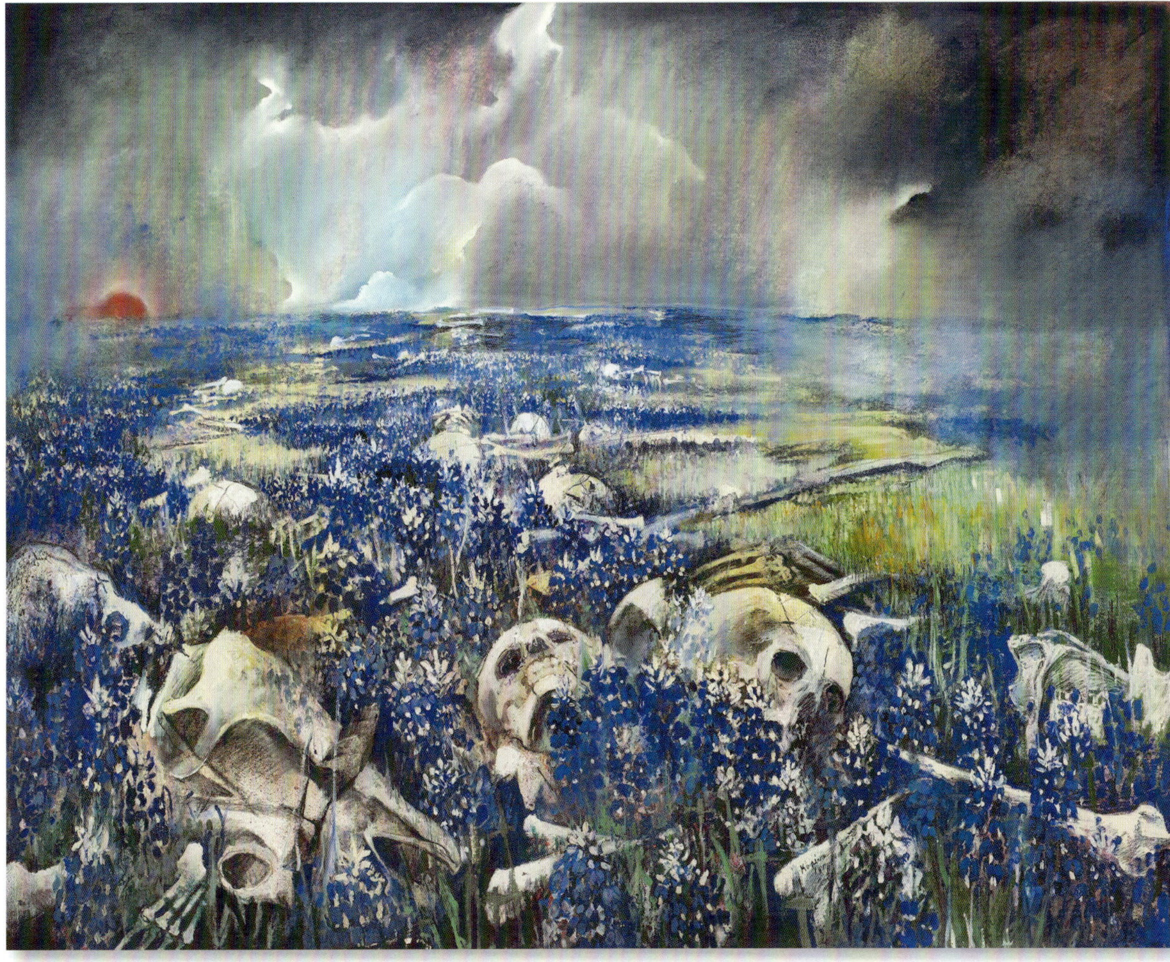

April 21, 1837, 1989,
Oil and mixed media on paper,
30 x 40 inches.
Collection of Meredith Cullen.

How and when did you first meet Sharon Kopriva?

I met her when she signed up for one of my classes. Sharon told me that she bagged groceries for a living. In actuality, she was a high-school art teacher. For some reason she thought I didn't like high-school art teachers.

What was your impression of her as a student?

Sharon's work – what she made and how she performed as an artist – was absolutely shocking in relation to her as a person. She could have easily been a third-grade teacher or a librarian. She was this nice, shy, quiet person … and then, all of a sudden, this stuff that she made was like "Whoa, what the hell is going on here?"

What was the art scene like in Houston, especially at the University of Houston, at time when you met Sharon, and how do you think it influenced her work?

Well, at the time there were two currents that affected the Houston art scene. One was the fact that the Museum of Fine Arts, Houston, had more power at that time than they do now. There just wasn't much other stuff going on. With very few galleries, there just wasn't much of an art scene.

But by the end of the '70s and into the '80s, of course, the art scene kind of exploded. At the time, the Museum of Fine Arts was consumed with Greenbergian ideas of color-field painting. The other thing is that there were a couple of galleries that were champions of the whole minimalist thing. Myself and Sharon Kopriva, in particular, were the antithesis – as was James Surls – of that kind of thinking. Ours was the polar opposite of Minimalism, or what I consider decorative art, this abstract color-field mentality of big, simple, stained canvases. So much of the faculty came out of that ideology.

Even from the very beginning, Sharon was very content-oriented in her work, and very unusual. As graduate schools are prone to be, the faculty tended to like people whose work is like their own. I always felt that folks who were way out there on the fringe were who we should be looking for in terms of our school, and me as a teacher, in particular. Also, don't forget the fact that the University of Houston had just had the great Julian Schnabel as a student, and he had a very big presence there. Surls as a teacher had a very big presence there, and I would like to think that I had a very big presence at the school. We represented a certain type of mentality, Surls and I, that was opposite of much of the other faculty.

Also, I would like to add, that outside of the Museum of Fine Arts and those few galleries, there was at that time an undercurrent in the art scene that was very edgy, and in a Southern tradition, very content-oriented. I would like to think that we had something to do with that, but I also think that there was just something in the air. It was a tough town– Houston kind of rose from the oil fields and bayous. It was not a sophisticated town to say the least, early on. I think the young artists really reflected that mentality. There was a big influence from the Mexican community on the young artists. There is a strong connection in all of South Texas to Mexico.

There was sensitivity to the narrative there that I think is very Southern. Yet the art establishment there – and I feel strongly about this – they had this need to connect to the art world of New York. Whereas the local people, the ones that came from that area, they rejected that. There was strong Texas, independent feeling that ... "We don't need to be influenced by the New York or European art scenes. We are making art about who and where we are at this particular time in our own lives and environment." It was a tough place, Houston, and I think that was reflected in the art. I think that was very important in Sharon's early development. Whether it was conscious or not, she clearly rejected the mentality of "Oh we are going to enlighten you poor crackers by bringing in these beautiful color field paintings."

I can't emphasize enough the influence at that time of curator Jim Harithas. He came in and took a bulldozer to that whole idea of looking to New York for guidance. He preached like some Southern Baptist evangelist. "You have a great thing going here. You have your own scene. You make art about your own community, your own lives, and make that as important as anything else." I think the young people in Houston at that time – we really bought into to that. The way to make great art is to look within, not to look to outside influences.

How was Sharon's early work received at the University of Houston?
I think that her work was received very poorly by much of the faculty, to say the least. Her work was just so different. Yet her work, even early on ... She was just a powerhouse. There was a very personal, content-oriented side to her work that was completely interesting and original.

To be fair to everyone at the school, as time went on and she was around more, she began to be accepted and highly respected by everyone. But in the beginning, it was very touchy.

What is the significance of Sharon meeting Ed and Nancy Kienholz?
It is good for everybody to have someone who they can look to as a mentor, kind of a spiritual comrade-in-arms, so to speak, as an artist. For me, clearly early on it was de Kooning, his whole presence, and his highly charged, painterly surfaces, and the emotional energy of de Kooning's work. For Sharon, because she was such an odd artist, she didn't fit into any category, any -ism. She certainly didn't come out of Impressionism or Romanticism or European Avant-garde ... She just came from outer space. Very few artists emerge like that, except occasionally you will see a great, like a Thornton Dial.

Ed and Nancy Kienholz came along. I mean, think about Ed. I mean, he has had big museum shows, but he was never given the credit like some of the Abstract Expressionist artists. To me, Ed is one of the most powerful artists of the 20th century.

He is very much someone like Sharon, or Thornton Dial, in that you can't pigeonhole them. There is no place to put them because they come from their own universe, their own world. There is some kind of strange creative force that comes from them personally and from their art that is incredibly unique, powerful and highly original. I mean, when those two kindred spirits met, it was just natural that they would migrate towards each other because there weren't very many people they could migrate towards.

In terms of their work, they were both so unique that you can't find anyone else to compare them to. I mean, who do you compare Ed and Nancy Kienholz to? You look at the last 35 years of American painting and sculpture, and who can you can compare Sharon to? That's why I mention Thornton Dial. I mean, one piece has a goat carcass in it, you know, and TV antennas and shit piled on top of each other, yet done in an absolutely poetic language that you have to understand the world of art and the whole creative process to fully appreciate the incredible genius of it.

Many people may go by a Dial or Kienholz and think that it is just some freak oddity or outsider junk art. The truth is that it moves toward something much higher. I think if you look at the best of Sharon's work, it does the same thing. Yet it is its own language. There is no other language to compare it to. It is like listening to some strange language you have never heard; this is the visual equivalent. It is a powerful visual statement with no point of reference because there has never been anything like it before.

That is the attraction between Ed and Nancy and Sharon. Now Ed was a tough curmudgeon. Sharon is the nicest person you will ever meet. Ed and Nancy really took to her, though, and took her under their wing. Naturally, I think they had a tremendous influence on her, not just on the work itself – how it was made and so forth — but also the idea of living in the environment from where your art comes from. If you look at Ed and Nancy's studio, it looks like one of their pieces. Entering Sharon's studio is like walking into one of her pieces. The entire environment becomes a piece. I am not sure that that came from Ed and Nancy, but they certainly paralleled each other.

What is one of your favorite works by Sharon Kopriva?
What about *The Cardinal* (pg. 37)? Two of the most iconic and powerful paintings in the history of art are Velázquez's *Portrait of Pope Innocent X* and Francis Bacon's *Study after Velázquez's Pope Innocent*. Now here this woman has taken on the challenge of not only painting these things, but making them three-dimensional. She has the spirit of this great Bacon copy of Velázquez, but she has done it in a three-dimensional form. Nobody, to my knowledge, has taken on this challenge and done it with the level of success as Sharon has.

As you have followed the work of Sharon throughout her career, what has changed? What has remained?
One of the things that has changed is that she is tougher. Early on, she was very idealistic. Because she is so nice, she didn't have that hard, professional side. I think her genuine sweetness kept her from reaching her full potential. As time has moved on, I think she has turned into a real hardened professional. She really has her eye on the target, which is the art itself. She is very dedicated and hard working.

She has never let all her travels, or her time in the art world, change her unique vision – which is all about something that I can't possibly explain – but it is about her Catholicism, her childhood, her personal history. It has to do with death, the church, the deep-rooted, dark side of Catholicism. Whatever it is, it has been a constant in her work. There is a consistency – and I think you will see it in this exhibition – that is present throughout her work.

How is Sharon unique in the context of contemporary art?
Most artists that work today look back at the history of art, but they never look *way* back. They look to the Renaissance or late-Renaissance, but they rarely look back to Egyptian or Paleolithic art, or cave paintings. We seem to have some sort of filter that keeps us limited to looking at the early Renaissance forward. Maybe it is the way we are taught in school; I don't know. Sharon looks back in her work to the earliest days of mankind. She looks at a global history that far precedes traditional Western art.

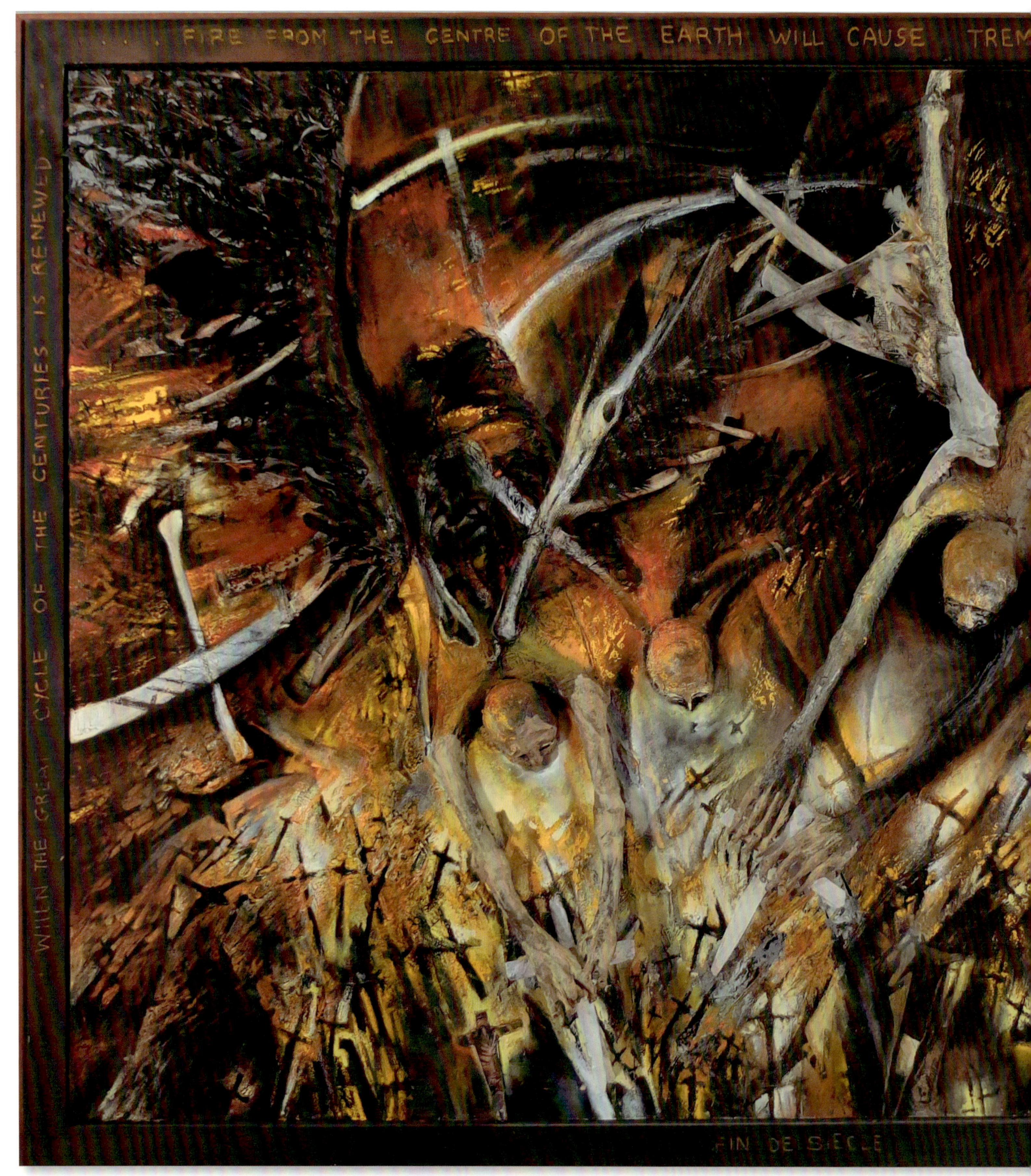

Fin de Siècle, 1987-2001,
Oil and mixed media on canvas, 80 x 115 x 11 inches.
Collection of the artist.

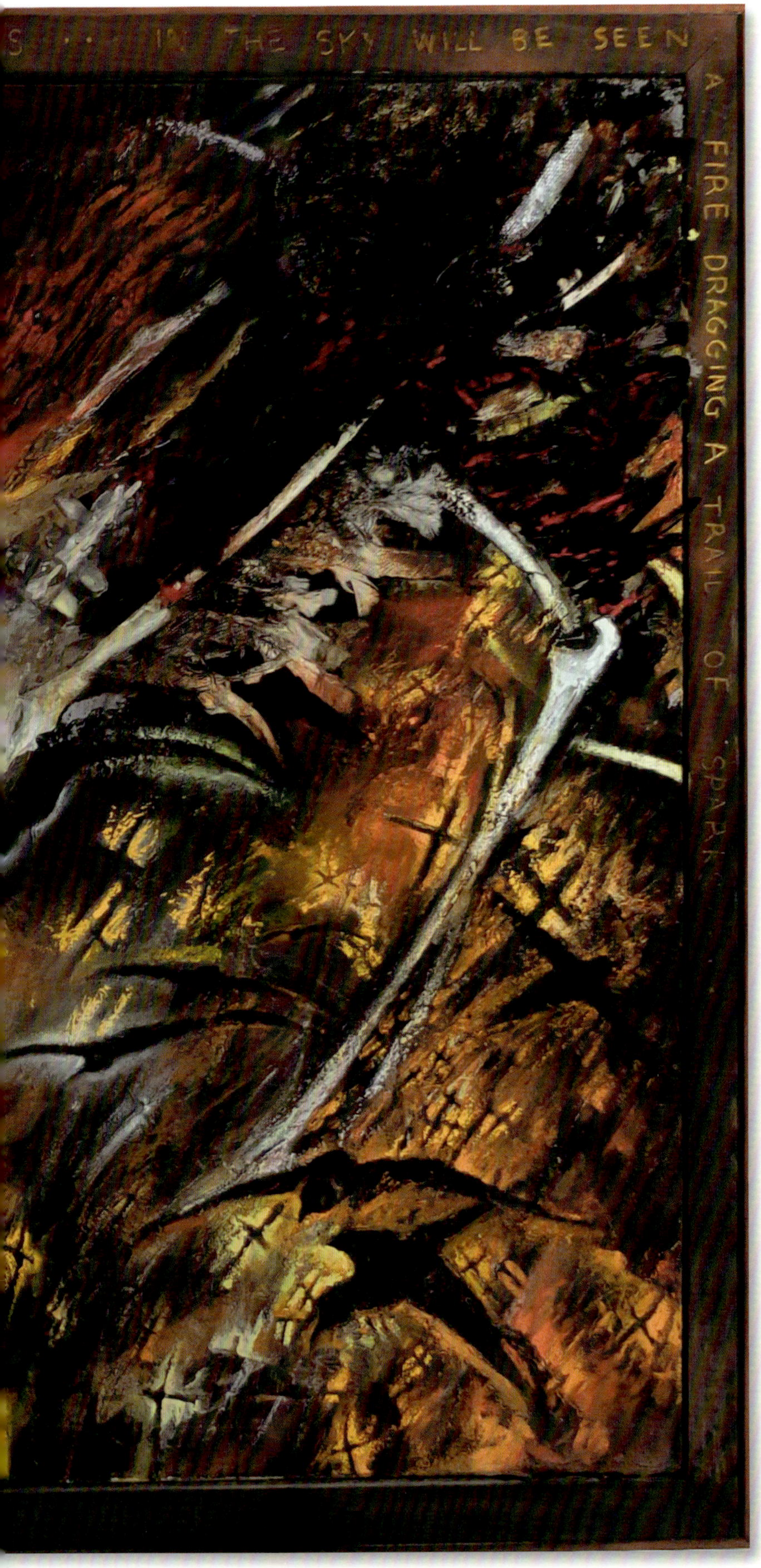

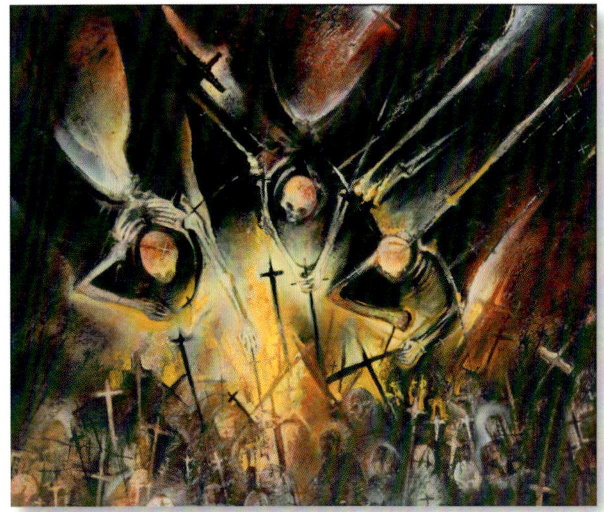

Study for Fin de Siècle, 1985,
Oil on paper, 18 x 22 inches.
Collection of Gus Kopriva.

The first marks were put onto the canvas that became *Fin de Siècle* on Aug. 16, 1987. It was to be the largest two-dimensional work I had attempted. I knew the theme was to be the conflict of good and evil – a universal theme with avenging angels and lots of fire. I think it was in the 1970s when I first started reading the translation of Nostradamus' prophesies. One in particular predicted an attack on New York, which he called the "New City." With that in mind, I began executing a painting about the anxiety and uneasiness accompanying the upcoming change of millennium.

There was a stir surrounding the Harmonic Convergence in the summer of 1987. Friends were traveling to spiritual places for the Aug. 16 event. I felt destined to begin the new work on that date. The painting took years to finish. It was worked, overworked and reworked – a process that did not want to be completed. In 1989 I first called *Fin de Siècle* finished, and that is when I named it. I was definitely at a stopping point, but it was not done. It was shown in Chicago in September 1989. When it returned to my studio, I continued to work on the piece. It was shown a second time in Dallas, opening on Sept. 8, 2001.

On Sept. 11, 2001, the Twin Towers of the World Trade Center were attacked by terrorists, seemingly fulfilling the prophesy of Nostradamus that had first informed this work.

In 2012, as I was planning to exhibit *Fin de Siècle* a third time, this time at the Ogden Museum of Southern Art, I revisited the ideas behind the Harmonic Convergence of 1987. The Mayan calendar was ending a phase and beginning a new – some believe "final" – phase, scheduled to end on Dec. 21, 2012.

– *Sharon Kopriva*

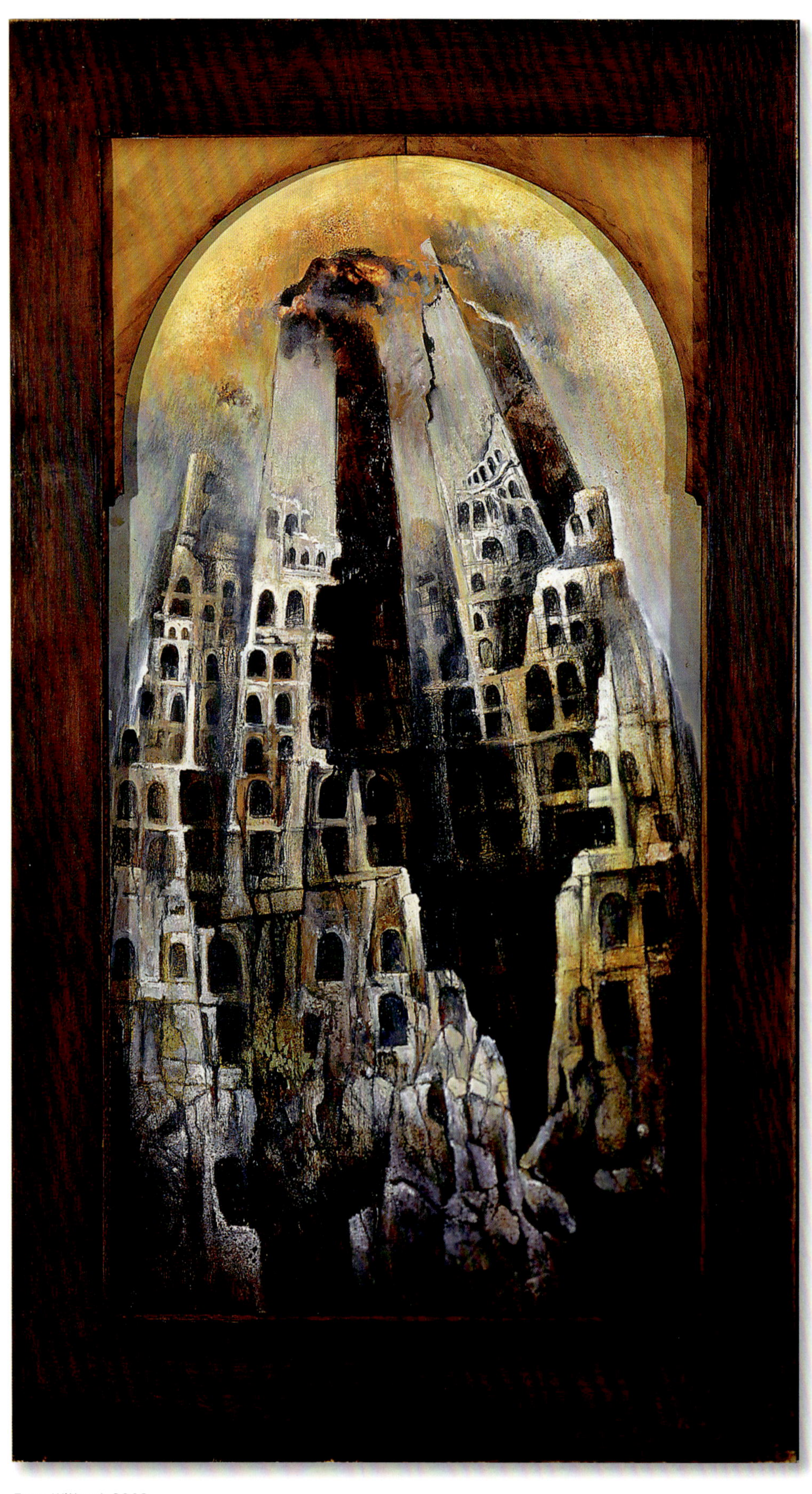

From Without, 2002,
Mixed media on clayboard, 41 x 24 inches.
Collection of Anne and Peter Brown.

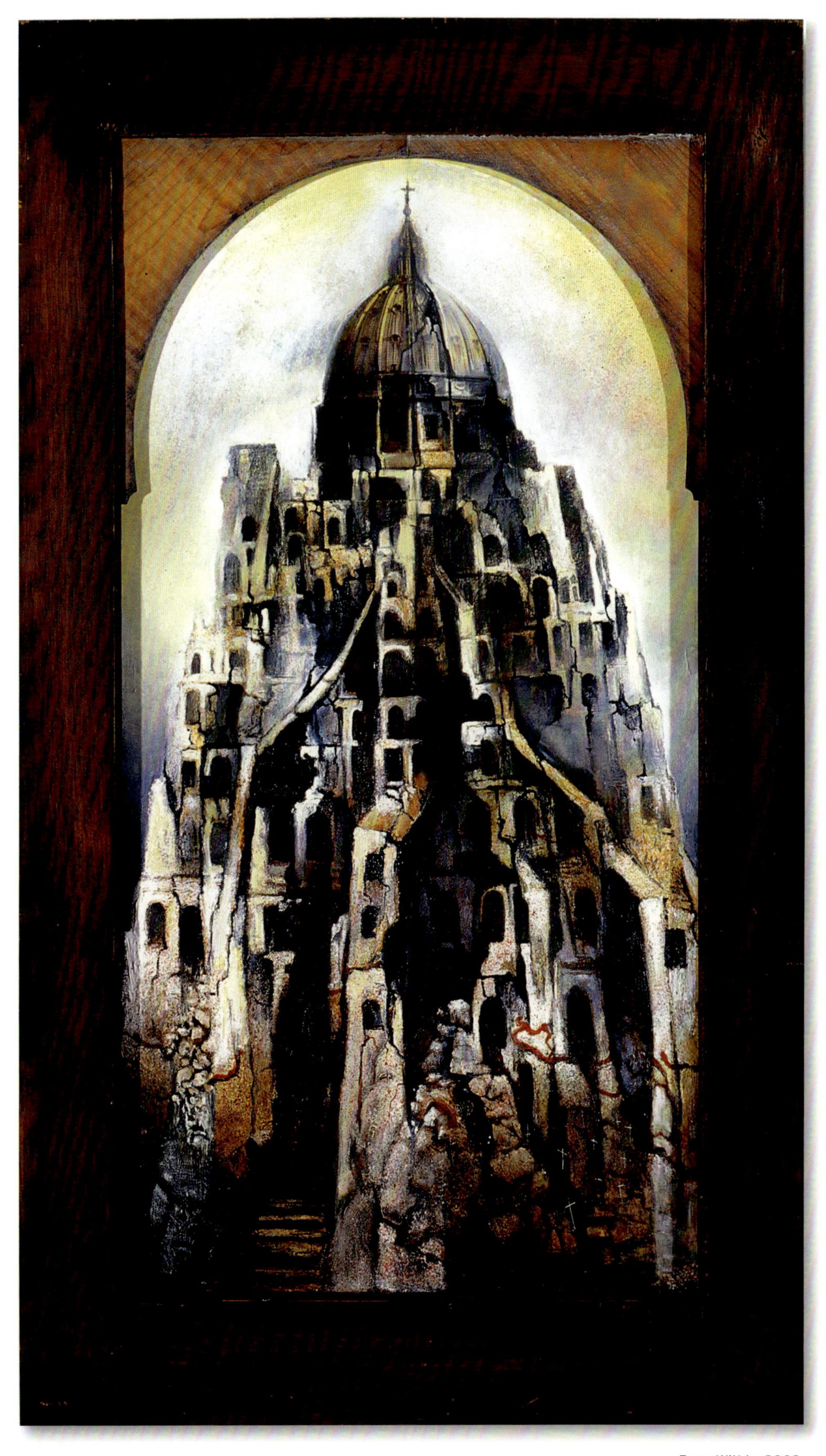

From Within, 2002,
Mixed media on clayboard, 41 x 24 inches.
Collection of Marilyn Oshman.

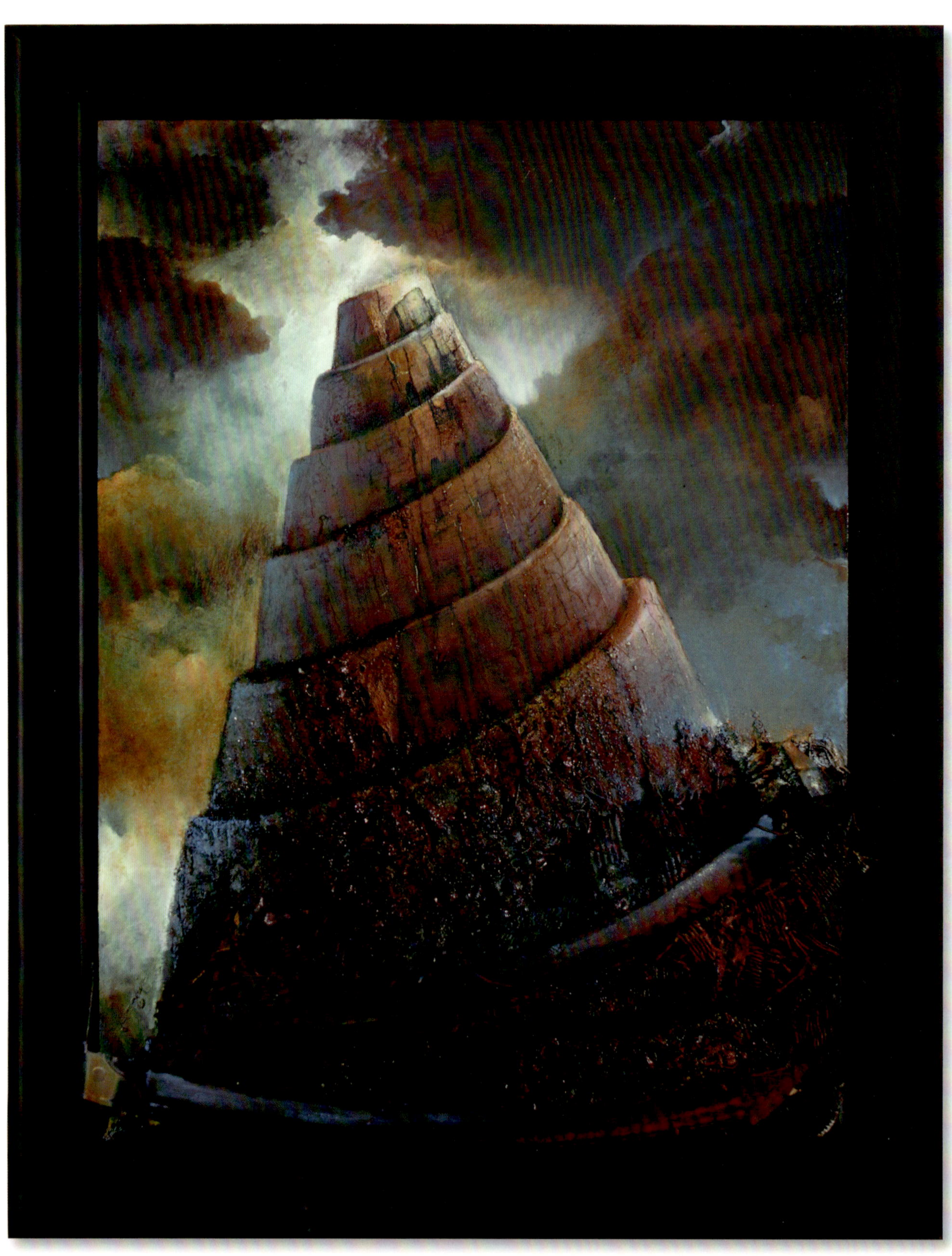

Spiral Ziggurat, 2003,
Oil and mixed media on clayboard, 47 x 37 x 5 inches.
Collection of Billie and Marvin Chasen.

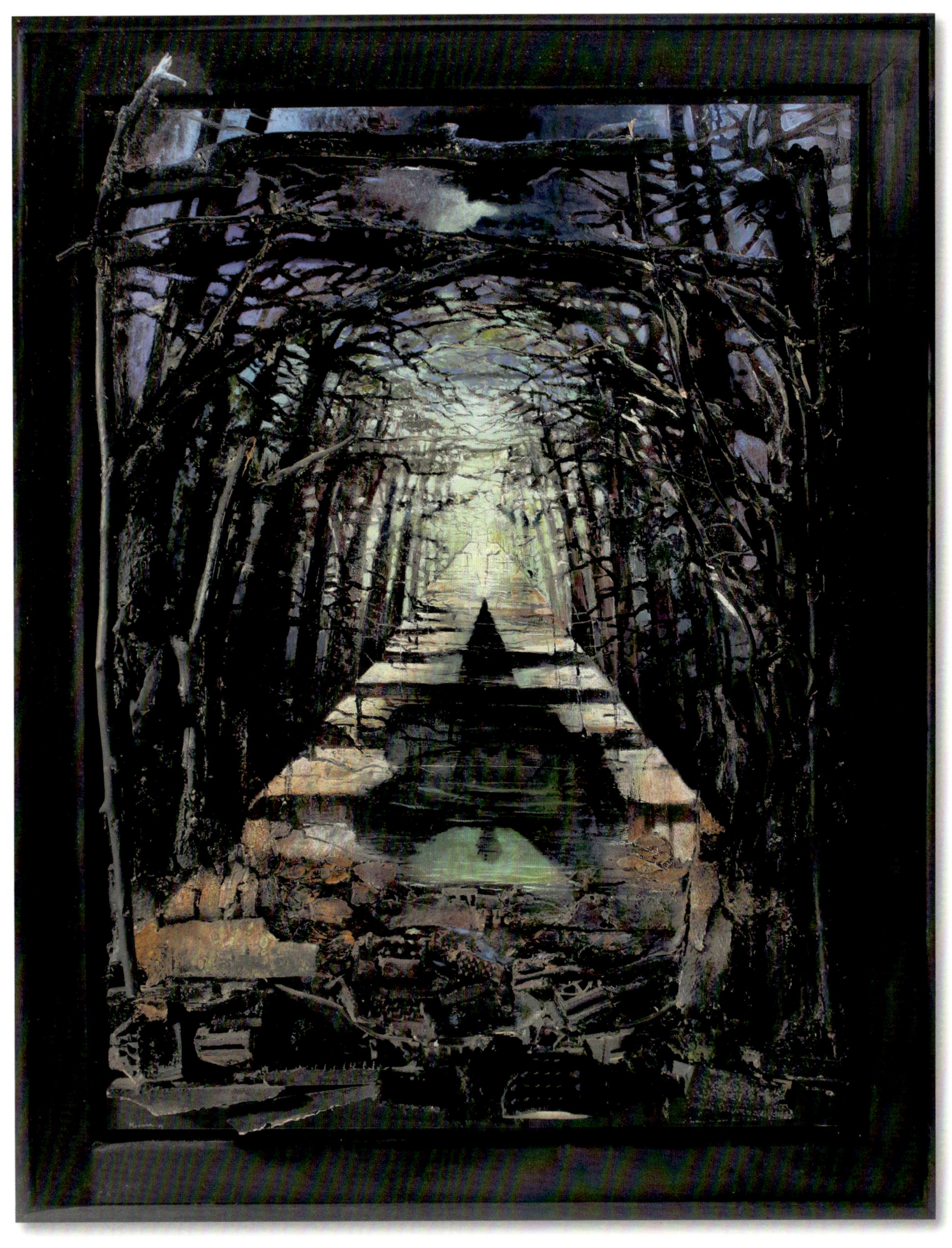

Inside of Night, 2007,
Oil and mixed media on clayboard, 47 x 37 x 4 inches.
Collection of the artist.

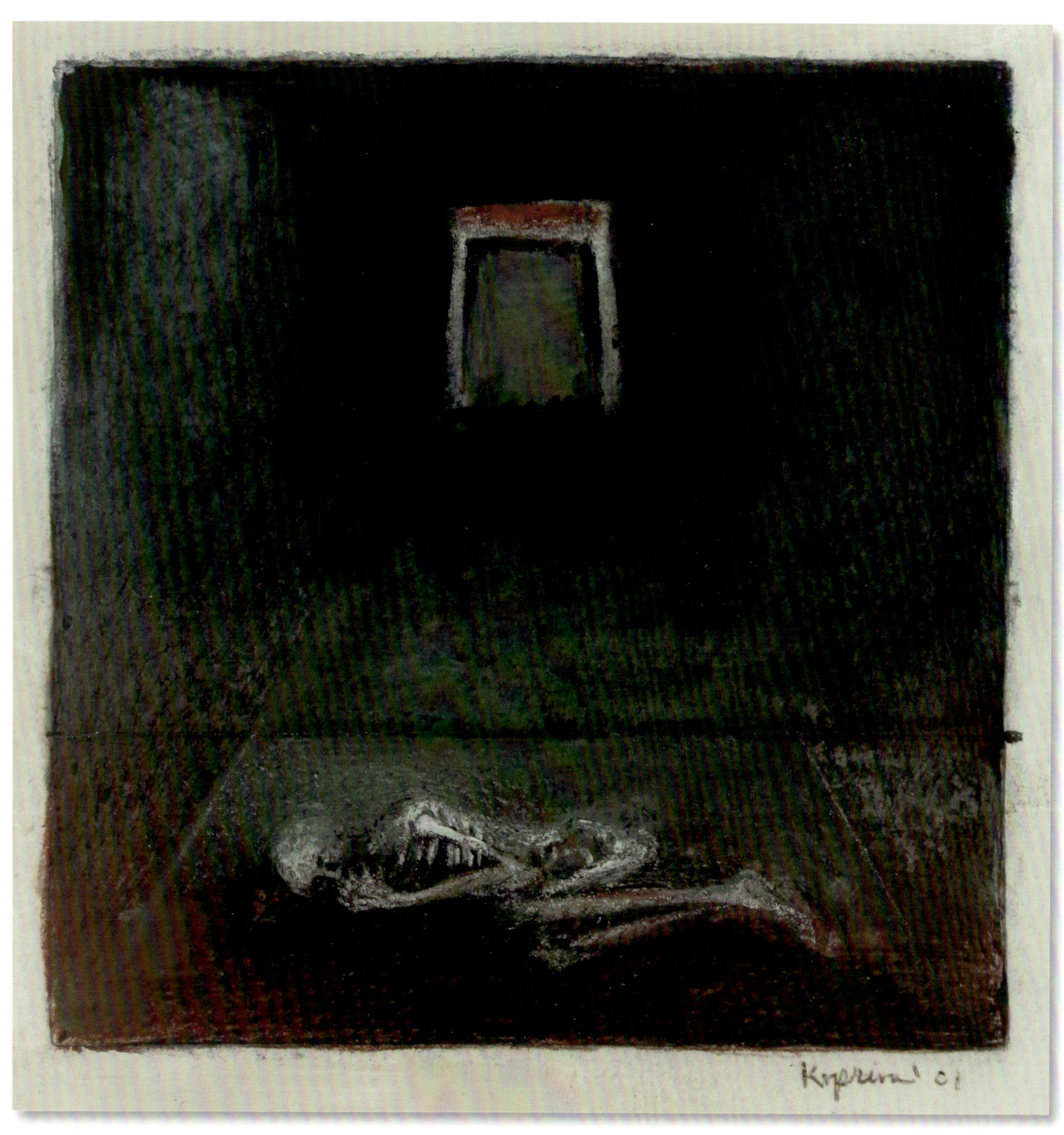

Death of the Firstborn - Plagues of Egypt, 2001,
Mixed media on paper, 5 x 5 inches.
Collection of the artist.

Opposite:
Plagues of Egypt, 2001,
Mixed media on paper, 5 x 5 inches.
Collection of the artist.

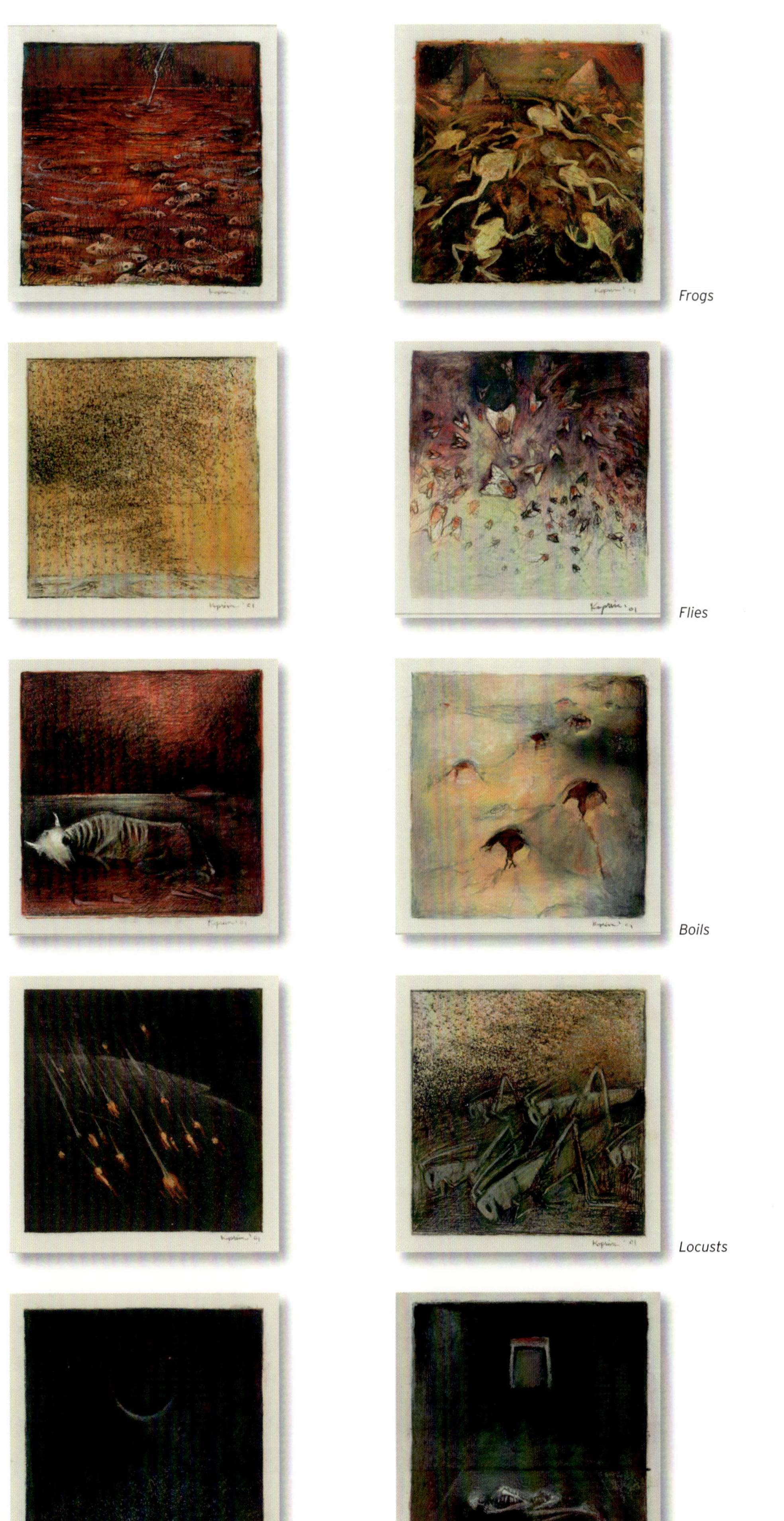

Blood of the Nile

Frogs

Gnats

Flies

Beasts

Boils

Fiery Hail

Locusts

Darkness

Death of the Firstborn

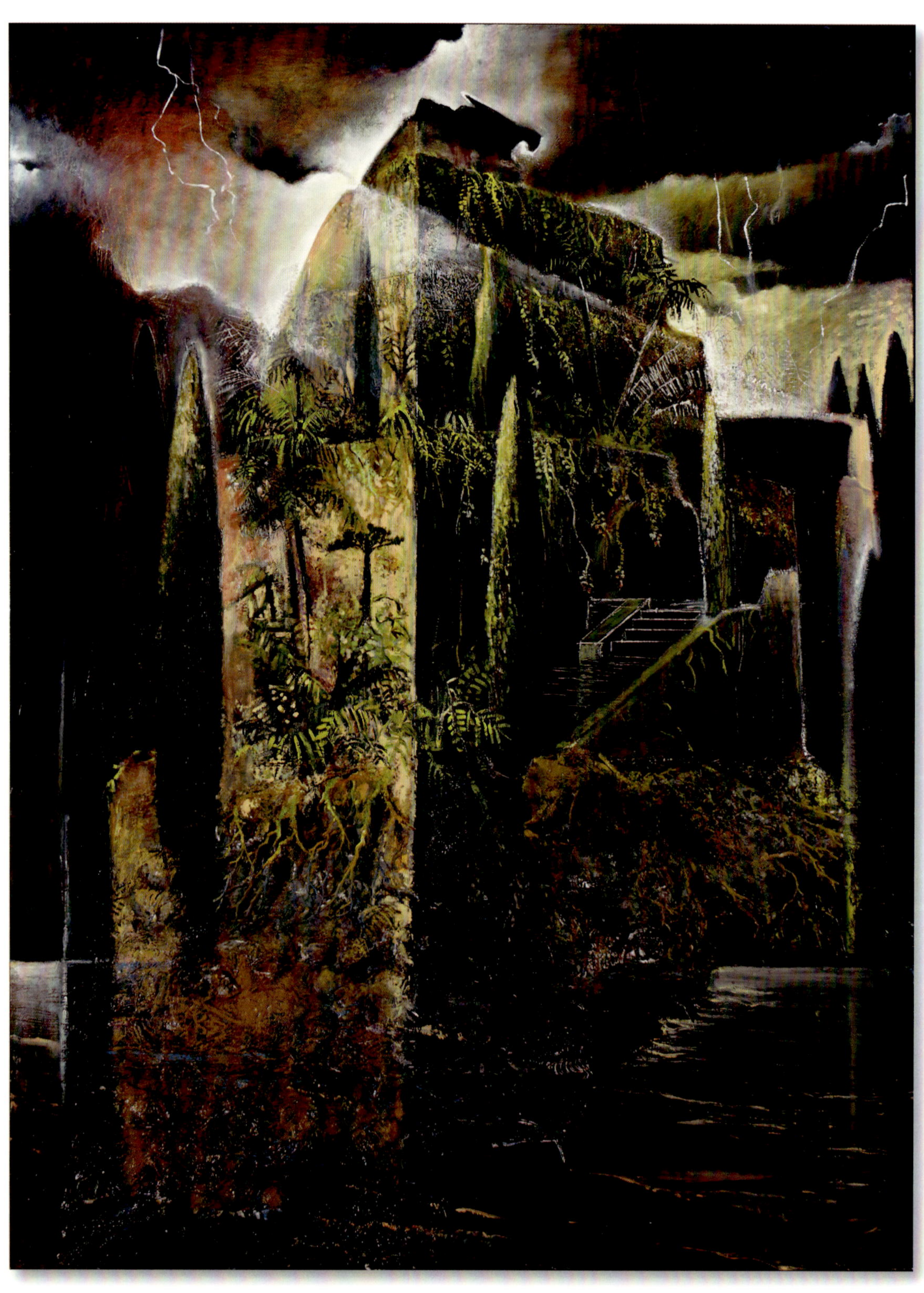

Garden of Semiramis, 2004,
Oil and mixed media on clayboard, 40 x 30 x 2 inches.
Collection of Karen Desenberg.

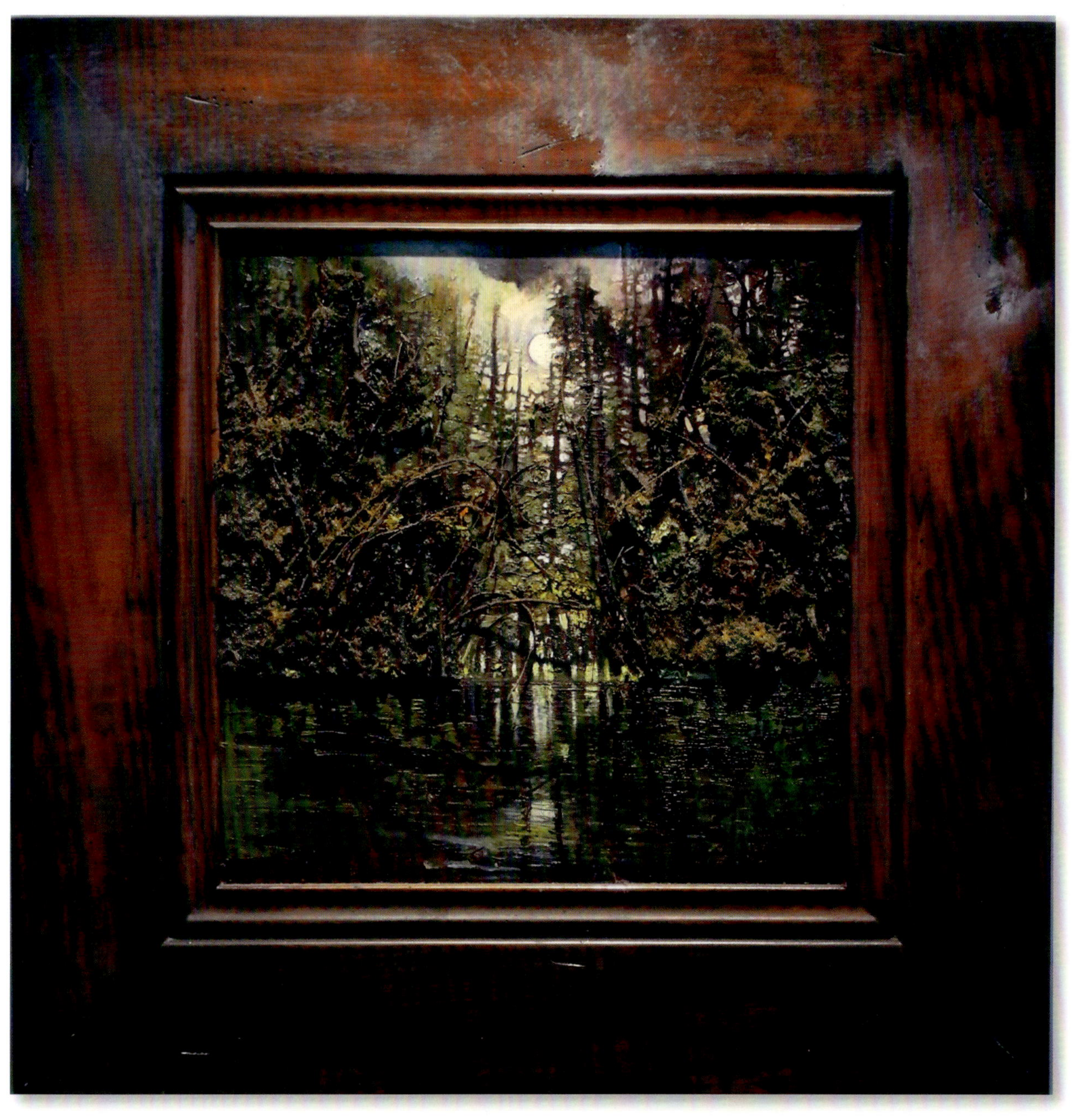

Rivermoon, 2010,
Oil and mixed media on board, 29 x 29 x 1.5 inches.
Collection of Marilyn Oshman.

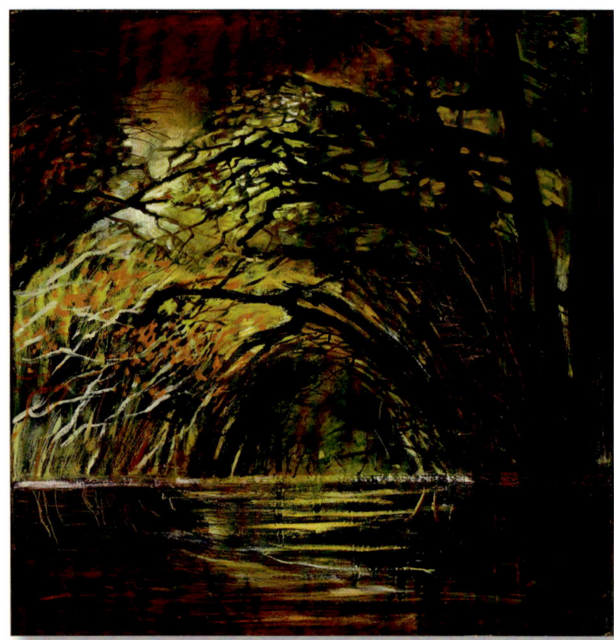

Brazos River, 2003,
Oil on board, 19 x 19 inches.
Collection of Marilyn Oshman.

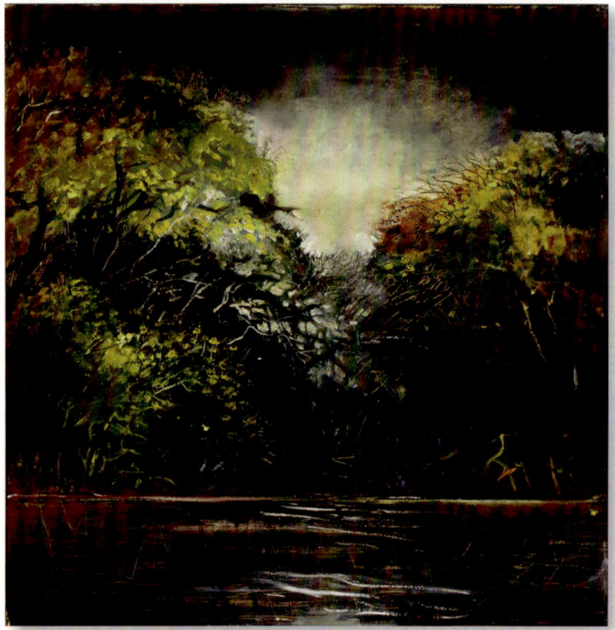

Old River, 2003,
Oil on board, 19 x 19 inches.
Collection of Barbara and Howard Hardin.

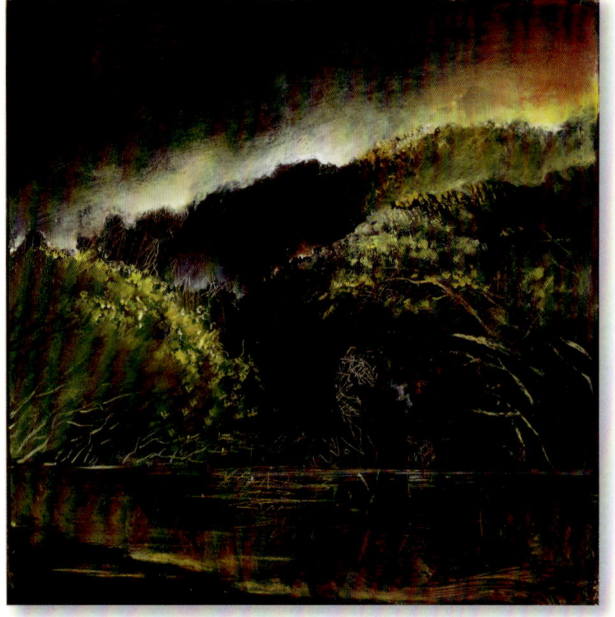

Lost River, 2003,
Oil on board, 19 x 19 inches.
Private collection.

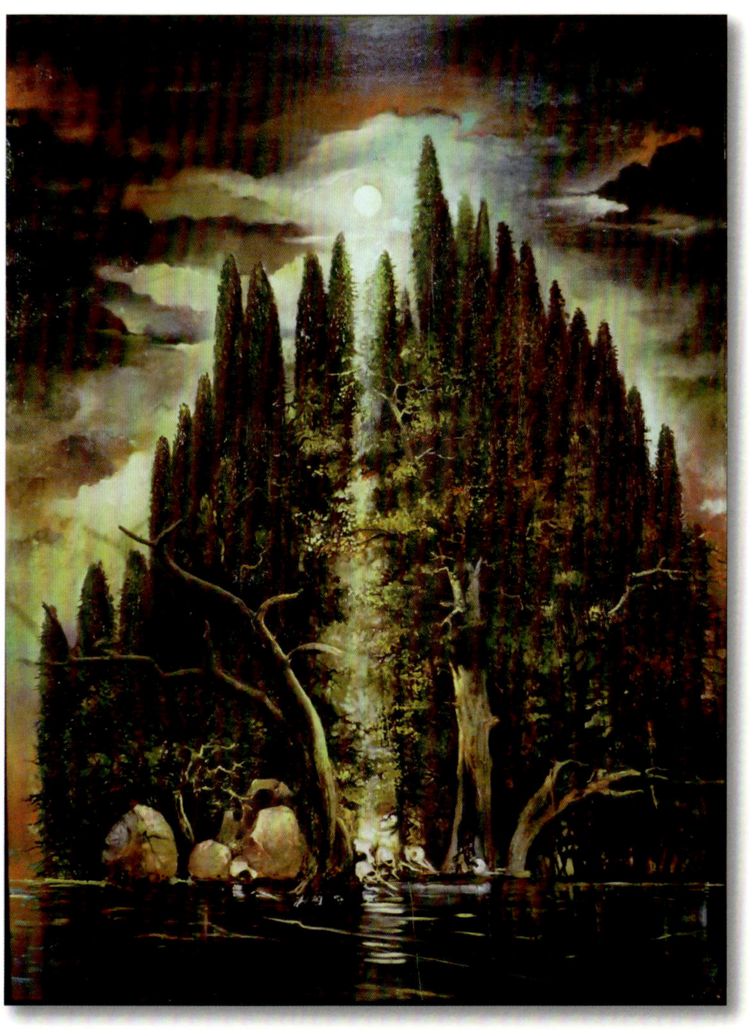

The Backside of Night, 2006,
Oil and mixed media on clayboard, 40 x 30 inches.
Collection of Jo Carole and Randy Long

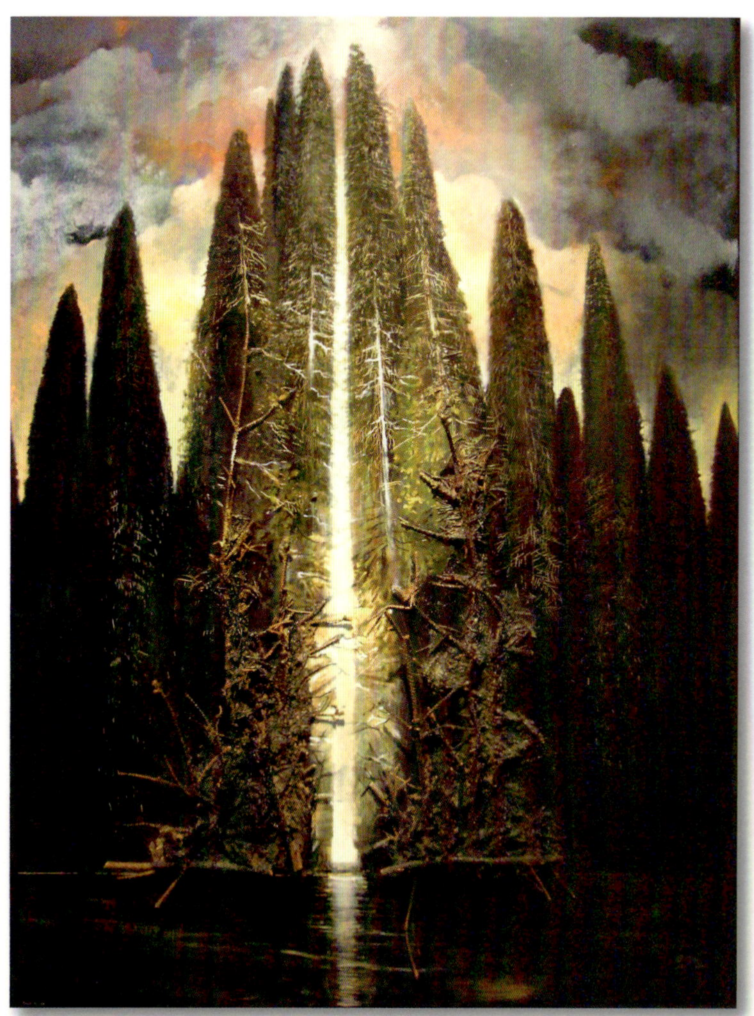

Helen's Gate, 2009,
Oil and mixed media on clayboard, 40 x 30 inches.
Collection of the Ogden Museum of Southern Art, New Orleans.

Matrimony, 2001 – 2012,
Papier-mâché and mixed media, 74 x 48 x 48 inches.
Collection of the artist.

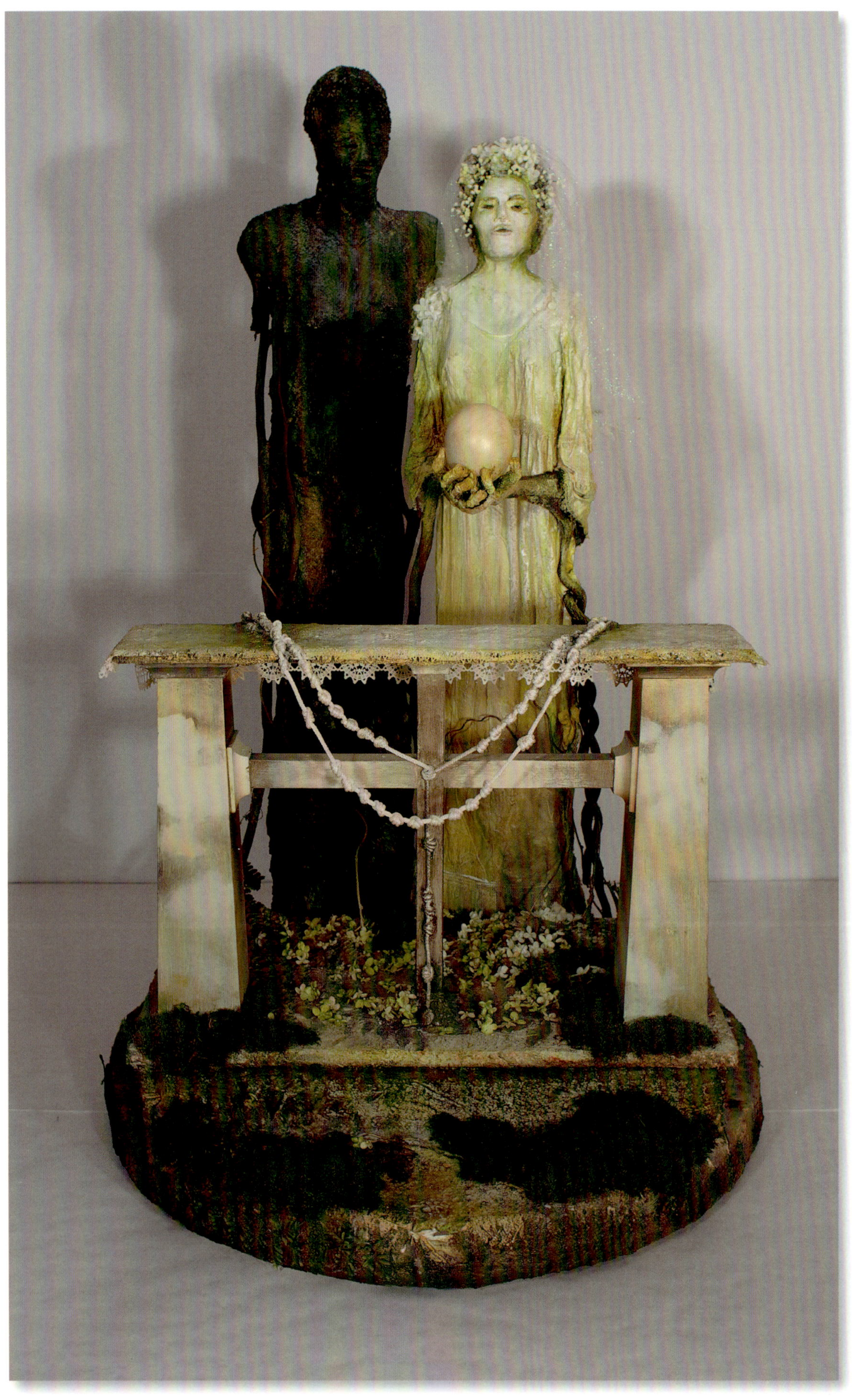

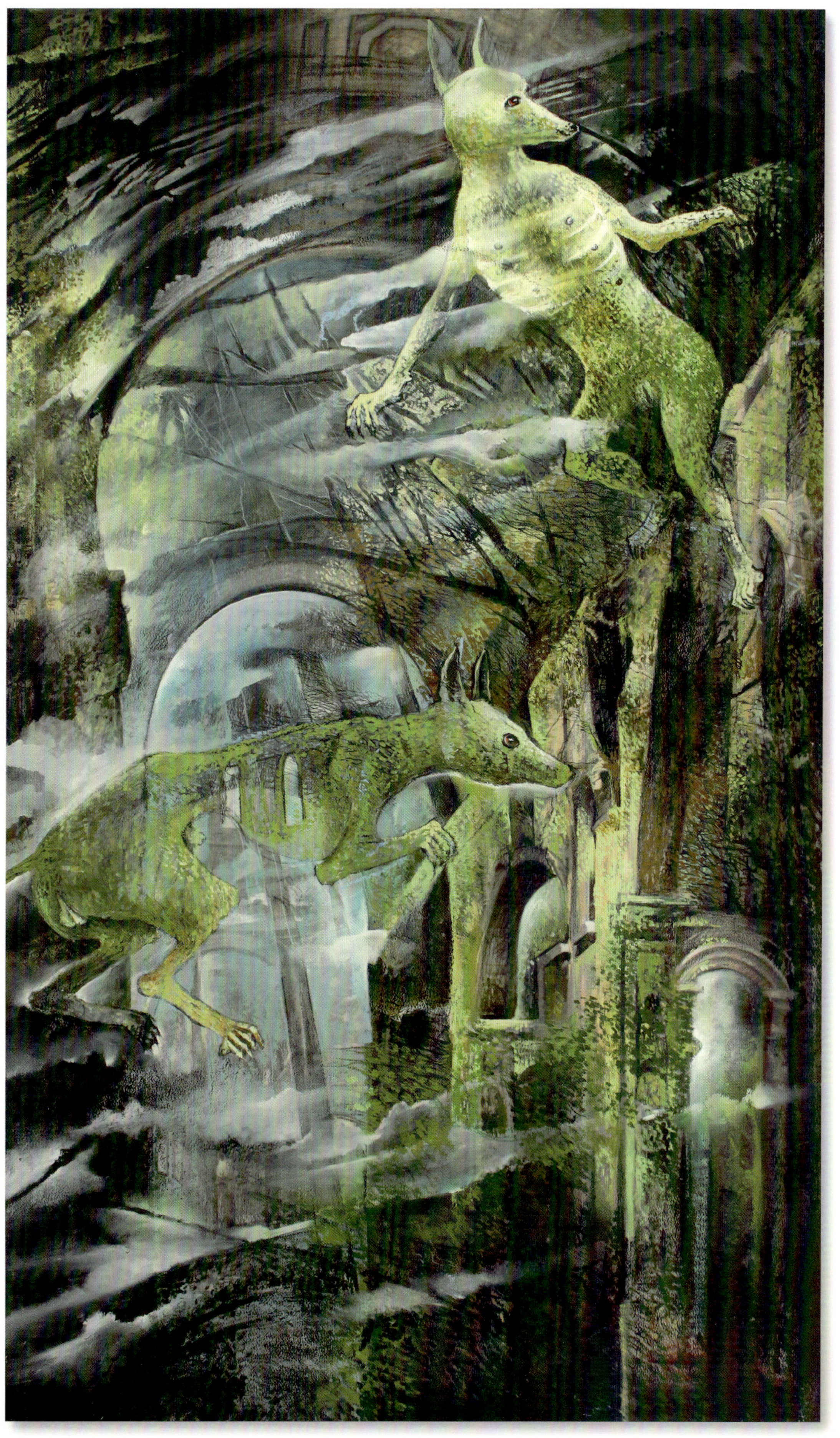

Emancipation of the Topiaries, 2012,
Oil and graphite on photo paper, 58 x 36 inches.
Collection of the artist.

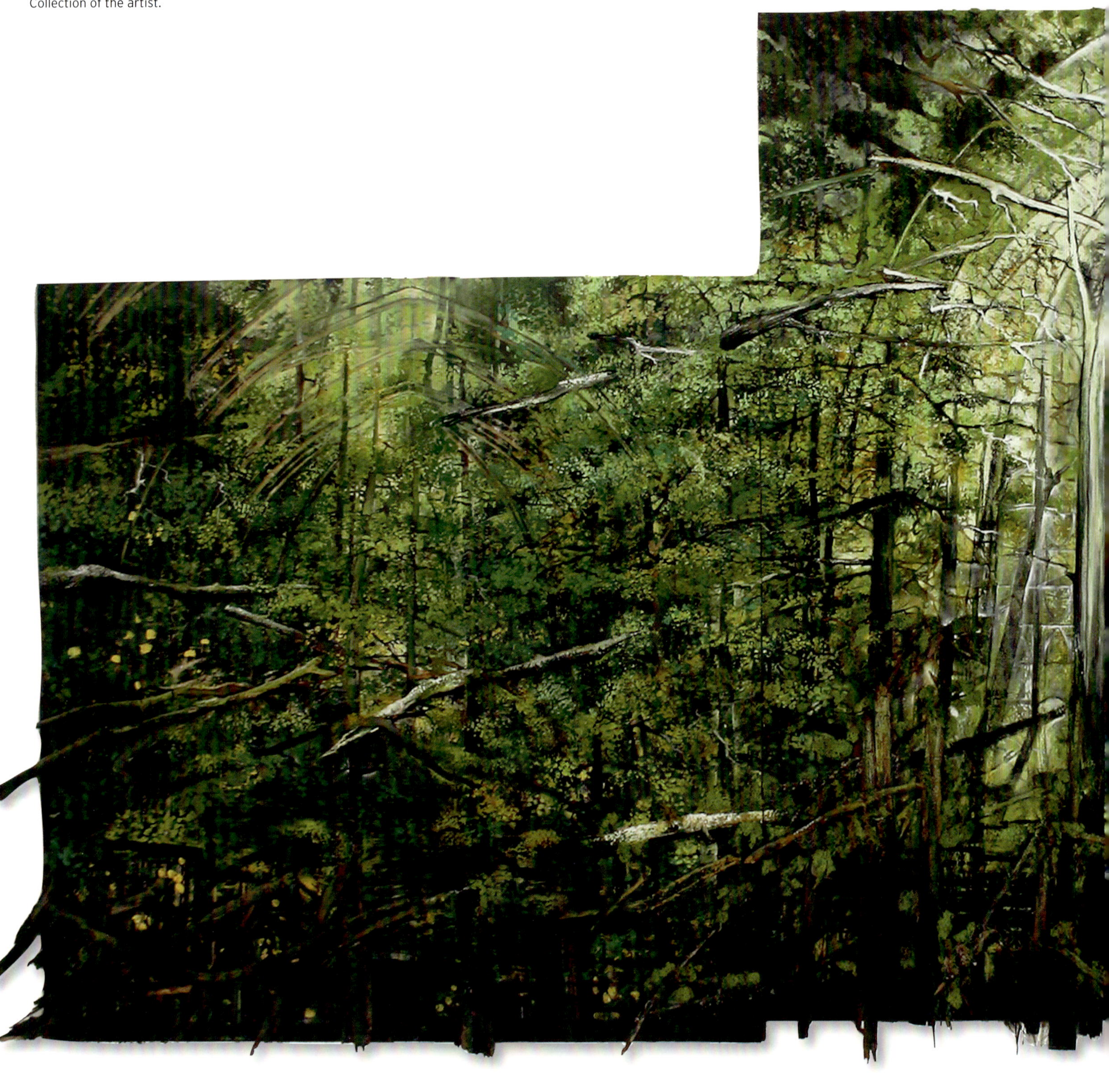

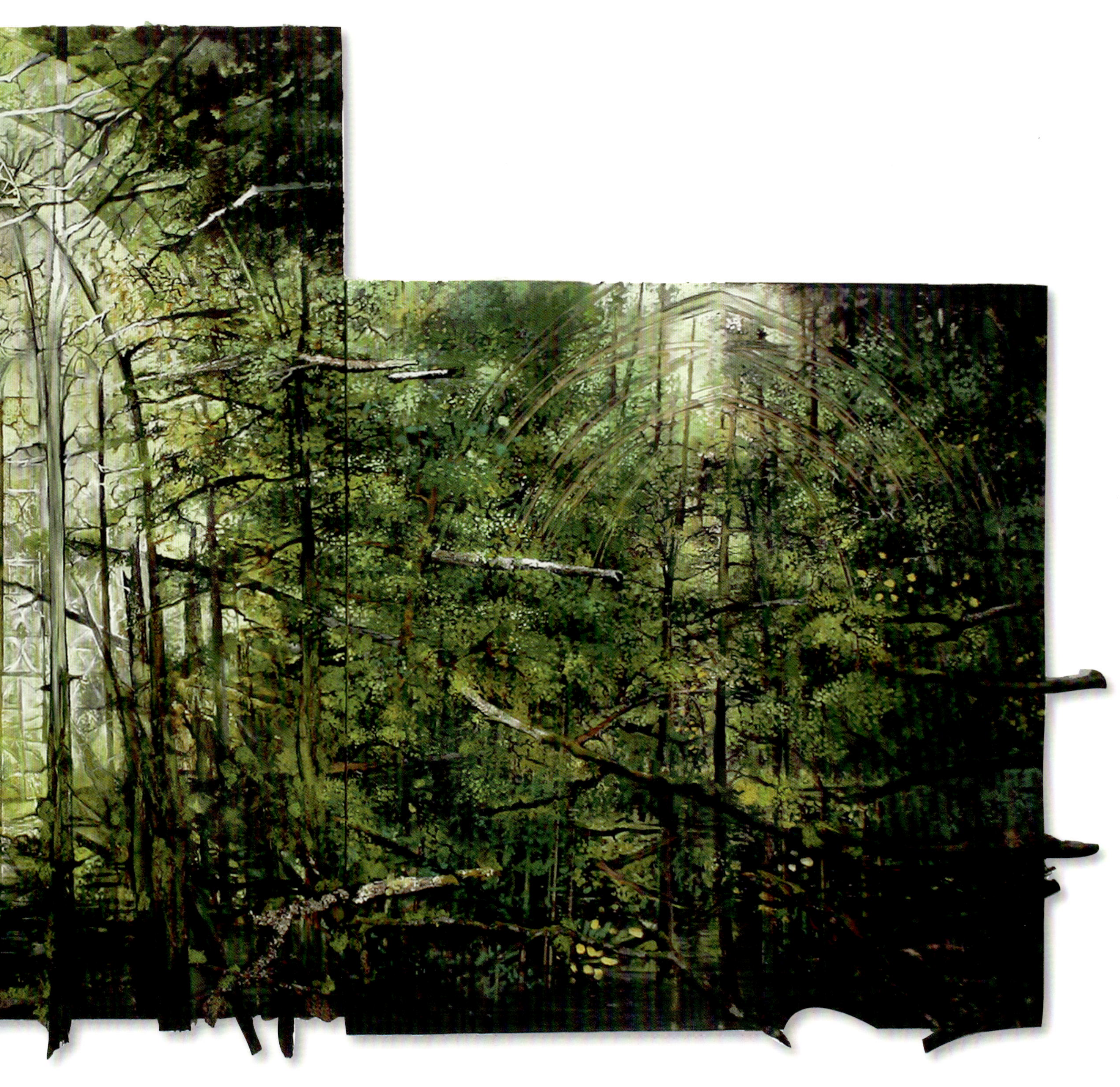

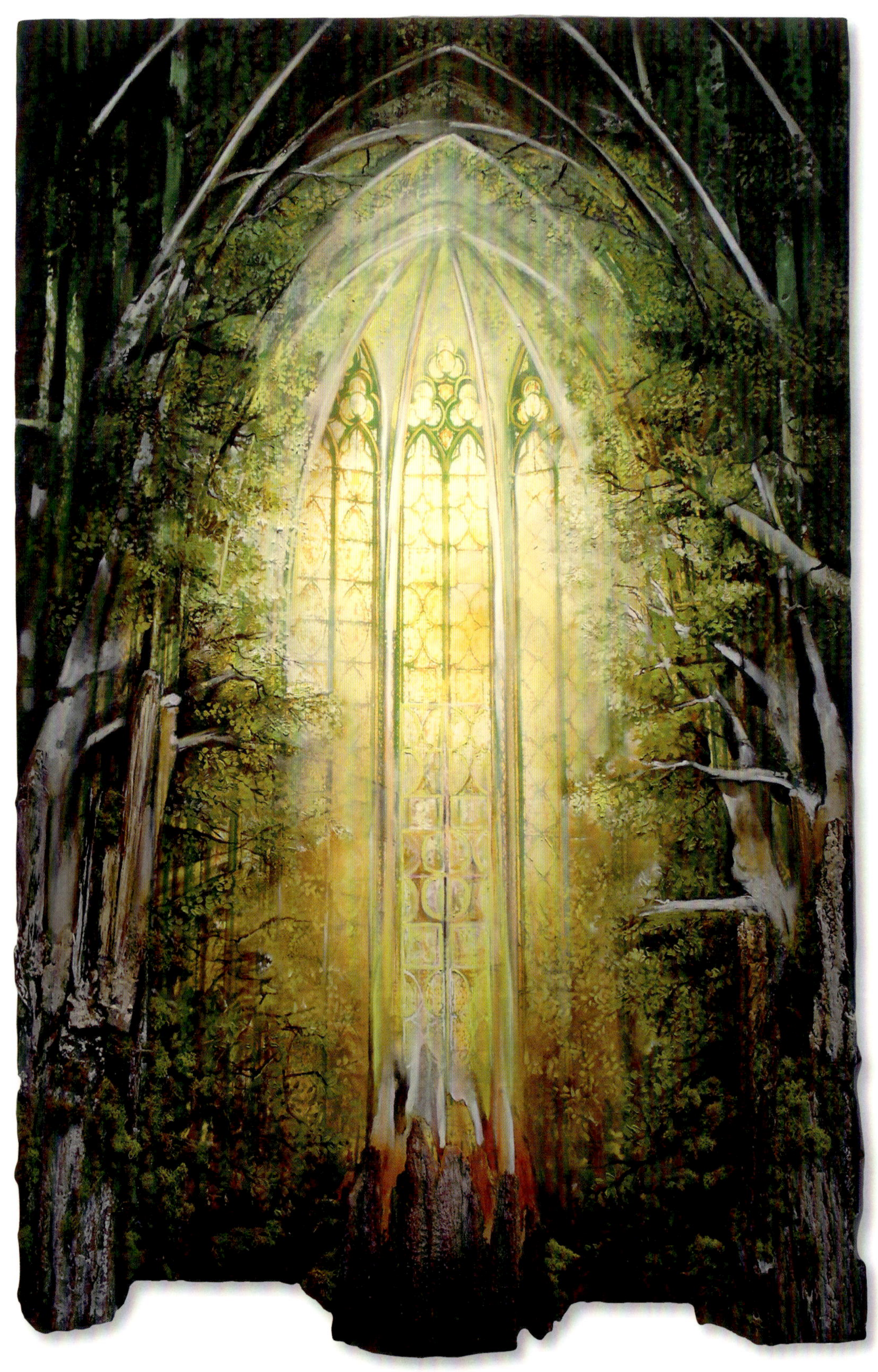

Sanctum, 2010-2011,
Oil and mixed media on photo canvas, 66 x 44 x 3 inches.
Collection of Dale Petrini.

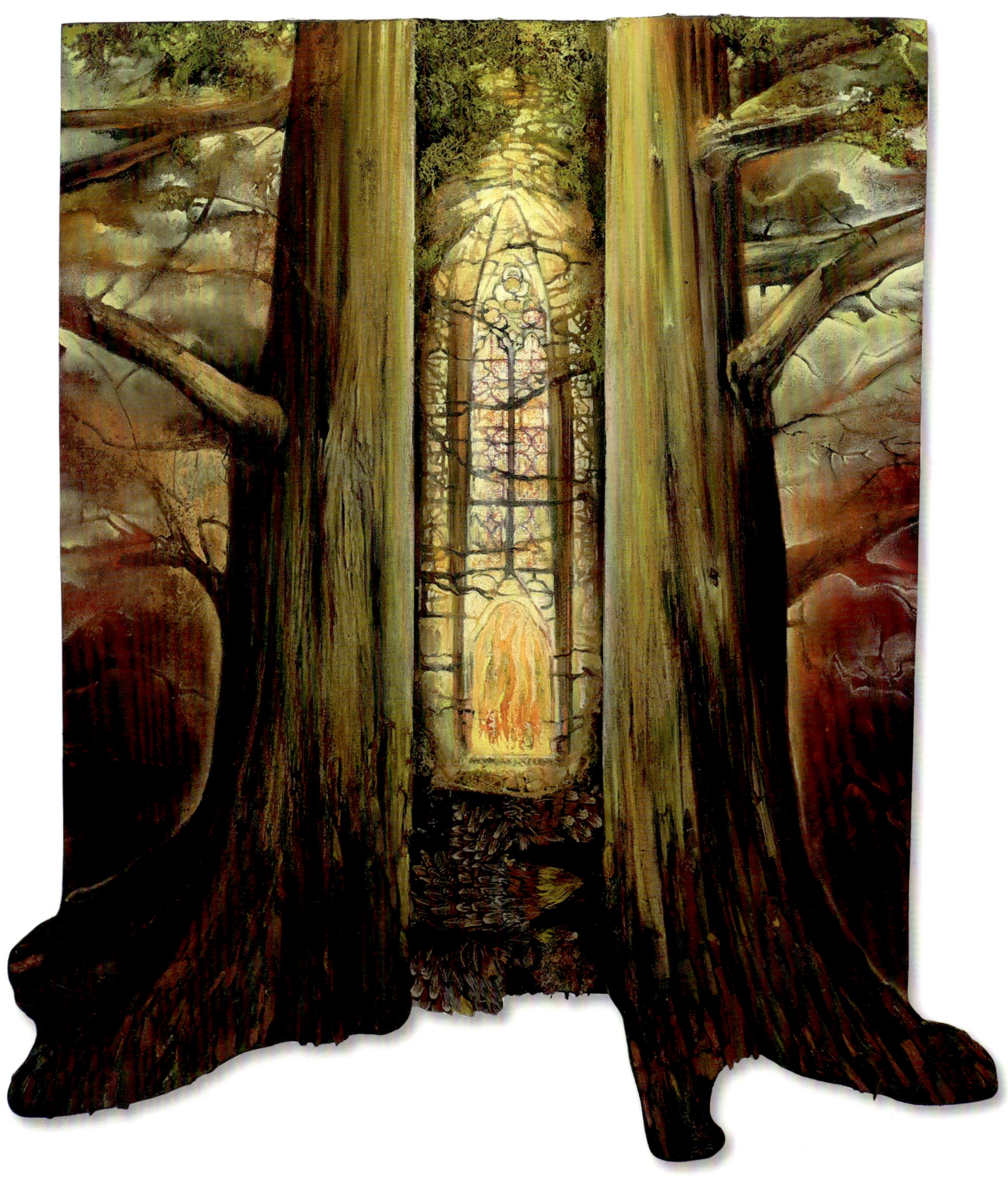

Alchemist's Tree, 2011,
Oil and mixed media on photo canvas, 40 x 36 x 2 inches.
Collection of Gwen and Dwayne Ortman.

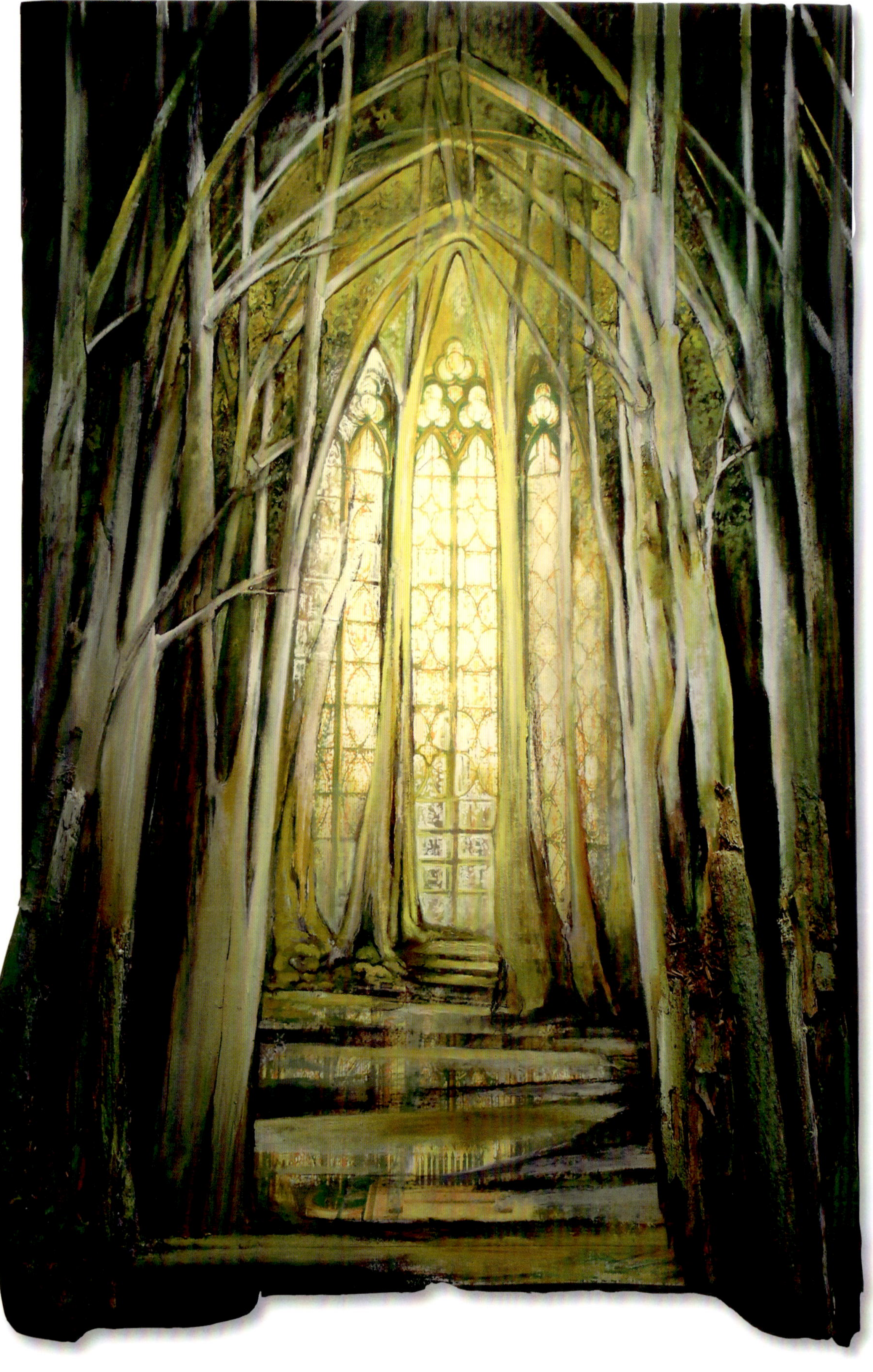

Hallowed Hall, 2011,
Oil and mixed media on photo canvas, 66 x 44 x 3 inches.
Collection of Christine Pillsbury.

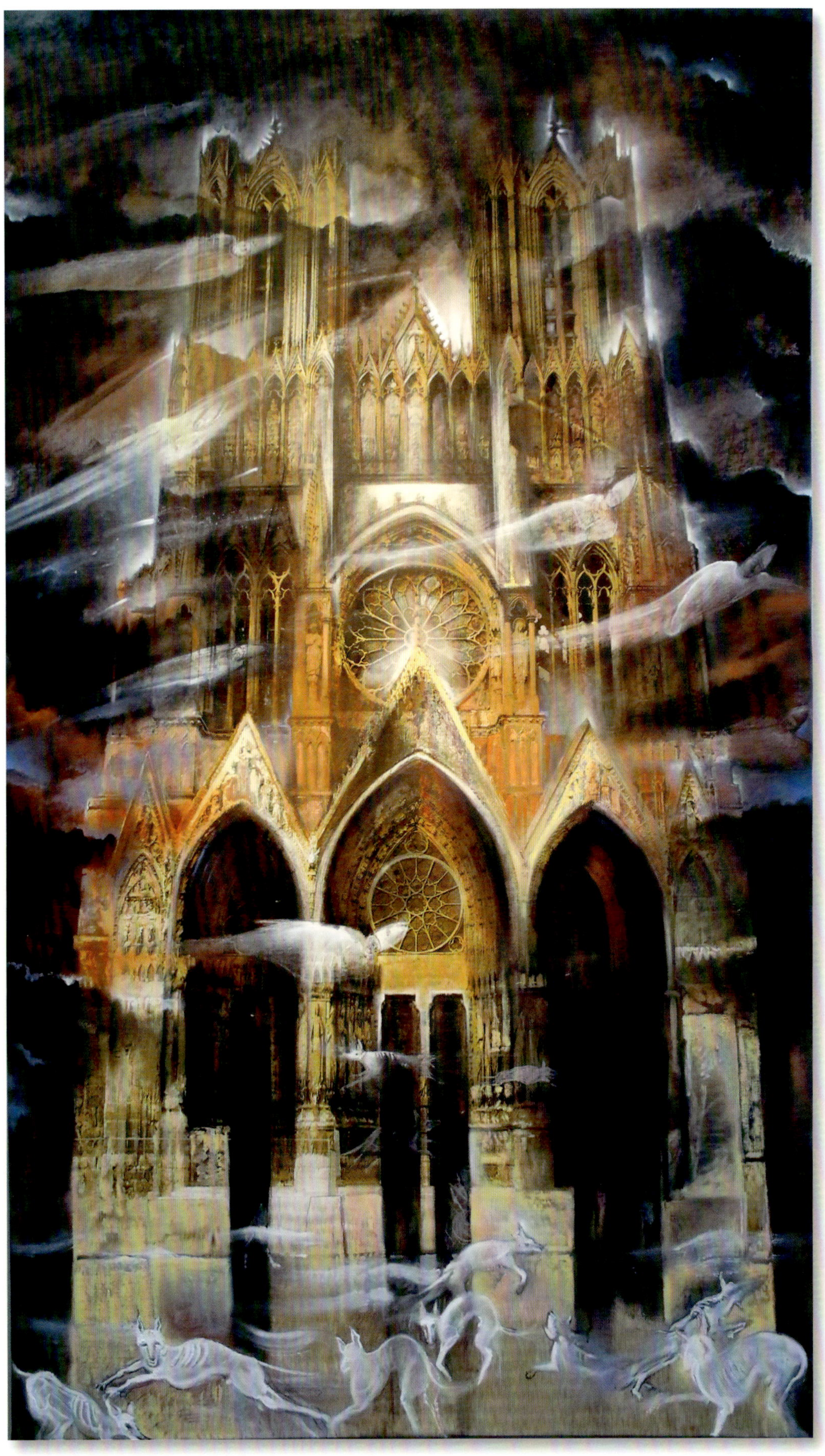

Night Sanctuary, 2010,
Oil on photo canvas, 68 x 40 inches.
Collection of Anne and Peter Brown.

Canis Major, 2010-2011,
Oil and mixed media on photo canvas,
75 x 48 x 11 inches.
Collection of the artist.

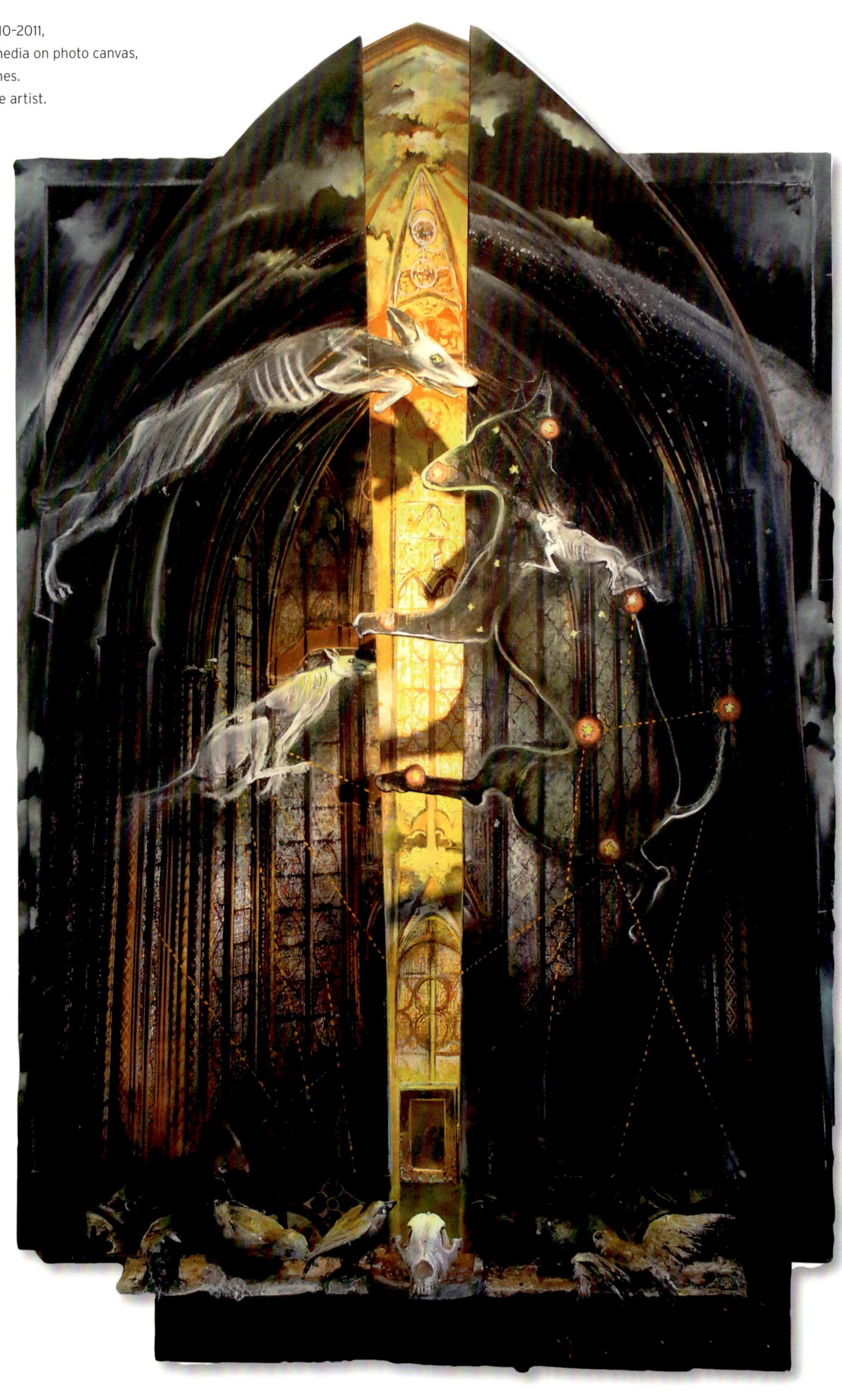

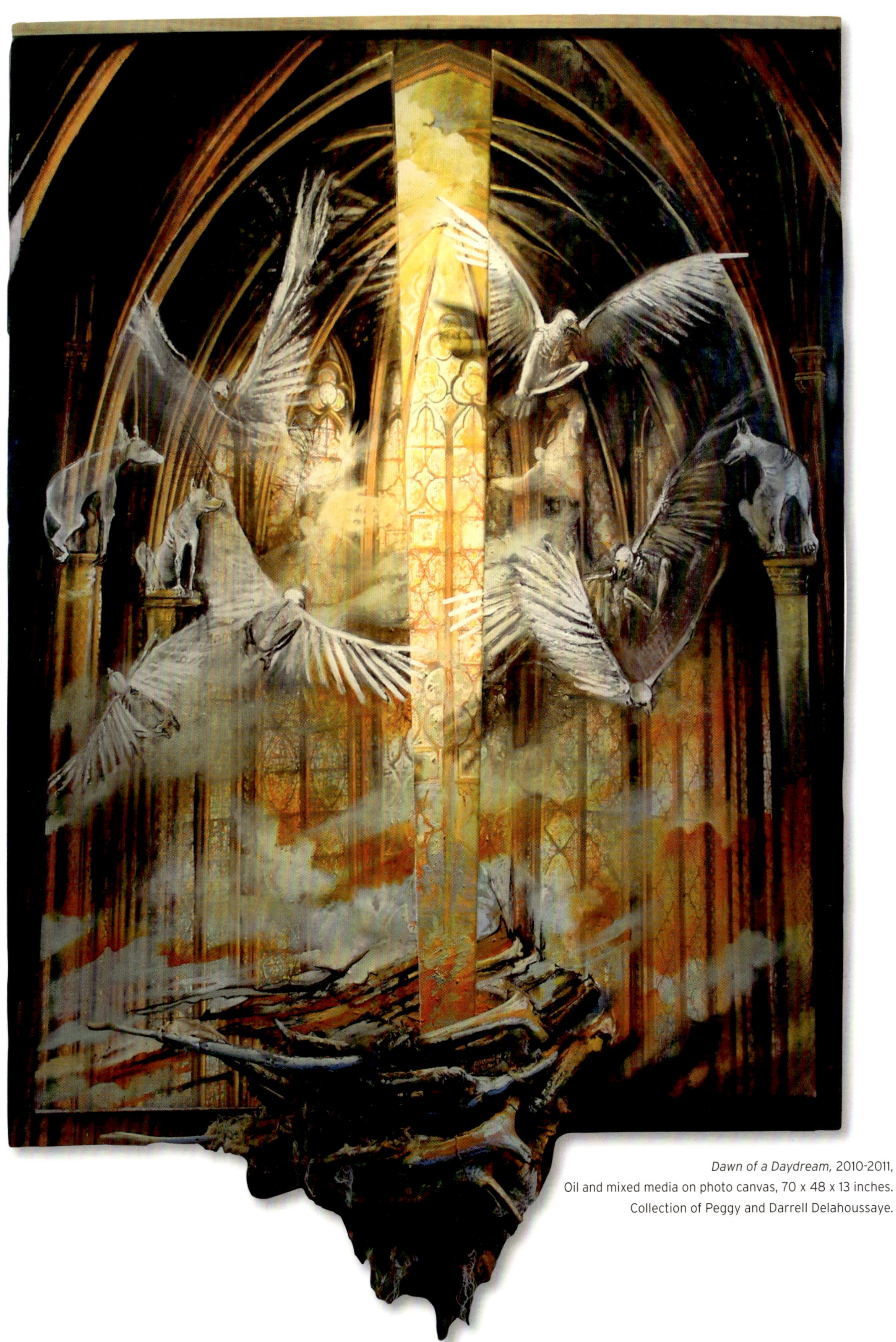

Dawn of a Daydream, 2010-2011,
Oil and mixed media on photo canvas, 70 x 48 x 13 inches.
Collection of Peggy and Darrell Delahoussaye.

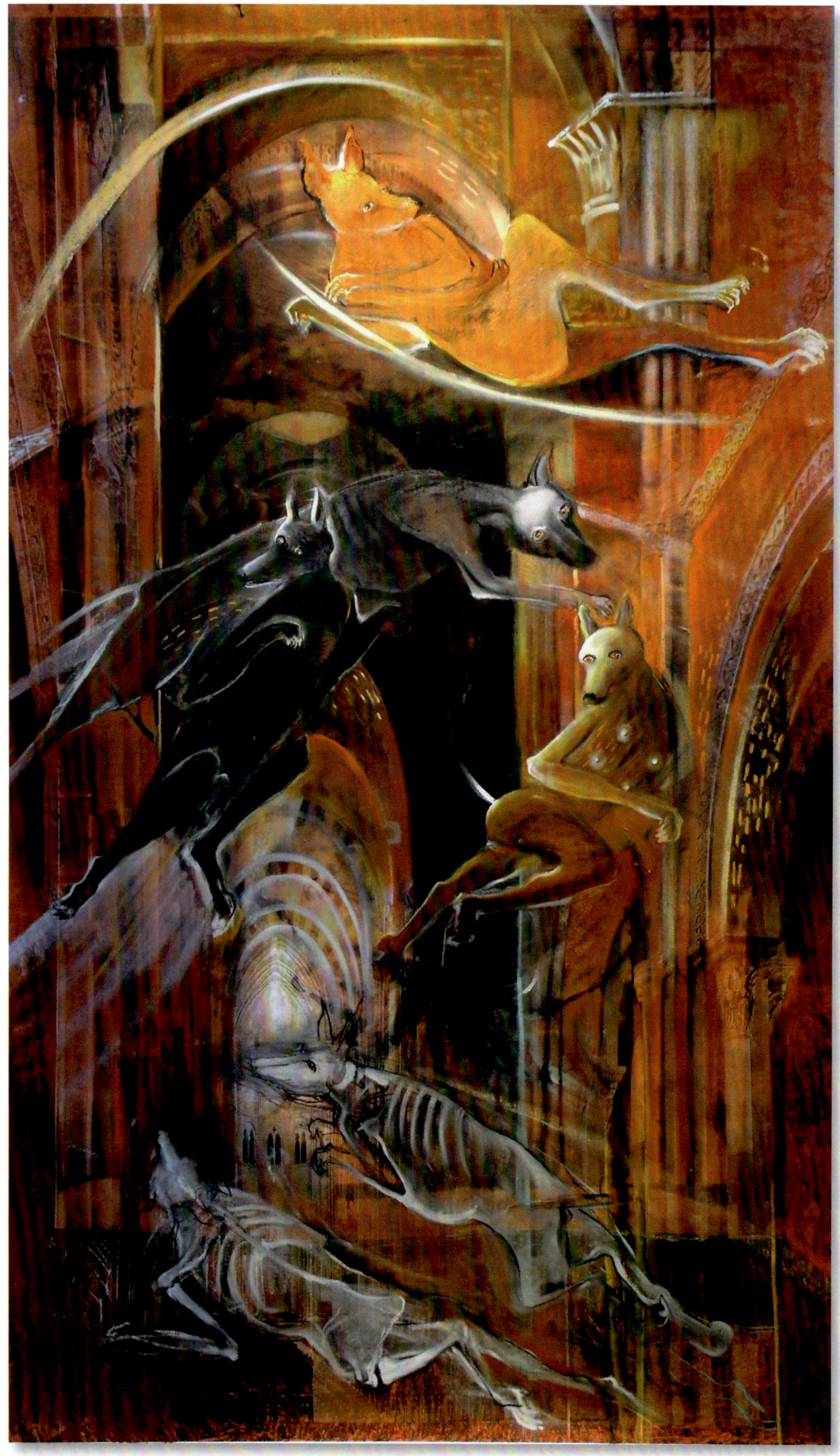

History of the World in Dog Years, 2011,
Oil and mixed media on photo canvas, 68 x 40 inches.
Collection of the artist.

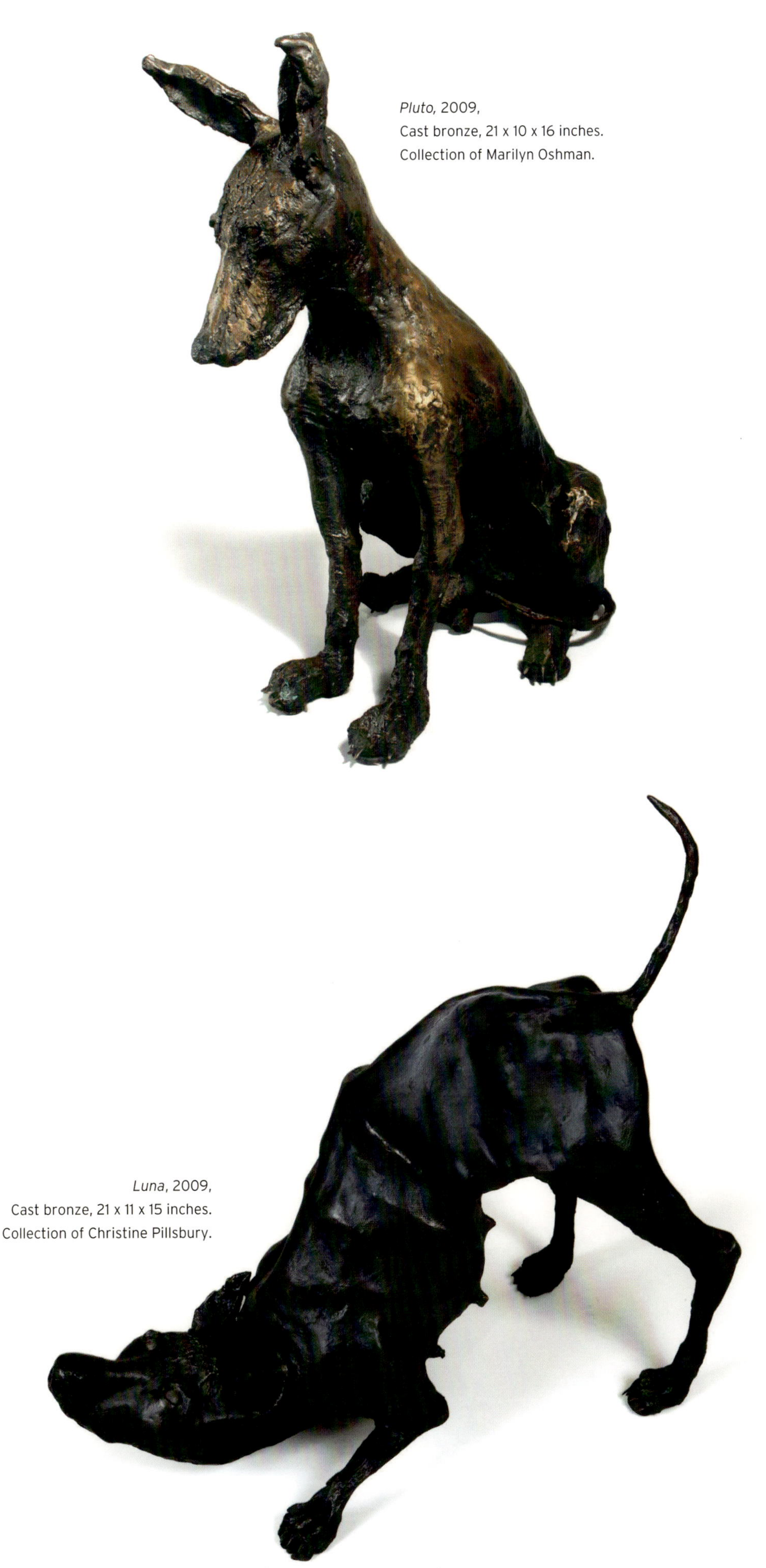

Pluto, 2009,
Cast bronze, 21 x 10 x 16 inches.
Collection of Marilyn Oshman.

Luna, 2009,
Cast bronze, 21 x 11 x 15 inches.
Collection of Christine Pillsbury.

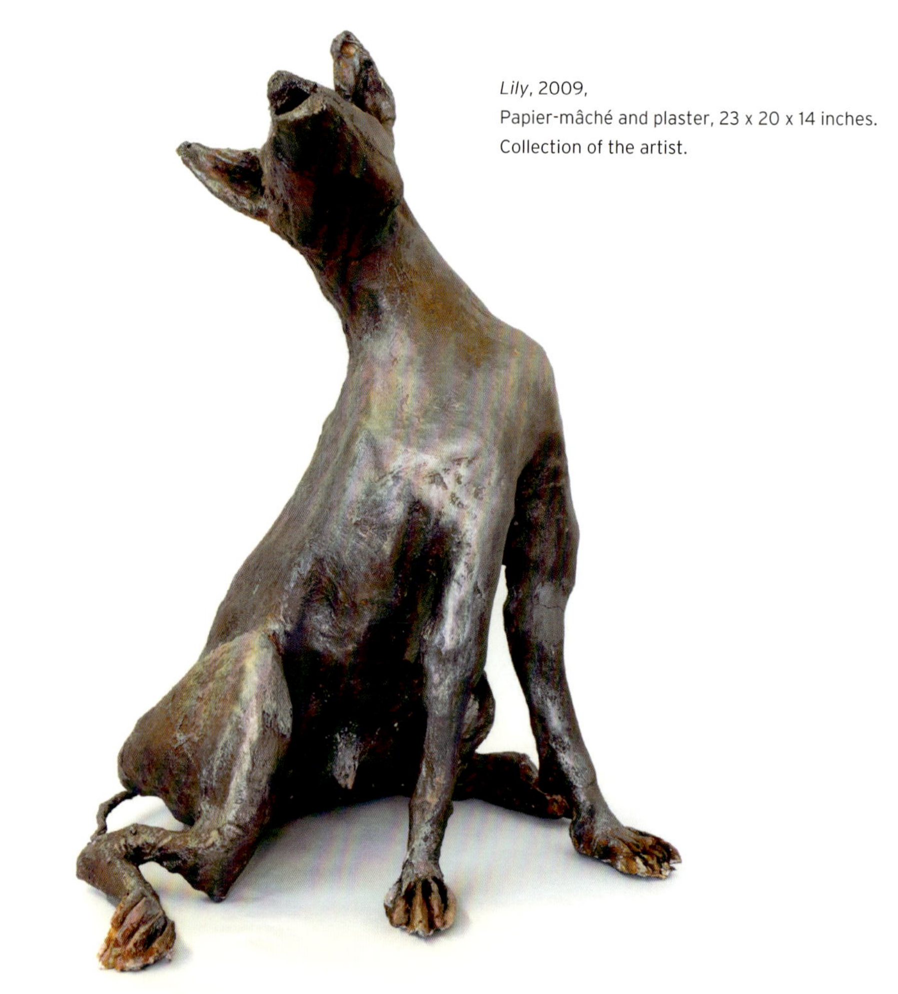

Lily, 2009,
Papier-mâché and plaster, 23 x 20 x 14 inches.
Collection of the artist.

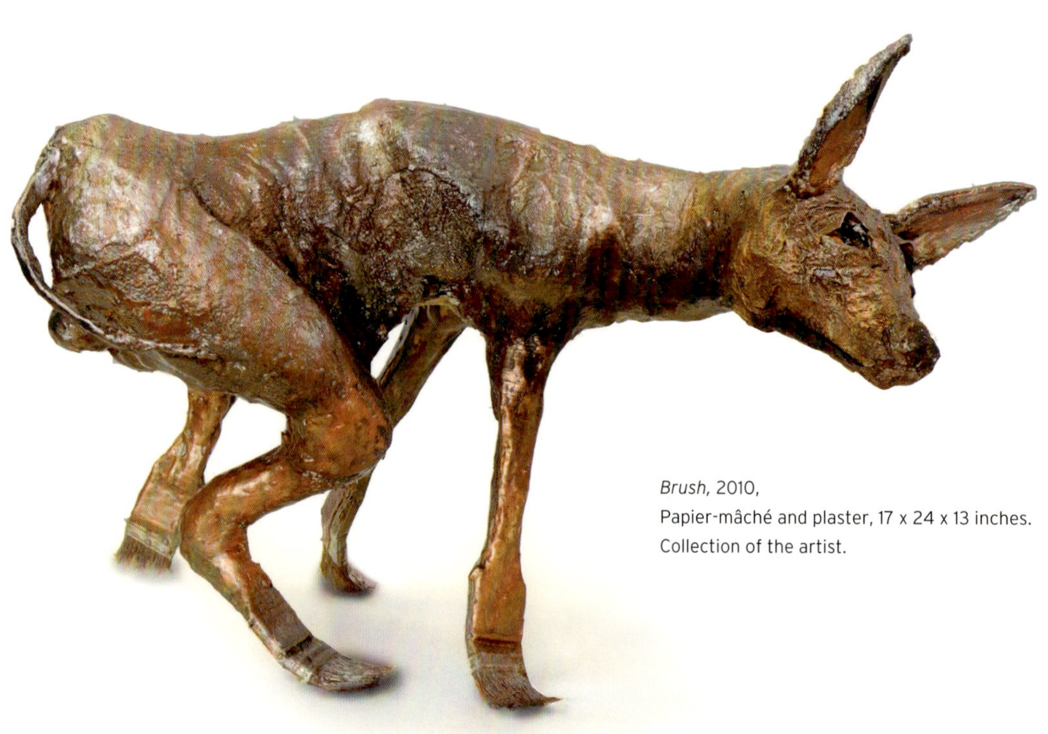

Brush, 2010,
Papier-mâché and plaster, 17 x 24 x 13 inches.
Collection of the artist.

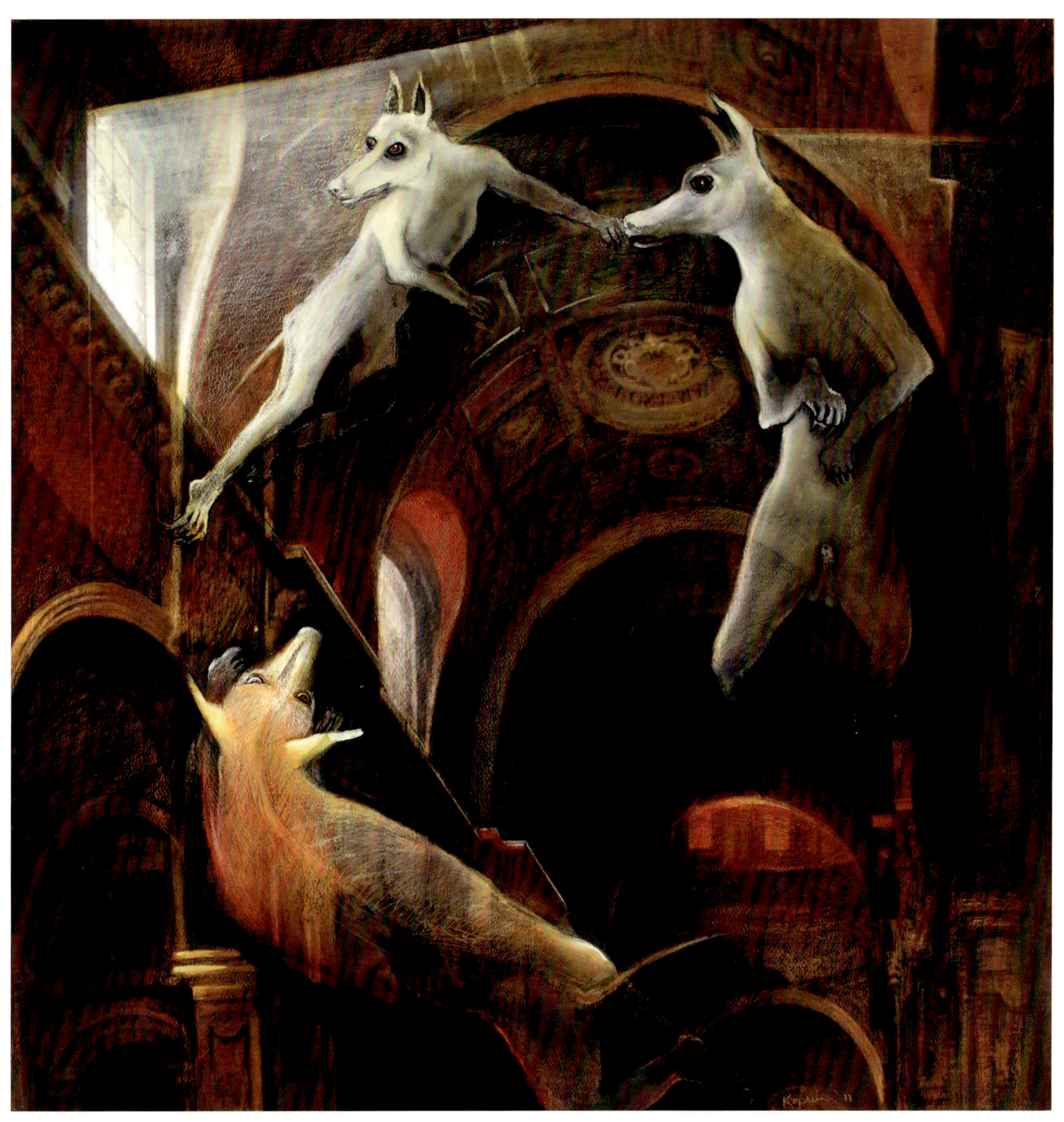

Vigilantes, 2012,
Oil and mixed media on photo paper, 44 x 44 inches.
Collection of Linda and James Clarke.

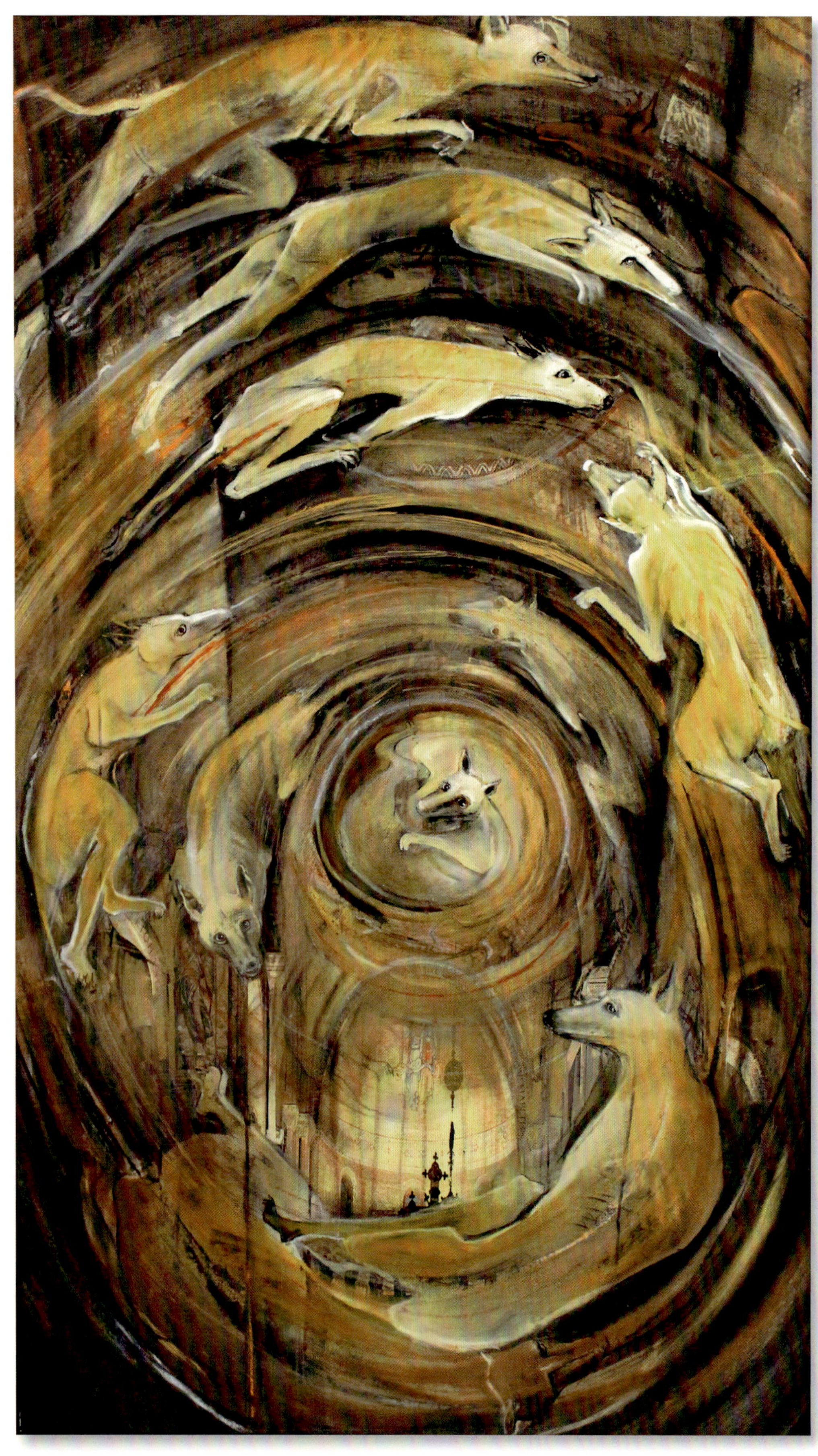

Solar Maelstrom, 2011,
Oil and mixed media on photo canvas, 68 x 40 inches.
Collection of the artist.

SHARON KOPRIVA'S MAGICAL REALISM

by Raphael Rubinstein

An artist who is best known for her sculptures of human figures and animals—mixed-media constructions that pair the sinewy grace of El Greco's saints and the decayed physiques of the catacomb or reliquary—Sharon Kopriva has placed architecture at the center of her vision in two recent series of paintings. This is not the first time Kopriva has availed herself of architectural form (her 2008 installation *The Conclave*, for instance, involves a giant birdcage shaped like a church cupola), but it is certainly her deepest investigation of the subject. The prevailing architectural style in one group of paintings is Gothic, specifically Gothic cathedrals, mostly French. In a second series of smaller paintings titled *Milestones*, the artist has focused on a more eclectic set of buildings and monuments.

On every occasion that a painter turns his or her attention to architecture it is worth remembering how, once upon a time, painting and architecture were not so separated as they are today. The early history of Western painting is essentially a history of how images were divorced from architecture, how frescoes and altarpieces evolved into easel paintings. Although there have been numerous instances of artists seeking to remarry painting and architecture (most notably with the Mexican muralists), these two mediums tend to go their separate ways. However, this primordial separation has not prevented painters from turning their vision to architectural structures; Kopriva's paintings are among the latest instances of this dialogue. Her choice of the Gothic cathedral as her subject places her in a line that we can trace back to Monet's sequential Rouen Cathedral paintings of the 1890s, to Turner's studies of Salisbury Cathedral around the turn of the 18th century and to Caspar David Friedrich's depictions of Gothic ruins in the early decades of the 19th century.

Of these three precedents, it is Friedrich's that is closest in feeling to Kopriva's work. Although her cathedrals are still intact, with even their stained-glass windows in perfect condition, and thus in dramatic contrast to Friedrich's panoramas of craggy remnants of once-grand edifices, Kopriva makes a visual connection between Gothic architecture and nature that is in perfect keeping with Friedrich's Northern Romanticism. In several paintings the cathedrals are being slowly taken over by encroaching forests: tall, tapering tree trunks; canopies of green leaves, zigzagging paths. In one painting, *The Alchemist's Tree*, a single massive tree encloses almost totally a cathedral interior, with only a single pointed-arch stained-glass window visible through a cleft in the tree. This ancient-looking tree is rendered even more impressive by the artist's decision to construct the work as a painting/relief sculpture, extending the base of the tree into three dimensions with her characteristic sculptural skill.

Kopriva begins these paintings by scanning vintage photographs of cathedrals. She then digitally alters the images in various ways: stretching them, flopping them, adjusting color and contrast. Finally, the digital image is transferred at a much larger scale to canvas with an ink-jet printer. One of the most impressive qualities of these paintings is how Kopriva achieves a seamless continuity between the mechanically reproduced image and the hand-painted image; it's impossible to say where one stops and the other begins. This lends a striking veracity to Kopriva's dreamlike scenarios, creating a mood of magical realism.

The natural imagery in Kopriva's work, especially the tree-thronged cathedrals, draws on her frequent visits to the vast forests and woods of Idaho. (Although based in Houston, Kopriva spends every summer in Idaho where she is part of an artistic community that first gathered around Ed Kienholz and Nancy Reddin Kienholz.) While the imagery in these mixed-media paintings is based on actual observation, it also emerges from venerable literary and artistic tradition of fusing forests and cathedrals through metaphor. In his 1905 essay "The Gothic in the Cathedrals and Churches of France," Rodin observed: "You enter a cathedral. You find it full of the mysterious life of the forest; and the reason of it is that it reproduces that life by artistic compression, so that the rock, the tree—Nature, in fine—is there; an epitome of Nature." Several decades earlier, the American poet Henry Wadsworth Longfellow published a sonnet titled "My Cathedral" in which he compared the "stately pines" of a forest with the towers of a cathedral.

Imbued with Romanticism's glorification of nature, and a pantheistic vision of America as an Edenic landscape unburdened by Europe's bone-filled sepulchers and "marble bishops," Longfellow preferred the forest's architecture because "Not Art but Nature traced these lovely lines/ And carved this graceful arabesque of vines." Similar themes emerge in William Cullen Bryant's "A Forest Hymn," a long poem which asserts that "the groves were God's first temples" where man, before he learned to "lay the architrave" or construct "the loft vault," could kneel in prayer "in the darkling wood,/ Amidst the cool and silence." (In an intriguing precedent to Kopriva's series, John A. Nums's frontispiece of the 1860 New York edition of Bryant's poem depicts a leafy wood framed by a vine-covered Gothic archway.)

In the cathedral paintings where the primeval forest is kept at bay something equally startling happens: the religious buildings become settings for scenes of strange choreography in which the Gothic interiors swirl with airborne dogs. These unusual-looking canines belong to the rare, ancient breed known as Peruvian Hairless that Kopriva has been passionately raising in recent years. Although Peruvian Hairless are featured in a number of paintings, Kopriva continually varies their appearance and mood. In *Insomniac's Nightmare* a half-dozen or so pale dogs curve sinuously through the dark, vaulted space of the Saint Madeleine Cathedral of Vezely, France. The feeling in *Solar Maelstrom* is very different: against the backdrop of Venice's Basilica di San Marco nearly a dozen Peruvian Hairless are arrayed in a vortex, circling a golden glowing orb within which a dog is curled fetus-like. The Saint Madeleine Cathedral reappears in the wonderfully titled *A History of the World in Dog Years,* but now the structure (and one of the dogs coursing through it) is bathed in a crimson light.

What the Peruvian Hairless offer to Kopriva, apart from the chance to celebrate the sleek forms and attentive visages of her beloved pets, is a kind of surrogate for the human figure. Because the musculature of their bodies is so evident, these dogs become occasions for the artist to paint what are essentially naked forms, figures with all the physical nuances of a Classical nude. There is also an implied religious message. If, in the cathedral/forest paintings Kopriva reconciles Pagan and Christian visions of holy space, in the Peruvian Hairless series she brings together animals identified with Incan culture (and renowned for their reputed healing powers) and the preeminent artistic achievement of Western European Christianity.

If the Cathedral paintings celebrate spiritual energy, the *Milestones* are largely concerned with its polar opposite, the destructive force of political conflict. Each work in the series is like a small votive painting, surrounded by an arched frame and featuring built-up relief elements along the bottom of the picture. The subjects range from legendary moments in ancient history (the destruction of the Tower of Babel, the building of the Trojan Horse) to iconic events of the 20th and 21st centuries, from Kristallnacht to Tiananmen Square in 1989 to the 9/11 attacks in New York City. Rather than evoking poetic reveries in the manner of Caspar David Friedrich's Romantic ruin-paintings, Kopriva's vanquished cities and crumbling monuments invite visions of terror and death. Their modest scale somehow renders the horrors they depict even more terrible at the same time that it challenges the artistic convention that history painting requires a large scale. And yet, these artfully crafted pictures do not offer a totally hopeless account of human history: one painting portrays the fall of the Berlin Wall and another a Whistleresque vignette of Mahatma Gandhi's 1930 Salt March. If Kopriva has a keen sense of mortality (of individuals and of civilizations), she is also ready to celebrate the persistence of hope and the new life that can grow amid the ruins of history—that is the real magic of her magical realism.

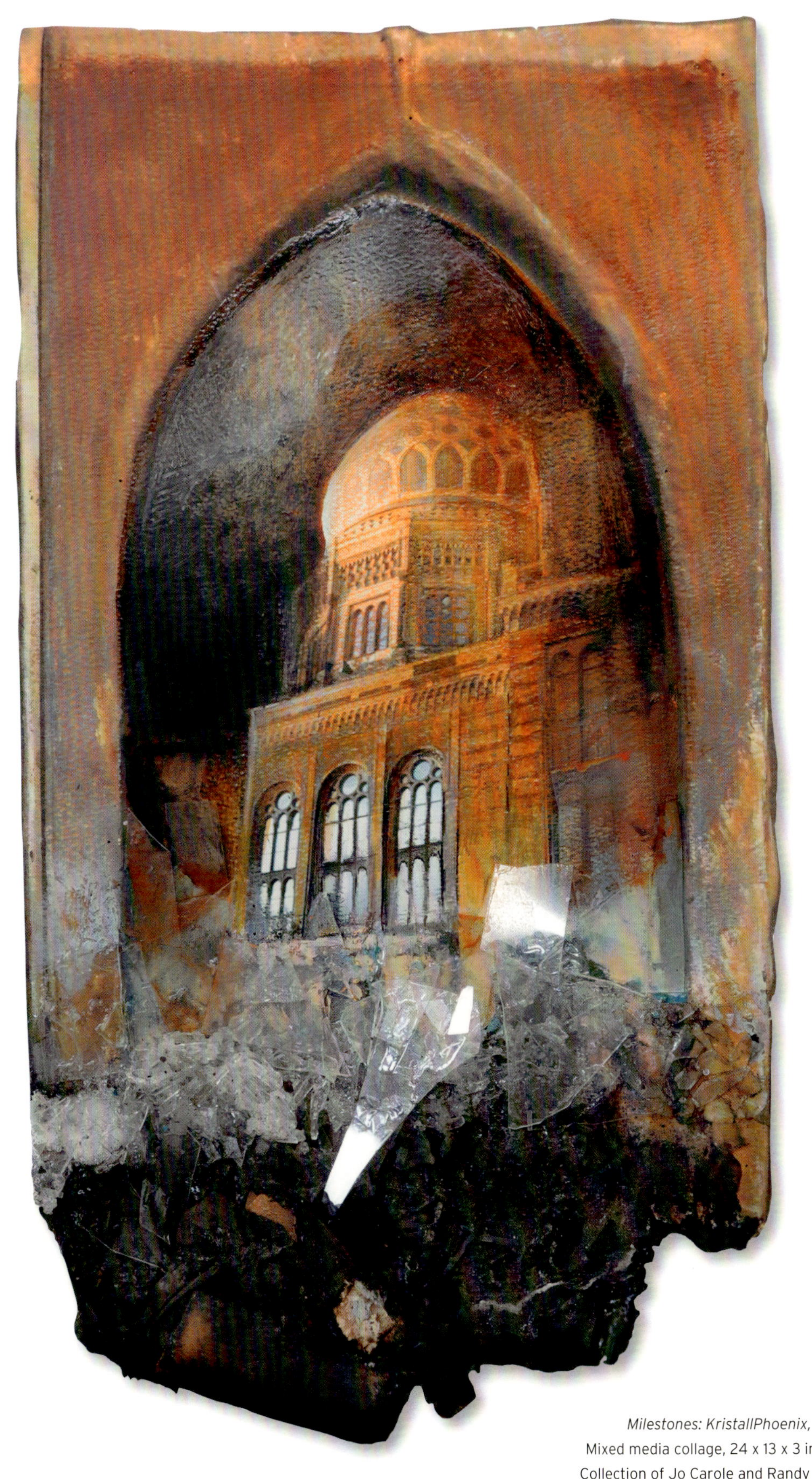

Milestones: KristallPhoenix, 2010,
Mixed media collage, 24 x 13 x 3 inches.
Collection of Jo Carole and Randy Long.

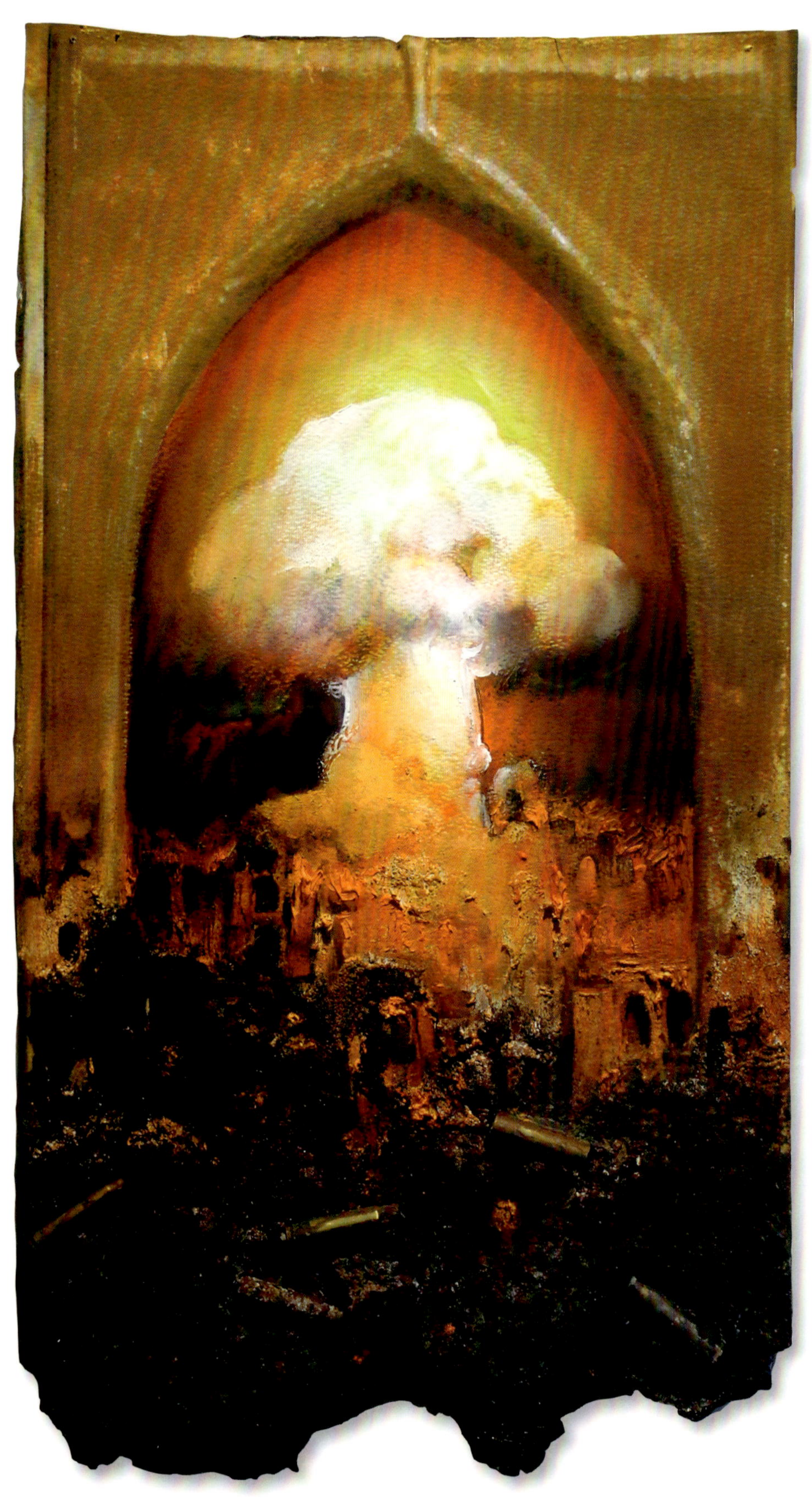

Milestones: 1945, 2009,
Mixed media collage, 23 x 14 x 3 inches.
Courtesy of Deborah Colton Gallery, Ho.

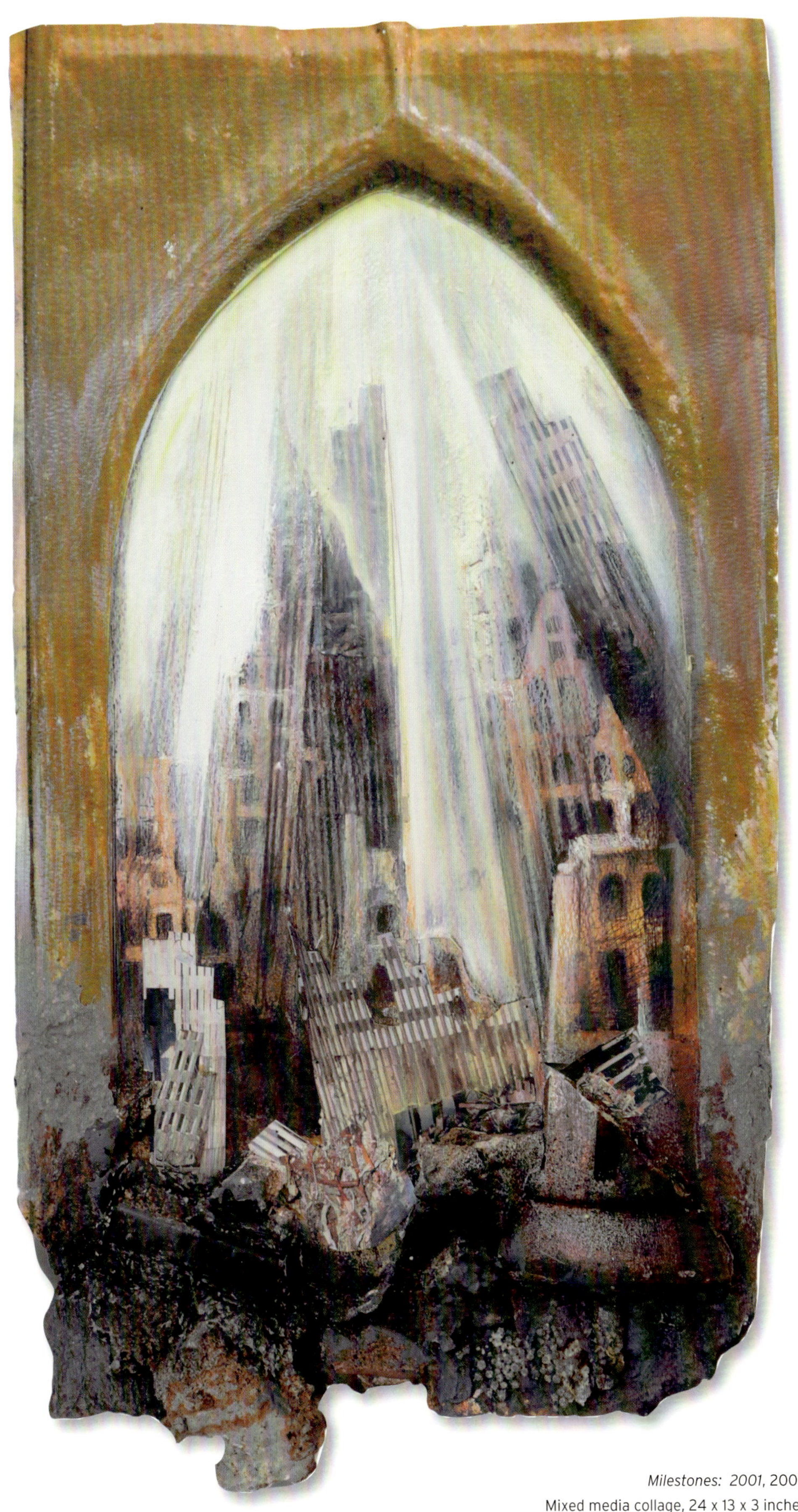

Milestones: 2001, 2009,
Mixed media collage, 24 x 13 x 3 inches.
Collection of Jo Carole and Randy Long.

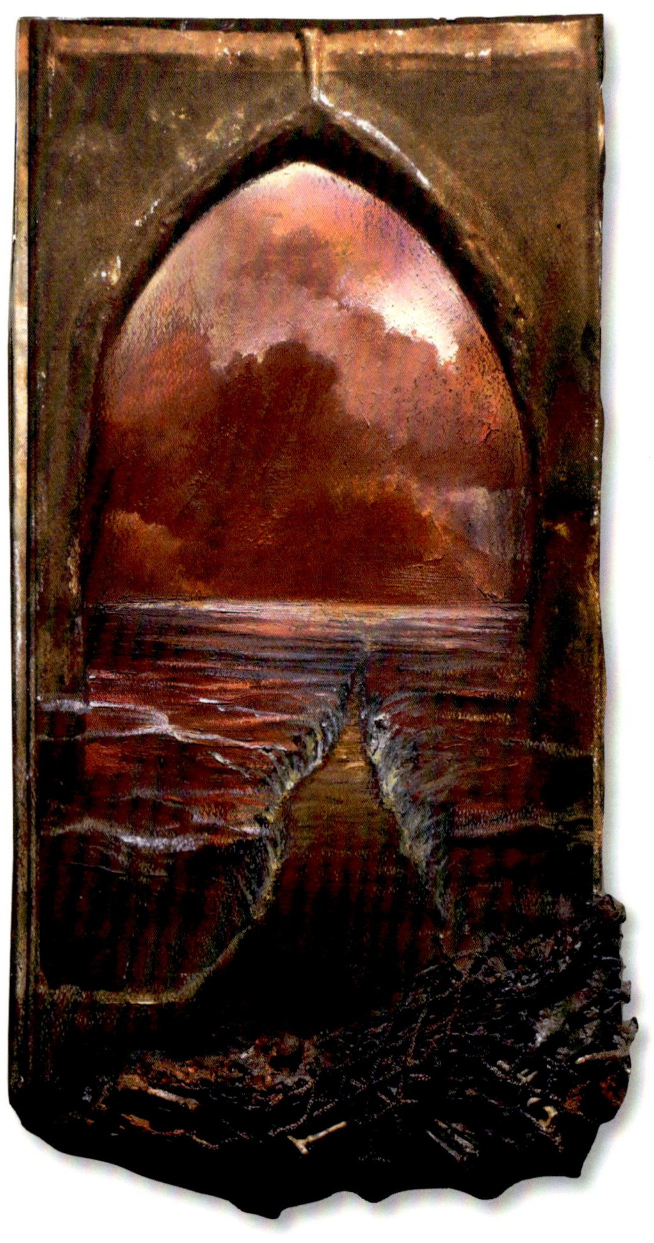

Milestones: Crossing the Red Sea, 2011,
Mixed media collage, 24 x 14 x 3 inches.
Courtesy of Deborah Colton Gallery, Houston.

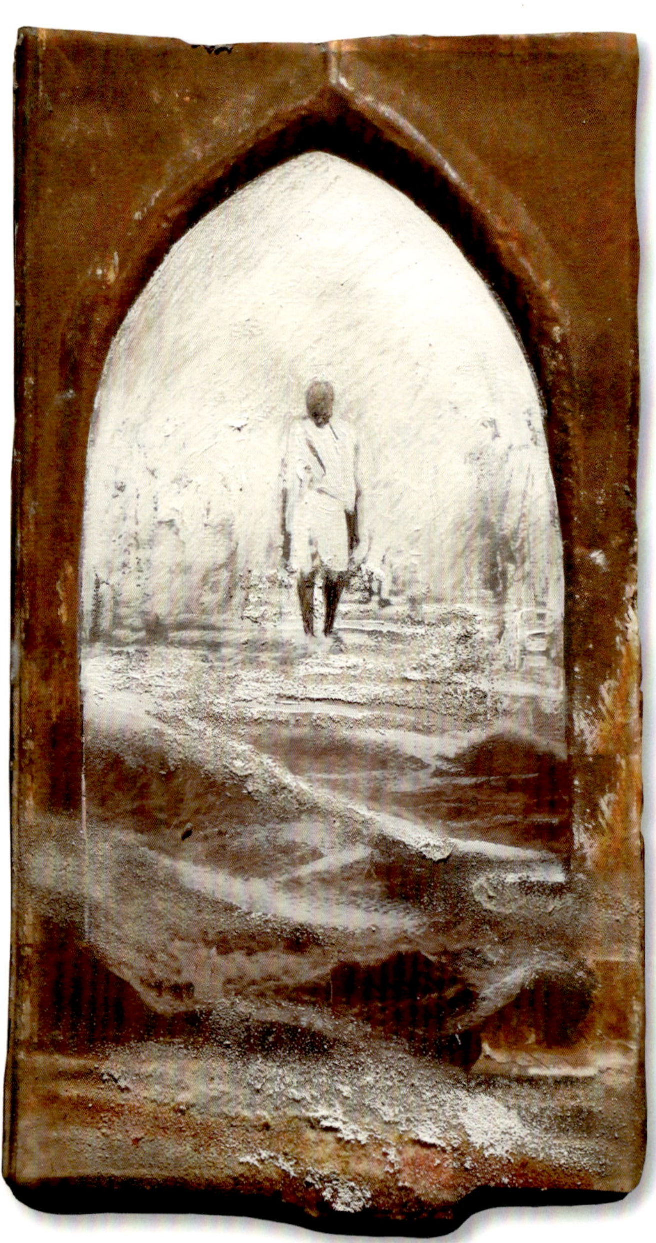

Milestones: Salt March, 2011,
Mixed media collage, 24 x 14 x 3 inches.
Collection of Dale Johnson.

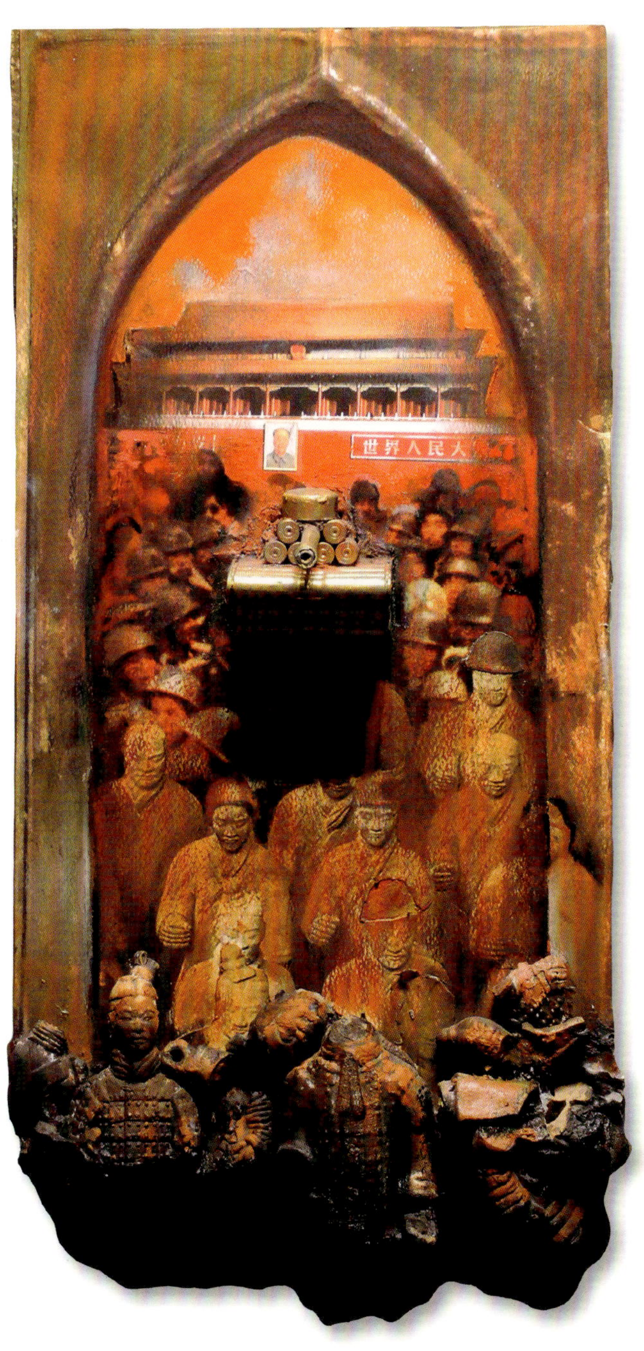

Milestones: Tiananmen Square, 2010,
Mixed media collage, 24 x 13 x 3 inches.
Collection of Ann and Jim Harithas.

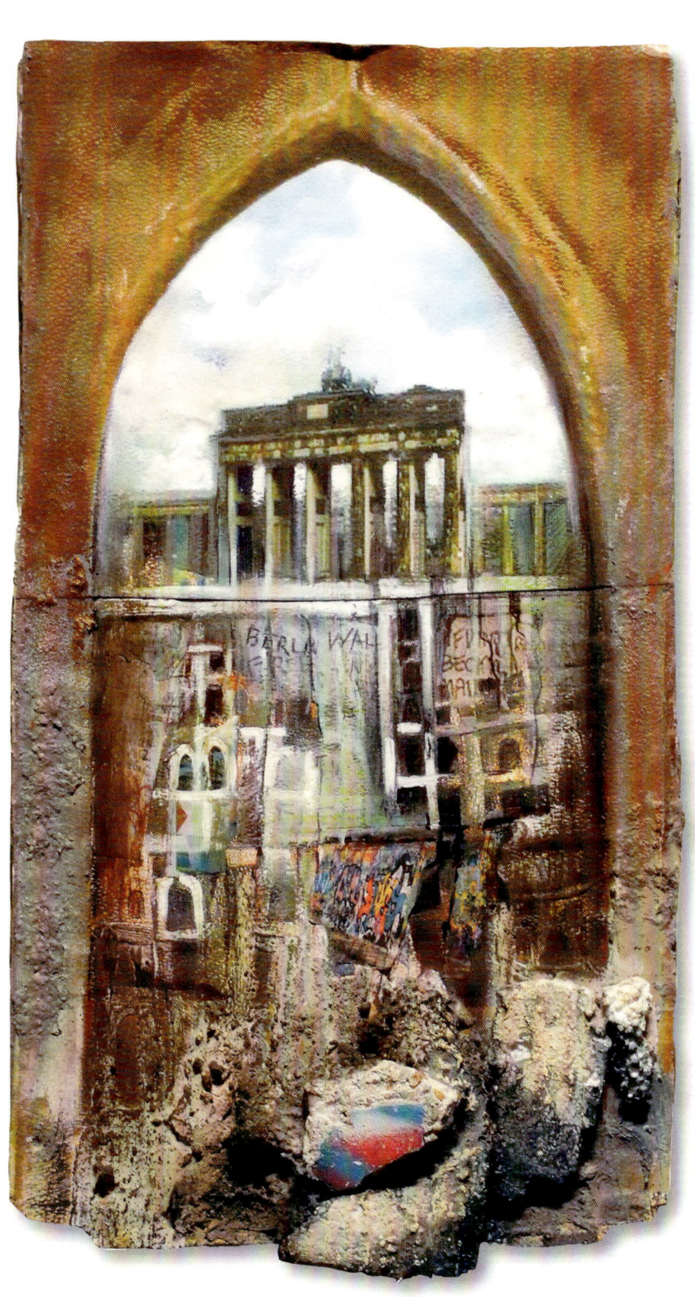

Milestones: Berlin Mauer, 2009,
Mixed media collage, 24 x 13 x 3 inches.
Collection of Rukshaan Krishna.

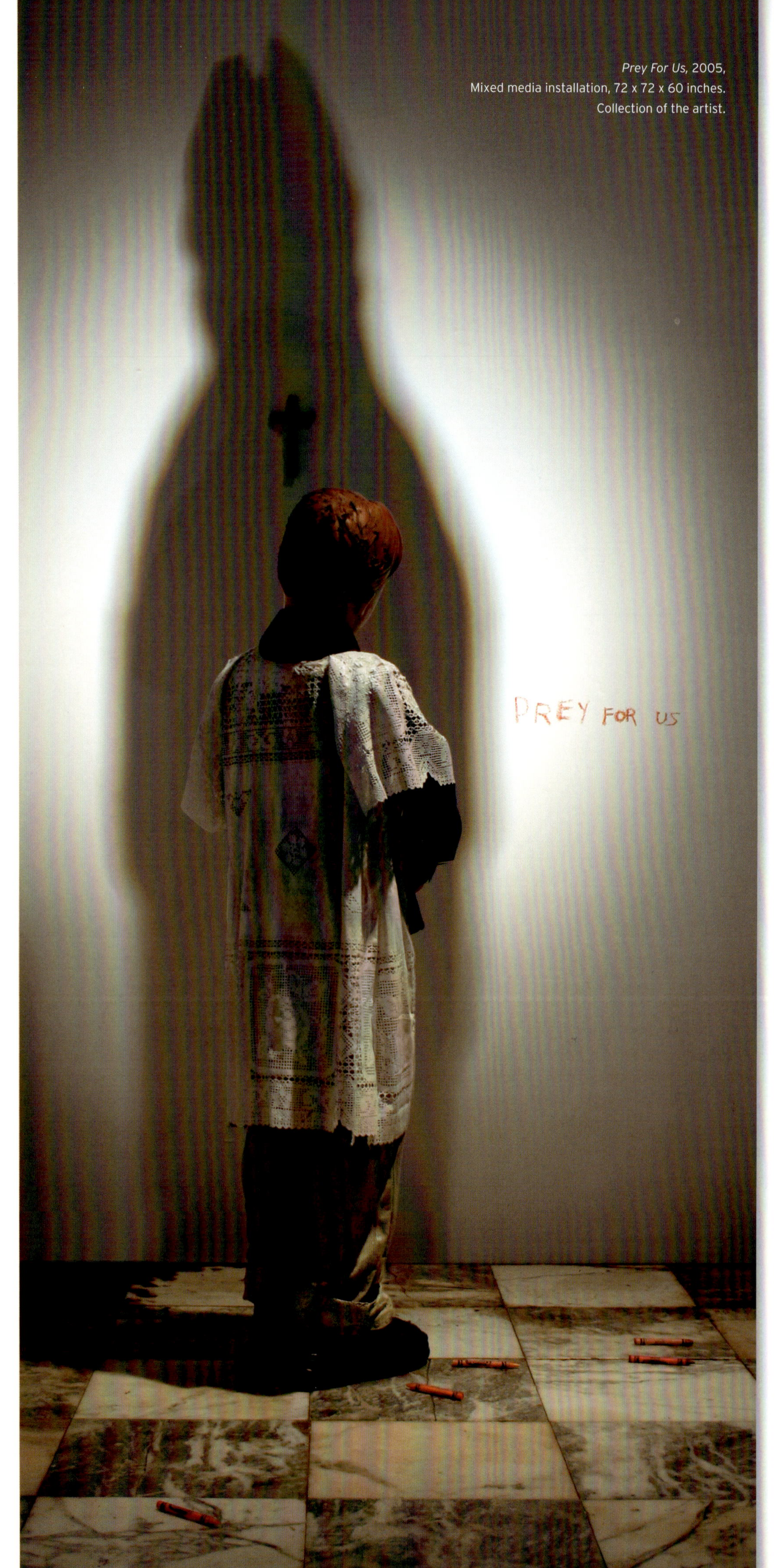

Prey For Us, 2005,
Mixed media installation, 72 x 72 x 60 inches.
Collection of the artist.

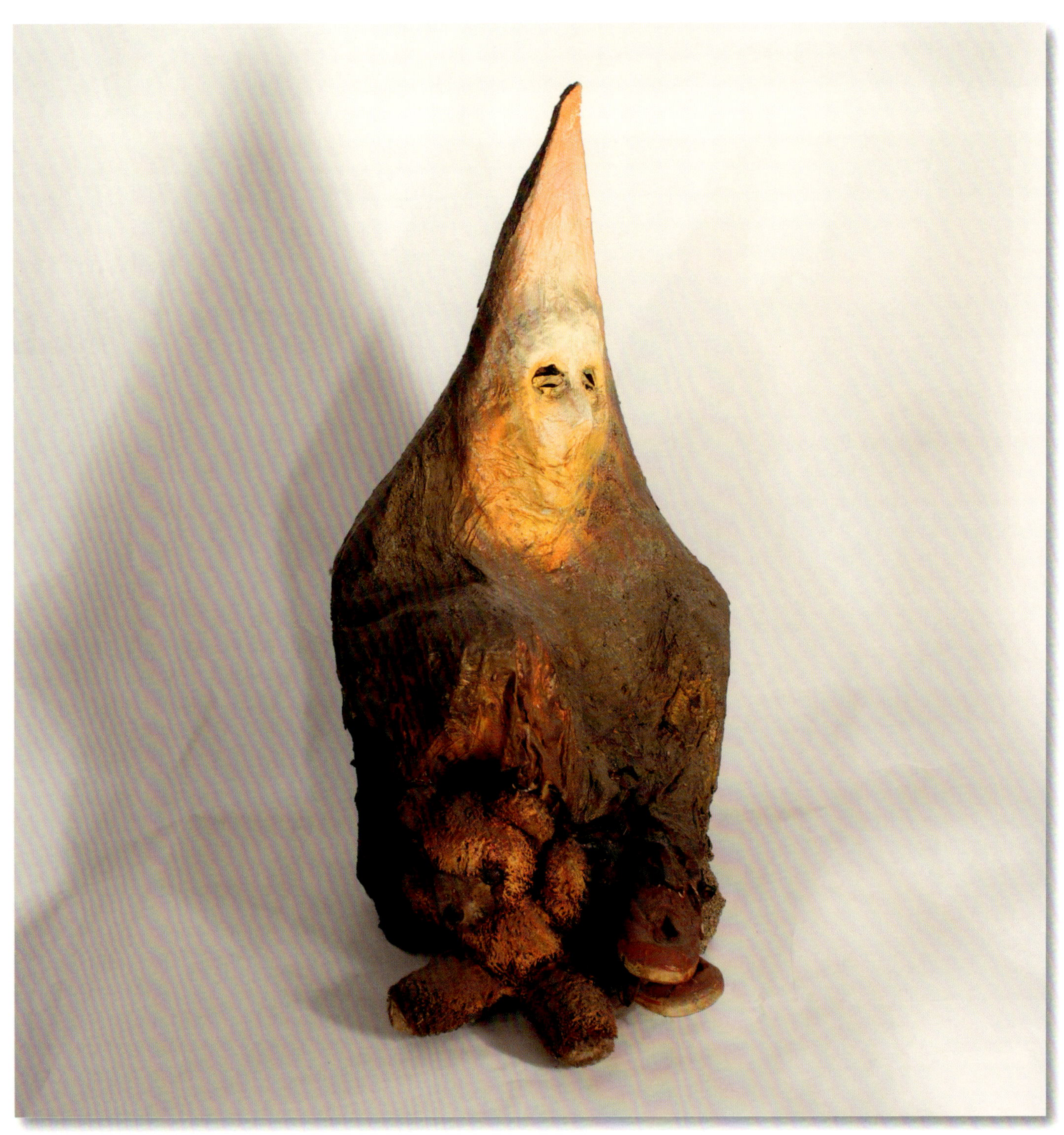

Klan Boy, 1994,
Papier-mâché and mixed media, 23 x 16 x 16 inches.
Collection of the Ogden Museum of Southern Art, New Orleans.

CHRONOLOGY

1948

Sharon Ortman is born in Houston, Texas, on Feb. 11. She is the middle child of three born to Lowell (Red) and Rosalie (Rosy) Ortman. Her brother Dwayne was born in 1946, and a sister, Jo Carole, is born in 1957.

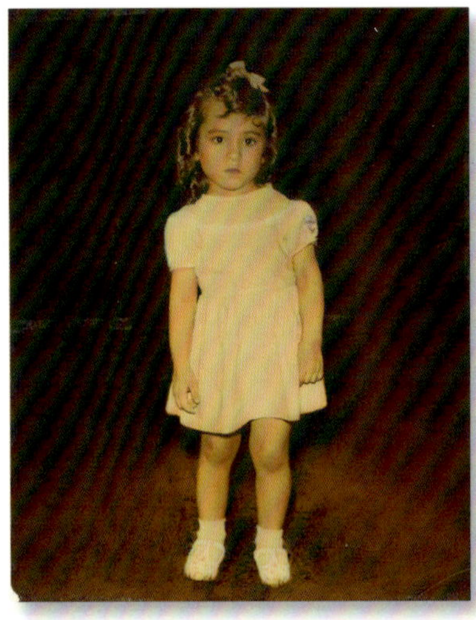

1951

Sharon wins her first – and last – beauty pageant at three years old at the Western Auto annual employees' picnic.

1954-1963

Sharon enters Christ the King Catholic School in Houston, Texas, and spends eight years immersed in a religion-infused educational environment. This Catholic upbringing influences her future artistic direction. After transferring to public school in 9th grade, Sharon's spiritual and cultural interests begin to expand and ultimately appear in her artwork.

1964-1966

Sharon meets Gus Kopriva in geometry class at Reagan High School in Houston. After high school graduation in 1966, Sharon enters the University of Houston.

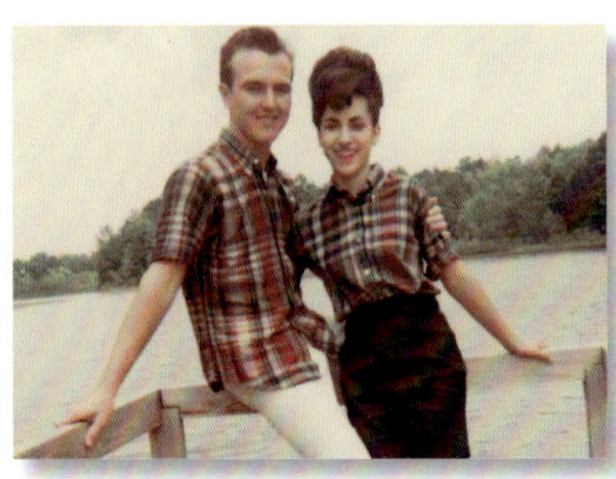

1970-1971

Sharon graduates from the University of Houston with a Bachelor of Science degree in education and begins teaching in the Aldine and Houston, Texas, public schools. She marries Gus Kopriva in Houston in 1971.

1979-1981

Sharon resigns from teaching to attend graduate school at University of Houston where she begins studies with John Alexander, Ed Hill, James Surls and others. She receives a Master of Fine Arts degree in painting in 1981.

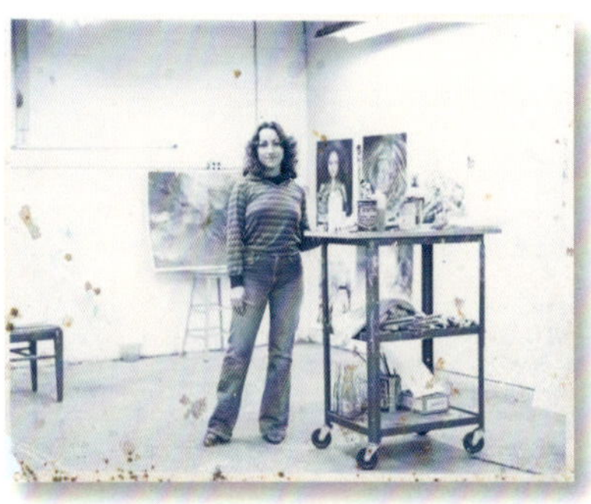

1982

Presents thesis exhibition in June at the University of Houston's Blaffer Gallery. Travels to Peru with Gus and friends Paul and Nancy Johnson following the exhibit opening. Their guide on the trip is Nancy's brother Richard Parker, and the experience is life changing for Sharon.

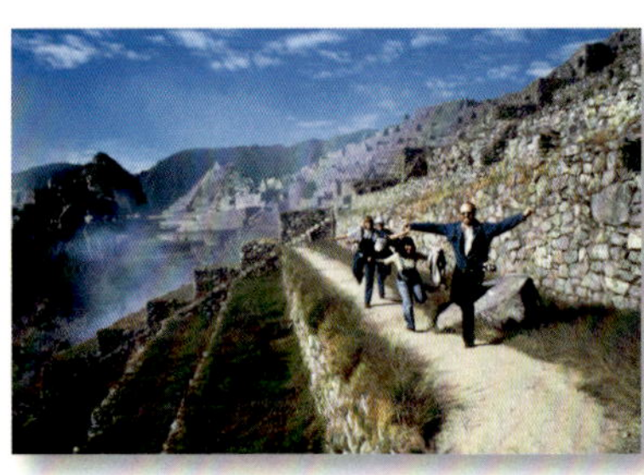

After returning from Peru, Sharon is introduced to Marilyn Oshman by John Alexander. Oshman becomes a life-long friend (and collector and supporter). Sharon begins volunteering with the Orange Show Foundation, and eventually becomes an employee for the organization from 1982 through 1989.

1982-1984

Sharon Kopriva completes her first "real" body of work during a two-year period after graduate school. She works in isolation in her studio and during this time of seclusion makes her first three-dimensional pieces, which develop naturally and directly from her highly textured paintings.

1984

In her first show after graduate school, Sharon participates in a three-person exhibition at the Midtown Art Center, curated by William A. Graham. Graham becomes Sharon's first art dealer in Houston.

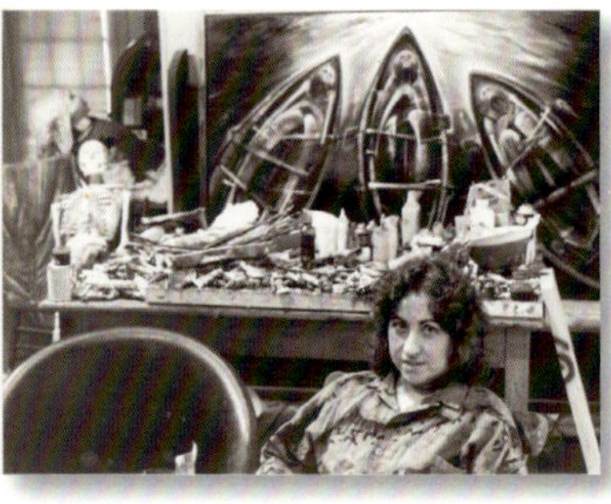

1985

Sharon's work is included in "Fresh Paint, The Houston School," an important exhibition that kicked off many artists' careers. Her piece *Bad Proud Ugly Disconcerned* is purchased by New York Art Dealer Allan Stone, beginning a relationship with the collector/dealer.

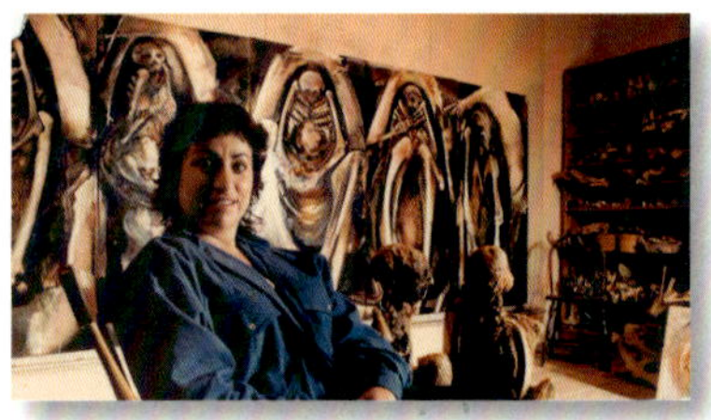

1986

Begins showing nationally and internationally, participating in exhibitions that include "Memento Mori" in Mexico City, "Empowered Painting" in Santa Fe, and several group exhibitions at Allan Stone Gallery in New York City. Sharon's painting *Seven Deadly Sins* is acquired by The New Mexico Museum of Art in Santa Fe.

1987

Meets Nancy and Ed Kienholz, who become friends and mentors. Sharon begins work on *Fin de Siècle*, as well as *Elvis,* on Aug. 16, the date of the Harmonic Convergence.

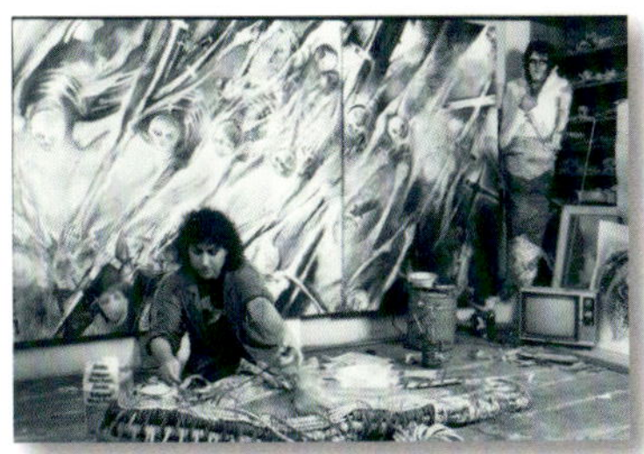

1988

Sharon's work *Cosmic Fish* is donated to The Menil Collection by the estate of Michael Duerr. She is one of 12 women selected to be in the "Texas Exhibition" at the National Museum of Women in the Arts. She participates in more Texas shows, with a first-place prize in the "Houston Area Exhibition." Meets Howard Barnett, a New Orleans art gallery owner, who becomes a friend and dealer.

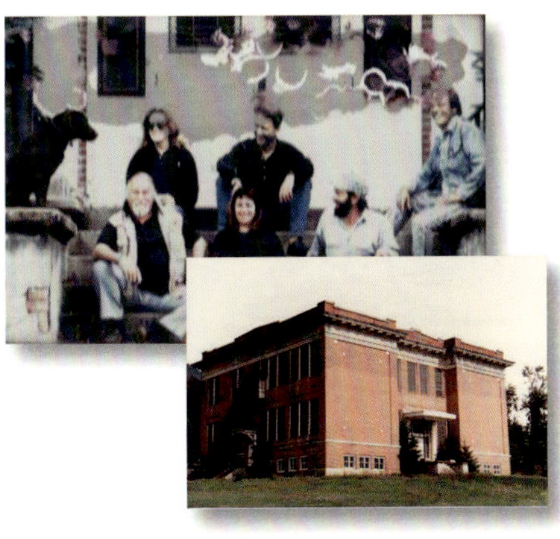

1989

Sharon continues to exhibit in the Texas area; is part of two group shows in New Orleans, at Simms Fine Arts and Hall-Bennett Gallery. Her work *Joan of Arc* is acquired by The Menil Collection, a gift of Nancy and Edward Kienholz. She starts spending summer months in an Idaho-based artist-in-residency program at The Hope School – as a guest of the Kienholzes. She feels an immediate connection to Hope, Idaho, and makes a trade with them: art for land. During the 10 years following that trade, Sharon

and Gus plan and build a residence and studio where they have been spending summers since.

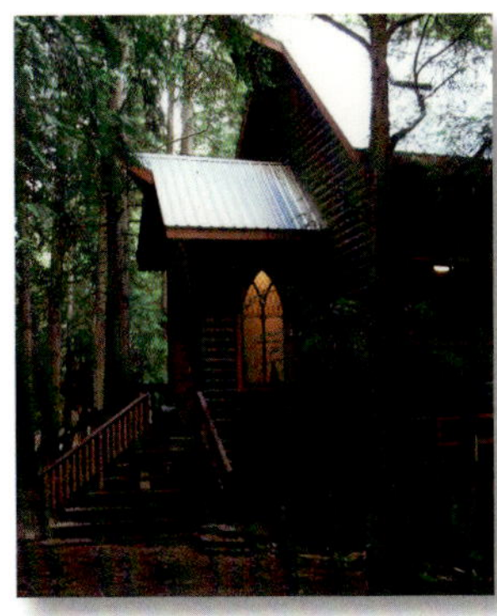

1990

Sharon's work *Sebastian* lands in the Harris County morgue after officials confuse the mummy-like sculpture with human remains. After a brief stay, the sculpture is returned to its owner.

1993

Sharon names a Crayola color – Asparagus – and becomes a member of the Crayola Crayon Hall of Fame. The Museum of Fine Arts Houston acquires her sculpture *Dusk*. Sharon participates in a residency in the Northern Territory of Australia, followed by a series of works on paper about aboriginal legends and mythology.

1994

Sharon and Gus are in Hope, Idaho, when Ed Kienholz dies suddenly of a heart attack. He is buried high upon Howe Mountain in the front seat of a latte-colored 1940 Packard coupe. That same summer, Sharon and Gus move into their Idaho home.

1995

Completes the first major bronze casting of *Rite of Passage* at the Walla Walla Foundry in Washington state. Has solo exhibition with Dutch Phillips gallery in Dallas.

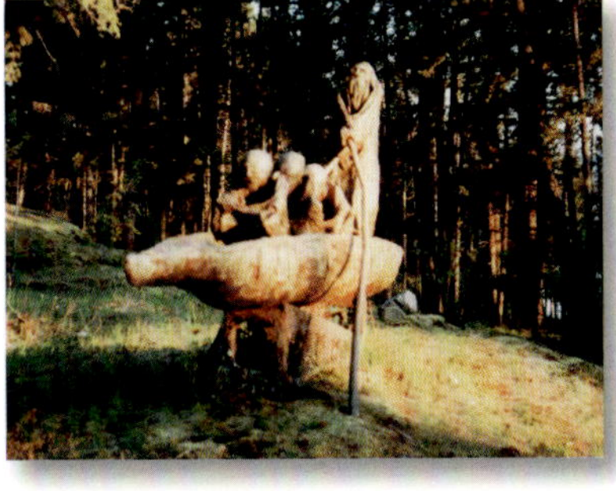

1996

Sharon's work *Catherine's Wheel* is acquired by Dominique de Menil for The Menil Collection. This follows having the original *Rite of Passage* piece featured in the group exhibition "American Kaleidoscope" at The National Museum of American Art. Sharon continues solo exhibitions, now with Barbara Davis Gallery in Houston.

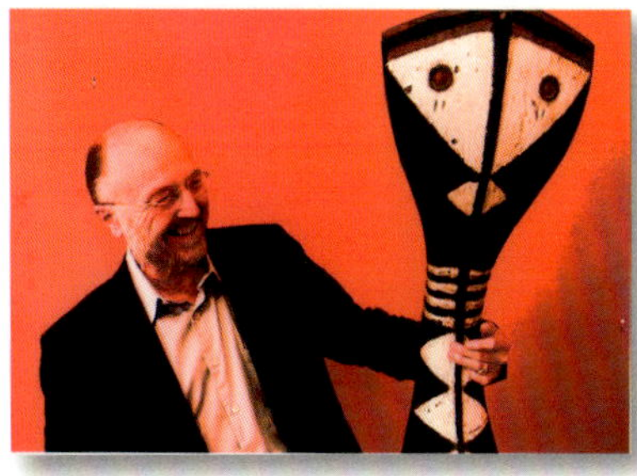

1998

Gus Kopriva opens Redbud Gallery at 303 E. 11th Street in Houston. Sharon begins developing a studio in the adjoining space.

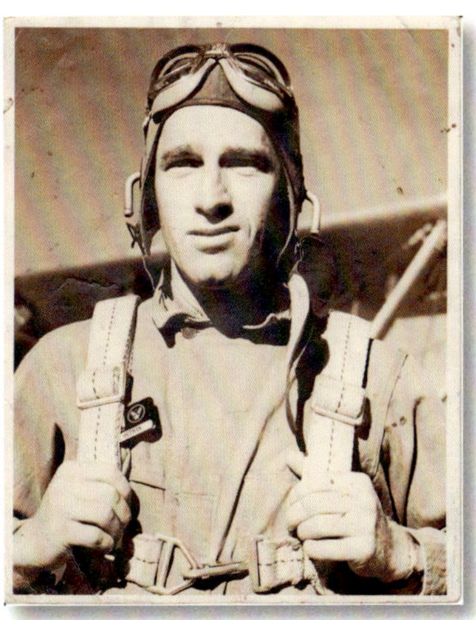

2000

Lowell Ortman, Sharon's father, dies in April in Houston. In May, she has a solo exhibition with The Menil Collection, curated by Walter Hopps.

2001

Collector, supporter and friend Ted Pillsbury begins representing Sharon and her works through Pillsbury Peters Gallery in Dallas. Sharon has solo exhibit at Pillsbury Peters later this year.

2002

Has first international solo exhibition at the Mönchskirche Museum in Salzwedel, Germany. Also participates in group show at Artco Gallery in Leipzig, Germany. In November, Sharon's mother Rosy dies.

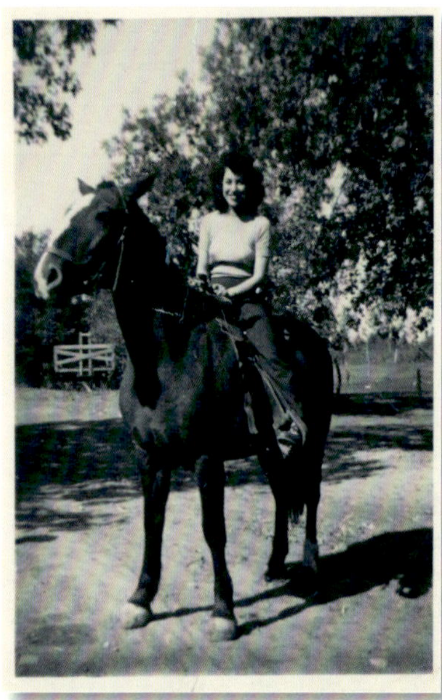

2003

Continues participating internationally in both group and solo exhibitions, including shows at the Humbolt Museum in Havana, Cuba, and Artco in Leipzig, Germany.

2004-2005

Sharon has another solo show, "Mounds and Monuments," at Barbara Davis Gallery, Houston. This exhibition represents a return to works depicting landscapes with architectural features. Sharon also has work in the New Orleans Triennial and wins the 2005 (Texas) State Visual Arts Award.

2005

Sharon's work *Mother Teresa* becomes part of the permanent collection at the Art Museum of Southeast Texas in Beaumont. It is a gift of Regina Rogers in loving memory of Sister Immaculata of the Sisters of the Blessed Sacrament.

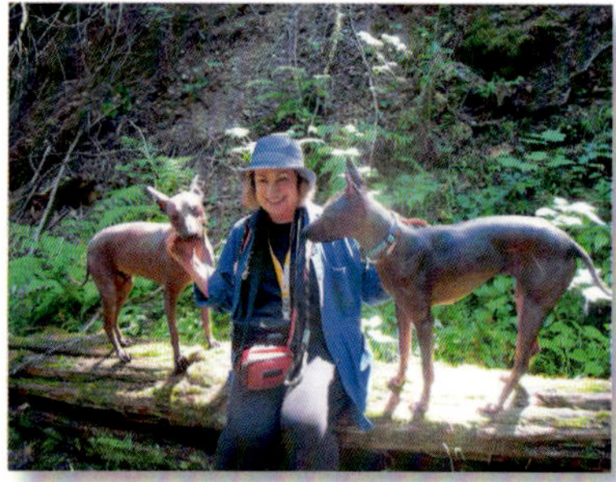

2006

Sharon makes a return trip to Peru and sees "Pero Sin Pello" dogs for the first time. She has two more international solos: at Zeitkunst Gallerie in Halle, Germany, and Museo de la Nación in Lima, Peru. Her *Saint Rose of Lima* sculpture is acquired by the museum.

2007

Sharon and Gus adopt Pluto (born September 2006), the first of her Peruvian Hairless dogs. Nine months later, they add another Peruvian dog, Luna, to the family.

2008

Continues showing internationally in Madrid, Sitges, and Seville, Spain.

2009

"I Have a Dream Exhibition" of Martin Luther King Jr. opens at the Carriage House Arts Center in New York City. The show travels three years in the U.S. and Europe. Has solo shows in Wittenburg, Germany, and Querétaro, Mexico (Museo de la Ciudad).

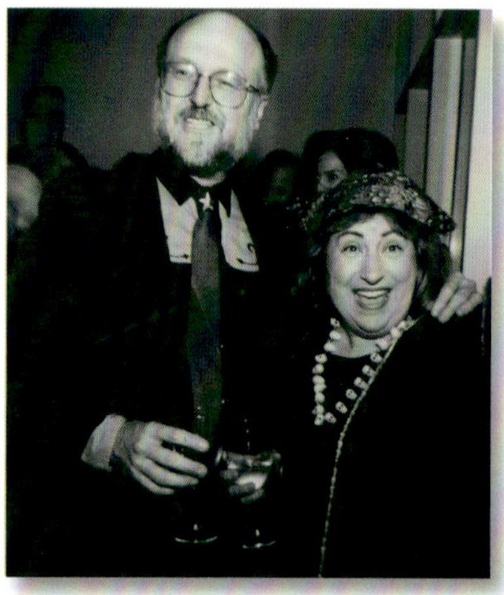

2010

Has solo show at Galerie Richard in Berlin, Germany. Pluto and Luna have puppies, and one, Thor, stays with the family.

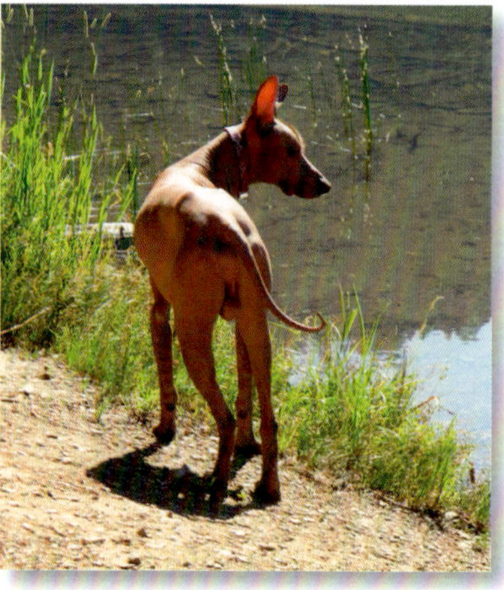

2011

Has solo shows in Mumbai, India, at the The Strand Art Room ("Phantoms and Milestones") and in Houston at the Deborah Colton Gallery ("Cathedrals, Phantoms and Naked Dogs") and at Houston Baptist University ("Forest Cathedrals"). Is invited to show in Project Row Houses' Group 35 show ("The Seven Deadly Sins in Dog").

2012

Sharon Kopriva opens a 30-year survey of her works at the Ogden Museum of Southern Art in New Orleans.

2013

Has solo show scheduled at Blue Star Contemporary Art Center in San Antonio, Texas, in June.

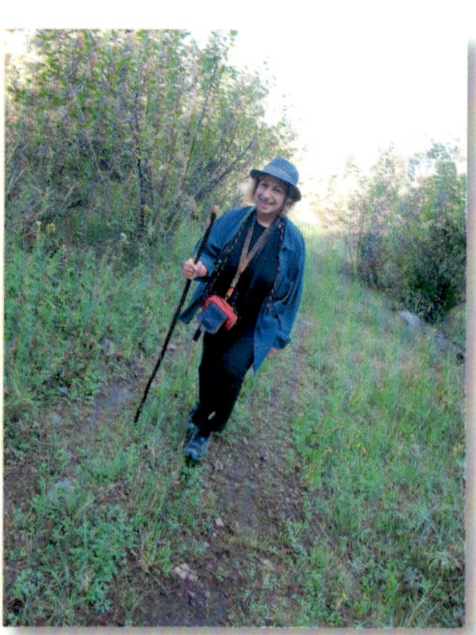

BIBLIOGRAPHY:

Alexander, Chris. "Houston Letter." *ArtSpace*, Summer 1985.

"American Kaleidoscope: Themes and Perspectives in Recent Art." *Washington City Paper*, Oct. 4-10, 1996.

Anderson, Mark A. *Extending the Artist's Hand: Contemporary Sculpture from The Walla Walla Foundry*. Pullman, Washington State University, September 2004.

Anspon, Catherine D. "Dallas Travel Notes." *Art & Antiques*, February 2002.

Anspon, Catherine D. "Morality, Mortality, the Church and Art: Sharon Kopriva's Reconciliations." *Public News*, Oct. 16, 1996.

Anspon, Catherine D. "The Mummies Have It: Sharon Kopriva at The Menil." *PaperCity*, June 2000, pg. 4.

Anspon, Catherine D. "Sharon Kopriva, Menil Collection, National Reviews." *Art News*, September 2000, pgs. 176, 178.

"ArtSpace Virginia Miller Galleries to Feature Sculpture of Sharon Kopriva." *Entertainment News and Views*, Jan. 12, 1996.

Balsamo, Dean. "Gallery Hopping." *Pasatiempo* (Santa Fe, New Mexico), Sept. 10, 1993.

Baria, Zeenia F. "Memories of the Past." *Bombay Times*, April 9, 2011.

Beck, Sharon. "Lives and Deaths of Saints." *Public News*, May 8, 1986.

Bell, David. "Empowered Painting at the Santa Fe Museum of Fine Arts." *Art in America*, January 1987.

Bennett, Steve. "Sculpture: The Spectrum, Works by Contemporary Artists Explore Light, Sound, Distance." *San Antonio Light*, Nov. 1, 1987.

Berkovitch, Ellen. "Kopriva's Sculptures Challenge Convention." *Journal North* (Santa Fe, New Mexico), Sept. 23, 1993.

Bloom, Suzanne and Hill, Ed. "Review: Sharon Kopriva." *Art Forum*, May 1989.

Bookhardt, D. Eric. "Darkness and Light." *Gambit Weekly*, March 12, 2002.

Bookhardt, D. Eric. "In the Season of All Saints." *New Orleans Weekly*, Nov. 15, 1994.

Bookhardt, D. Eric. "Sharon Kopriva: Sculpture." *Art Papers*, March/April 1995.

Bott, Margaret. "Texas Artists Today." *Origins*, July 2011, pg. 24.

Bravo, Armando Alvarez. "Deronda, Sobre Arte Algo Mas." *El Nuevo Miercoles*, Jan. 31, 1996.

Briggs, Peter. "The Art of Faith and War." *Art Lies*, Spring 2007.

Brown, Betty Ann and Raven, Arlene. *Exposures, Women & Their Art*. New Sage Press, 1989.

Chadwick, Susan. "Corpse-like Sculptures Raise Questions of Life Cycle." *The Houston Post*, Jan. 18, 1989.

Chadwick, Susan. "The Dark Religious Imagery of Sharon Kopriva's Art." *The Houston Post*, May 4, 1986.

Chavez, Gerardo. Exhibition catalogue, *Amistad*, Trujillo, Peru: Museo de Arte Moderno de Trujillo, November 2007.

Chavez Jr., Lupe. "Houston Artist's Mummies Help Her Express Her Inner Struggle with Religion." *The Monitor, Festiva*, Aug. 27, 1999.

Collins, Michael. Exhibition catalogue, *Faith and War: The Art of Sharon Kopriva and Ed Wilson*, Lubbock, Texas: Landmark Gallery, Texas Tech University, December 2007.

Colpitt, Frances. "Report from Houston." *Art in America*, October 2000, pgs. 67-75.

Curtis, Gregory. "Behind the Lines." *Texas Monthly Magazine*, December 1988.

Daniel, Mike. "Group Exhibition at Pillsbury Peters." *Dallas Morning News*, July 28, 2000.

Danko, Pat St. John. "More Thoughts on a Houston School." *New Art Examiner*, April 1986.

Delgadillo, W. "Arte Narrative, Momias…." *Semanario* (Juarez, Mexico), April 20, 1992.

Demchak, Susanne. "An Interview: Sharon Kopriva." *Public News*, Oct. 25, 1984.

Dobay, Louis. "Sculpture that Works." *Public News*, June 20, 1987.

Edwards, Jim. Exhibition catalogue, *Forest Cathedrals and the Stations of the Cross*, Houston, Texas: Houston Baptist University, Dec. 2, 2011.

Edwards, Jim. "Sharon Kopriva's Cathedrals, Phantoms and Naked Dogs." Exhibition catalogue, *Cathedrals, Phantoms and Naked Dogs*, Houston, Texas: Deborah Colton Gallery, 2011.

Ellis, Simone. "Critical Reflections." *The Magazine* (Santa Fe, New Mexico), October 1993.

Exhibition Catalogue. *Raices*, Lima Peru: Museo de la Naciòns, September 2006.

Farb, Carolyn. "Religious Experience." *Brilliant Magazine*, November 2005, pgs. 50-51.

Fauntleroy, Gussie. "Fine Art and Life Cycles." *Pasatiempo* (Santa Fe, New Mexico), May 3, 1996.

Foster, Steven. "The Art of Sharon Kopriva." *The Mesa Journal*, Nov. 21, 2000.

Fullerton, Deborah. Exhibition catalogue, *Earthbound*, Corpus Christi, Texas: Corpus Christi Museum of Art, March 25-May 16, 2010.

Gall, Frank C. "Sharon Kopriva/Barbara Davis Gallery." *Art Lies*, Winter 1998-99.

Gambrell, Jamey. "Texas: State of the Art." *Art in America*, March 1987.

George, Ron. "Vigor Mortis." *Corpus Christi Caller-Times*, Sept. 29, 1992.

Goddard, Dan R. "Death Prominent in Sculptor's Work." *San Antonio Express-News*, June 24, 1993.

Goddard, Dan R. "Macabre." *Sunday Express News* (San Antonio, Texas), Nov. 9, 1987.

Goddard, Dan R. "Texas Artists Visit Another Reality." *The Sunday Express News* (San Antonio, Texas), July 1, 1990.

Greene, Alison de Lima. *Texas: 150 Works from the Museum of Fine Arts*. Museum of Fine Arts, Houston, 2000.

Green, Roger. "Sacred Works Have Rewards, if Not the Religious Kind." *Times-Picayune*, April 1, 1990.

Harithas, James. Exhibition Catalogue, *450 Fronteras*, Houston, Texas: Station Museum, February 2008.

Hobbs, Robert. "The Reality of Illusion: Thoughts on Houston and Some of its Women Artists." *No Bluebonnets, No Yellow Roses*, Midmarch Arts Press, New York, New York, 1988.

Holliday, Kate. "Religions Commentary." *The New Orleans Art Review*, November 1994.

Hopps, Walter. Exhibition catalogue, *Sharon Kopriva: 1986-1998*, Houston, Texas: The Menil Collection, June 2000.

Johnson, Patricia C. "Artist of the Year." *Houston Chronicle*, March 31, 2001.

Johnson, Patricia C. "Gallery Exhibits Show Growth of Two Artists." *Houston Chronicle*, Nov. 2, 1996.

Johnson, Patricia C. "Kopriva Turns Icons of Faith into Provocative Theater." *Houston Chronicle*, June 14, 2000, pgs. 1D, 10D.

Johnson, Patricia C. "Mounds and Monuments." *Houston Chronicle*, March 2004.

Johnson, Patricia C. "Shows Offer a Mix of Reality, Experimentation, Physicality." *Houston Chronicle*, May 11, 2000, pg. 1D.

Johnson, Patricia C. "Strong Art in Small Spaces." *Houston Chronicle*, May 3, 1992.

Johnson, Patricia C. "Stretching the Frame," *Houston Chronicle*, Nov. 10, 1998.

"KOAN Critics Roundtable Must See— American Kaleidoscope: Themes and Perspectives in Recent Art." *KOAN Magazine*, November 1996.

Krishna, Rukshan. Exhibition catalogue. *Phantoms and Milestones*, Mumbai, India: The Strand Art Room, April 2011.

Kutner, Janet. "Skeletal Sculpture Designed to Shock." *Dallas Morning News*, April 28, 1995.

Martin, Deborah. "Texas Dialogue." *El Paso Herald Post*, May 14, 1992.

McBride, Elizabeth. "A Writer Looks at Art: Kohlmeyer, Clarke, Kopriva, Morales." *ArtScene*, Fall 1986.

McEntire, Frank. *Dreams and Shields: Spiritual Dimensions in Contemporary Art*, Salt Lake Art Center, February 1992

Michael, Nadia. "Cathedrals, Phantoms and Naked Dogs." *002 Magazine* (Houston), June 2011, pgs. 22-23.

"Mixed Mediums: Cycles of the Spiritual." *KOAN Magazine*, October 1997.

Modak, Nasrin. "Subtle Landmarks, Phantoms and Milestones." *Verve Magazine*, April 2011.

Nitz, Corinna. "Die Ruckkehr des Martin Luther." *Mitteldeutsche Zeitung* (Wittenburg, Germany), July 3, 2009.

"Palo Santo." *Caretas* (Lima, Peru), Sept. 21, 2006.

Pillsbury, Edmund P. *Texas Vision: The Barrett Collection—The Art of Texas and Switzerland*. Dallas, Texas: Southern Methodist University Press, 2005. pgs. 107, 174.

Planas, Enrique. "Polvo Somos." *El Comercio* (Lima, Peru), Sept. 26, 2006.

Reese, Elizabeth. "Contemporary Outdoor Sculpture in Meditation Part." *Art Lies*, Summer 2001.

"Rezos and Penitencias." *Diario, Querétaro, Qro*, photographs, Jan. 19-20, 2009.

Rose, Barbara and Kalil, Susie. Exhibition Catalogue, *Fresh Paint: The Houston School*, Houston, Texas: Museum of Fine Arts, Houston, 1985.

Rubenstein, Raphael. "Sharon Kopriva's Magical Realism," Exhibition catalogue, *Cathedrals, Phantoms and Naked Dogs*, Houston, Texas: Deborah Colton Gallery, May 2011.

Rushing, W. Jackson. "Houston: Sharon Kopriva, The Menil Collection." *Sculpture*, November 2000, pgs. 72-73.

Sanchez, Felix. "Mummy Unwinds at Morgue." *The Houston Post*, March 15, 1990.

Sandoval, Emiliana. "Wood Sculpture, Rainforest Art and Catholicism Mix in Exhibit." *Santa Fe New Mexican*, Sept. 3, 1993.

Schiche, Ericka. "Empty Shells." *Public News* (Houston, Texas), Oct. 26, 1994.

Serrano, Gabi. Exhibition catalogue. *I Have a Dream*. New York, New York: Gabbaron Foundation, Fall 2009.

Serwer, Jacquelyn Day. *American Kaleidoscope: Themes and Perspectives in Recent Art*, October 1996.

Shields, Kathleen. "Empowered Painting at the Museum of Fine Arts, Santa Fe." *ArtSpace*, Fall 1986.

Tennant, Donna. "Sharon Kopriva at Graham Gallery, Houston." *ArtSpace*, Fall 1986.

Watson, Randall. "Work 1986-1998 at The Menil Collection." *Art Lies*, Fall 2000, pg. 95.

Wilson, Wade. "Mysteries of Death are Explored by Sharon Kopriva." *Fort Worth Star-Telegram*, April 30, 1995.

Zhu, Christopher. *Houston Contemporary Art at the Shanghai Museum of Art*. Shanghai, China: Shanghai Museum of Art, July 2006.

Zhu, Christopher. "Sharon Kopriva." *Art Today* (Shanghai, China), January 2007.

SELECTED EXHIBITIONS AND COLLECTIONS

SOLO EXHIBITIONS

2012
From Terra to Verde: The Work of Sharon Kopriva, The Ogden Museum of Southern Art, New Orleans, Louisiana, United States, book

2011
Cathedrals, Phantoms and Naked Dogs, Deborah Colton Gallery, Houston, Texas, United States, catalogue

Phantoms and Milestones, The Strand Art Room, Mumbai, India, catalogue

2010
Martyrs, Ministers and Milestones, Galerie Richard, Berlin, Germany

2009
The Voice of Silence, Taylor/Bercier Fine Art, New Orleans, Louisiana, United States

Rezos, Museo de la Ciudad, Querétaro, Mexico

2006
Roots, Museo de la Nación, Lima, Peru, catalogue

Lost Rivers, Zeitkunst Galerie, Halle, Germany

2004
The Backside of Night, Gerald Peters Gallery, Dallas, Texas, United States

Mounds and Monuments, Barbara Davis Gallery, Houston, Texas, United States

2002
Kreuz Weg, Mönchskirche, Salzwedel, Germany

Marguerite Oestreicher Fine Arts, New Orleans, Louisiana, United States

2001
Pillsbury & Peters Fine Arts, Dallas, Texas, United States

Texas Artist of the Year Award, Art League of Houston, Houston, Texas, United States

2000
Sharon Kopriva: Works from 1986-1998, The Menil Collection, Houston, Texas, United States, catalogue

1998
Birds of Pray, Barbara Davis Gallery, Houston, Texas, United States

1997
From Dust Thou Art, Dutch Phillips Gallery, Dallas, Texas, United States

Contemporary Art Month – Sharon Kopriva Drawings and Sculpture, Parchman Stremmel Gallery, San Antonio, Texas, United States

1996
Vessels and Reliquaries, ArtSpace Virginia Miller Galleries, Coral Gables, Florida, United States

Reconciliations, Barbara Davis Gallery, Houston, Texas, United States

1995
New Sculpture, Paintings and Constructions, Dutch Phillips Gallery, Dallas, Texas, United States

1994
New Constructions and Paintings, Hall-Barnett Gallery, New Orleans, Louisiana, United States

1993
LewAllen Gallery, Santa Fe, New Mexico, United States

1992
Conflicting Rituals, Corpus Christi State University, Corpus Christi, Texas, United States, catalogue

1991
Rite of Passage, The Art Center, Waco, Texas, United States, catalogue

Penances, Art Museum of Southeast Texas, Beaumont, Texas, United States

1989
Sharon Kopriva: Sculpture and Paintings, J. Rosenthal Gallery, Chicago, Illinois, United States

Sculpture and Paintings, Graham Gallery, Houston, Texas, United States, catalogue

SELECTED GROUP EXHIBITIONS

2010
Museo de Arte Moderno de Trujillo, *Texas cae en un trozo de tela*, Sept. 25, Trujillo, Peru (catalogue)

Various Spaces, *I Have a Dream*, Sitges (Barcelona), Marbella, Madrid, Valladolid, Zarragoza, Andorra, Aviles, Sevilla, Granada, Murcia, Gran Canaria, and Lanzarote, Spain (catalogue)

Corpus Christi Museum of Art, *Earthbound*, March 25-May 16, Corpus Christi, Texas, United States (catalogue)

2009
Altes Rathaus, *Rebels and Reformers*, July 7-Aug. 18, Wittenberg, Germany

2008
Mercat Vell, *8 Donnes, 8 Paisos*, March 8-April 27, Sitges (Barcelona), Seville, and Madrid, Spain (catalogue)

2007
Museum of the Nations, *Amistad*, Sept. 5-30, Lima, Peru (catalogue)

2006
Texas Tech University, *Faith and War*, Dec. 7-Jan 18, 2007, Lubbock, Texas, United States (catalogue)

Station Museum, *Frontera 450+*, Oct. 21-Jan. 28, 2007, Houston, Texas, United States

2005
New Orleans Museum Of Art, *New Orleans Triennial*, Aug. 6-Oct. 16, New Orleans, Louisiana, United States

Meadows Museum, *Texas Vision*, works on paper from The Barrett Collection, Southern Methodist University, February-March, Dallas, Texas, United States (catalogue)

2003
Humboldt Museum, *Ambos Mundos*, Havana, Cuba

2001
Texas Art at the Museum of Arts, *Crossing State Lines*, Houston, United States

1997
Dimock Gallery, *Mixed Mediums: Cycles of the Spiritual*, George Washington University, Washington, D.C., United States

1996
National Museum of American Art, Smithsonian, *American Kaleidoscope – Themes and Perspectives in Recent Art*, Washington, D.C., United States

1995
Contemporary Arts Museum, *Elvis + Marilyn = 2 x Immortal*, Houston, Texas, United States

Museum of Fine Arts, *Texas: Myth and Reality*, Houston, Texas, United States

1993
Assistance League of Houston, *Texas Art Celebration '93* (Second Place, Juried by David Ross), Houston, Texas, United States

The Museum of Fine Arts, Houston, *Texas Contemporary Acquisitions of the '90s,* Houston, Texas, United States

Texas Biennial, Dallas, Texas, United States

1992
Salt Lake City Art Center, *Dreams and Shields*, Salt Lake City, Utah, United States (catalogue)

1989
The Huntington Museum, *A Century of Texas Sculpture*, Austin, Texas, United States (catalogue)

Hooks-Epstein Gallery, *Another Reality*, Houston, Texas, and Little Rock, Arkansas, United States

1988
Blaffer Gallery, University of Houston, *Houston Area Exhibition* (First Place, Juried by Edward and Nancy Reddin Kienholz, Richard Koshalek, and Alison de Lima Greene), Houston, Texas, United States

National Museum of Women in the Arts, *1988 Texas Exhibition*, Washington, D.C., United States (catalogue)

1987
Allan Stone Gallery, *Estes and Others*, New York, New York, United States

1986
Centro Cultural Arte Contemporaneo, *Memento Mori* (Curated by Richard Flood), Mexico City, Mexico (catalogue)

Museum of Fine Arts, *Empowered Painting*, Santa Fe, New Mexico, United States

1985
Museum of Fine Arts, *Fresh Paint: The Houston School*, Houston, Texas, United States

GRANTS/AWARDS

Commission for *Cool Globes* sculpture, Vestes, Houston, Texas, United States, 2009

Texas State Visual Artist of the Year (Awarded by the Texas Legislature), Austin, Texas United States, 2005-2006

Texas Artist of the Year, Art League of Houston, 2001

Houston Millennium Makers Award, 2000 Individual Artist Grant, Cultural Arts Council, Houston, Texas, United States, 1997

Residency Grant, Museum of Northern Territories, Darwin, Australia, 1994

Mid-America Arts Alliance/National Endowment for the Arts Fellowship Award in Sculpture, United States, 1993

PERMANENT PUBLIC COLLECTIONS

The Art Museum of South Texas, Corpus Christi, Texas, United States (2)

Art Museum of Southeast Texas, Beaumont, Texas, United States

Dallas Museum of Art, Dallas, Texas, United States (5)

Lowe Art Museum, Miami, Florida, United States

The Menil Collection, Houston, Texas, United States (3)

Mourtala Diop Collection, Dakar, Senegal. (2) Museo de Arte, Lima, Peru

The Museum of Fine Arts, Houston, Texas, United States (2)

New Mexico Museum of Art, Santa Fe, New Mexico, United States

New Orleans Museum of Art, New Orleans, Louisiana, United States

Ogden Museum of Southern Art, New Orleans, Louisiana, United States (2)

University of Houston, Houston, Texas, United States

Vestes, Houston, Texas, United States

espan
ACKNOWLEDGEMENT

Special thanks for inspiration and support from all of my friends and those who made this publication possible, especially Marilyn Oshman, Bradley Sumrall, John Alexander, Catherine Anspon, Elisa Rochford and, as always, Gus Kopriva (my "eternal bliss"). Thanks to the staff of the Ogden Museum of Southern Art, Phillip Collier Designs, Garrity Print Solutions, Aker Imaging Photo Lab, Digital Imaging Group and all of my photographers.

To my lenders:

Art Museum of Southeast Texas

Nancy Allen

Kirk Baxter and David Waller

Bill Bowman and Adriene Parks

Anne and Peter Brown

Michele and Joe Carte

Billie and Marvin Chasen

Gayle and Michael Collins

Mary and Roy Cullen

Meredith Cullen

Deborah Colton Gallery

Karen Desenberg

Ron Garcia

Nancy Reddin Kienholz

Jo Carole and Randy Long

Cindy and Andrew Lubetkin

Tony Markey

The Ogden Museum of Southern Art

Gwen and Dwayne Ortman

Marilyn Oshman

Jennifer and Scott Palermo

Dale Petrini

Redbud Gallery

Taylor/Bercier Gallery

Carol and Andy Vickery

Renee Wallace

To the writers, editors and contributors:

Bradley Sumrall, Raphael Rubenstein, John Alexander, Jim Edwards,
Walter Hopps, Ted Pillsbury, Allan Stone
and Elisa Rochford

To
Marta C. Dougherty
(October 6, 1958-February 22, 2012)

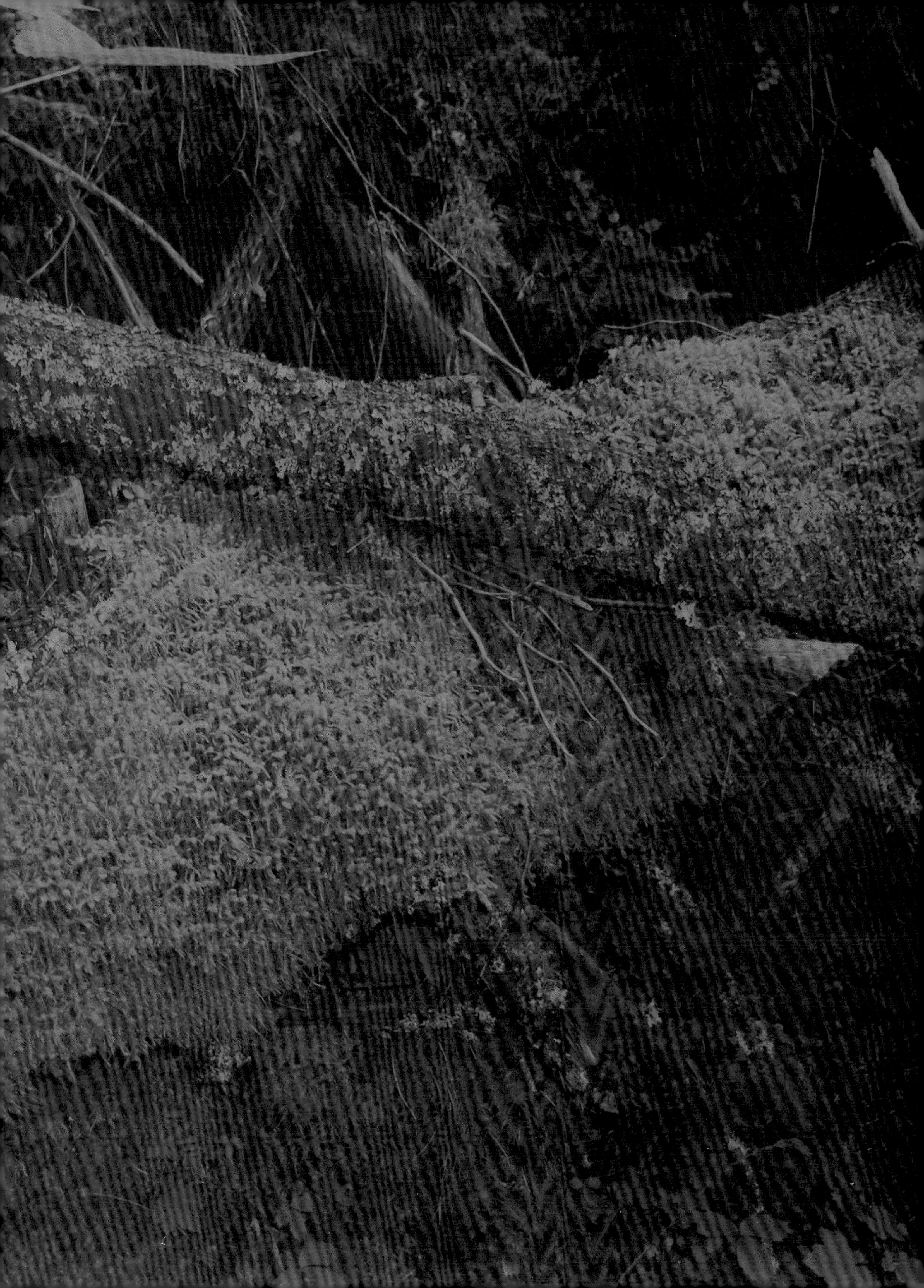